D1598659

BLACK GHETTO RIOTS & CAMPUS
DISORDERS: A SUBCULTURAL AND
PHILOSOPHICAL STUDY OF DEMOCRATIC LEGITIMACY
AND AMERICAN POLITICAL VIOLENCE, 1964-1970.

Roger B. Canfield

R. & E. RESEARCH ASSOCIATES
San Francisco
1973

Copyright 1973 by Roger B. Canfield

R AND E RESEARCH ASSOCIATES
4843 Mission St., San Francisco 94112
18581 McFarland Ave., Saratoga, CA 95070

Publishers and Distributors of Ethnic Studies

Editor: Adam S. Eterovich

Publisher: Robert D. Reed

Library of Congress Card Catalog Number
73-82399

ISBN
0-88247-239-9

TABLE OF CONTENTS

iii

CHAPTER SEVEN

LIST OF CHARTS

CHAPTER I

AN INTRODUCTION TO AMERICAN POLITICAL VIOLENCE
DESCRIPTION, HYPOTHESES, AND CONCEPTS

The study of areas of conflict and patterns of violence
would help in understanding the political system of any
society. Such study would, by necessity, probe into
the innermost fabric of the society upon which the
political system is founded.[1]

Epochs sometimes occur in the life of a nation when the
old customs of a people are changed, public morality is
destroyed, religious belief shaken, and the spell of
tradition broken. ...The citizens then have neither the
instinctive patriotism of a monarchy nor the reflecting
patriotism of a republic; ...they have stopped between
the two in the midst of confusion and distress.[2]

The Problem of Political Violence

Public Reactions to Violence

During the 1960's, the average American voter,
politician, and social scientist were startled and disturbed
by the unexpectedly widespread incidence of political demonstrations, protests, and riots in America's streets, college
campuses, and predominantly black urban centers. In a continuing series of studies on public opinion of fears and hopes
for the nation, public concern over national unity and political stability has increased substantially. "As a hope for
the nation, national unity jumped from only 1% in 1959 to

---

[1]Francisco Jose Moreno and Barbara Mitrani (eds.),
Conflict and Violence in Latin American Politics (New York:
Thomas Y. Crowell Co., 1971), 1st page of unpaginated preface.

[2]Alexis de Tocqueville, Democracy in America, trans.
Henry Reeve, ed. Phillips Bradley (New York: Vintage Books,
1945), Vol. I, pp. 251-252.

1

9% in 1964, and] [3] to 15% in 1971."[4] As a _fear_ for the
nation, only 8% mentioned disunity and political instability
in 1964,[5] compared to 26% in 1971.[6] Attempting to probe
further, in 1971 Cantril and Roll discovered that "unrest
in our country and ill feeling between groups was believed"
to be increasing to the extent that 62% of the American people
believed either that "a real breakdown in this country"
was likely, or they were uncertain that it might "blow
over soon."[7]

Number of Urban and Campus Incidents

From June 1963 to May 1968, over 450 civil rights and
anti-war demonstrations, involving nearly two million participants, resulted in nearly 20,000 arrests and 800 casualties.[8]
During the same period, there were 91 student protests,
demonstrations, and riots, involving over 100,000 participants.
These events resulted in nearly 2,000 arrests and
122 casualties.[9] An increasing percentage of schools--
6.1%, 10.8%, and 14.0%-- had student protests from 1967-68
to 1969-70. During the spring of 1970, there were protests
against the President's Cambodian incursion on 57% of the
nation's campuses, according to the Carnegie Commission on
Higher Education.[10] In the supposedly quiet fall of 1971,
the American Council of Education reported that at least
460 institutions of higher education had experienced at

---

[3]Lloyd A. Free and Hadley Cantril, The Political
Beliefs of Americans: A Study of Public Opinion (New York:
Clarion Books, Simon and Schuster, 1968), p.104.

[4]Albert H. Cantril and Charles W. Roll, Hopes and
Fears of the American People (New York: Universe Books,
1971), p. 24.

[5]Free and Cantril, p. 105.

[6]Cantril and Roll, p. 24.

[7]47% breakdown, 15% don't know, and 38% blow over
(Ibid., p. 68).

[8]Ted Robert Gurr, "A Comparative Study of Civil
Strife," History of Violence in America, ed. Ted Robert
Gurr and Hugh Davis Graham, A Report to the National
Commission on the Causes and Prevention of Violence (New
York: Bantam Books, 1969), p. 576.

[9]Ibid.

[10]Seymour Martin Lipset, Rebellion in the University
(Boston: Little, Brown and Co., 1971), p. 46.

least one serious protest resulting in personal injuries, property destruction, building occupations, and class disruptions. Over half of all campuses nationally were involved in peaceful protests. [11] In one study, over 56% of the nation's junior high schools reported some form of protest.[12]

Both the violence and the public reaction was even greater over rioting in America's predominantly black urban centers. From June 1963 to May 1968, there were 239 disturbances in the black urban centers. These disturbances involved probably 200,000 participants and resulted in nearly 50,000 arrests and over 8,000 casualties.[13]

Apparent Motivations and Purposes
of Violence

A Violence Commission staff report on the apparent motivations and purposes of the incidents, as compared with earlier violence in American history, illustrates the potential political significance of this contemporary violence. The Violence Commission has conducted a newspaper study of the magnitude of particular motivations and purposes of violence in America by thirty year periods.[14] The Commission divided motivations into six general categories of political violence: (1) personal action, (2) action against authority, (3) protest against foreign affairs, (4) action to change official leadership, (5) group antagonisms and

---

[11]"Were Campuses Really Quiet," Time, October 4, 1971.

[12]Marc Liberale and Tom Seligson (eds.), The High School Revolutionaries (New York: Random House, 1970), pp. xii-xiv.

[13]Gurr, "A Comparative Study...." Other figures about events where the political significance is unknown are: during 1971, over 1,000 bombings in California (California Attorney General, "Report on Bombings in California during 1971" [Reported on ABC, "News Scene," San Francisco, January 29, 1972, 6:30 P.M.]); from January to June, 1972, 607 bombings nationally, and 63 of federal installations ("Age of the Bomb," National Review, Vol. XXIV, No. 22 [June 9, 1972], p. 629).

[14]See James F. Kirkham, Sheldon G. Levy, and William J. Crotty, Assassination and Political Violence, A Staff Report to the National Commission on the Causes and Prevention of Violence (New York: Bantam Books, 1970), pp. 234-235. These figures were adjusted for changes in population and newspaper size according to number of pages. The adjusted figures range from an index figure of 0.0 to 235.4 per general category per period.

protests, and (6) reactions of official groups.[15] Generally
from 1819 to the present (1968), group antagonisms have
resulted in the highest number of injuries and deaths in
every thirty year period.

Yet the highest number of group incidents (235.4)
for any single period is for the present (1939-1968).[16]
Actions against authority in response to social conditions
have increased seven times (57.2 compared to 8.8) over the
previous period. Similarly, violence involving group
differences in social viewpoint have increased six times
(13.2 compared to 2.2) over the previous period. Racial
conflicts nearly quadrupled from from 37.4 to 116.6.[17] In
no other period as that of 1939-1968 has foreign affairs
protests been politically significant. All other periods
were assigned a magnitude of zero![18] Overall from 1939 to
1968, violence with personal political objectives also
increased eight times (35.2 compared to 4.4) over the
previous period.[19] Though group or class antagonism
dominate political violence, individual political interests
seem also to be increasingly salient in contemporary
motivations for political violence.

---

[15]The Violence Commission found it useful to subdivide these categories. The personal motivations include
economic gain, personal revenge, political disagreement,
and efforts to gain political advantage. The Action against
authority category involves political goals, social conditions, protests against police, and protest against local
officials. Group antagonism includes religious, labor,
racial, political, and social viewpoints and internal group
antagonisms. The reaction of official groups category
primarily involves police violence.

[16]Within the group antagonism category, racial conflicts have consistently been the most severe throughout
American history, except during two periods. During these
two periods, the labor category was most severe. Labor
antagonisms were slightly ahead (69.4 to 68.8) of race for
1879-1908 and nearly triple the racial category (103.4 to
37.4) for 1909-1938. Generally, racial antagonisms and
violence have been omnipresent and increasing. The highest
incidences of racial violence occurred during the following
two periods: 68.8 during the period of white Southern reta-
liation against blacks in the Reconstruction Era, 1879-1908,
and 116.5 for the current period, which includes vigorous
civil rights movements. All of the index figures come from
Kirkham, Levy, and Crotty, tables 3 and 4, pp.234-235.

[17]Ibid., p. 235.

[18]Ibid.

[19]Ibid.

In the protest against authority categories
(adjusted for population and newspaper size), three out of
four of the categories are higher for the present period
than for any other period in American history. The highest
subdivisions of the protests against authority category are:
actions directed toward a political goal (13.2), over social
conditions (57.2-- seven times earlier period), and over
police actions (15.4). The total for all these categories
of protest against authority was 123.2 versus 77.0, 18.4,
11.0, and 0.0 for other thirty year periods since 1819.

In summary, during the present period, 1939-1968,
ideological and class issues seem to have come into their
own. Kirkham comments on the data by saying, "Group antagonisms and action against authority have been an increasing
basis for politically violent events."[20]

> It would thus appear that personal motivations for poli-
> tically violent events have in general been replaced by
> more deep-seated controversies over the role of govern-
> ment.
> ....
> The general impression is that protests currently are
> more impersonal; that is, they involve protests against
> actions of authorities, group antagonisms, or, in the
> later period, foreign affairs protests.[21]

The above data are only a description of the changing motives
and purposes of political violence. A good part of the rest
of this study is an attempt to explain and understand these
data.

Violence and Political Science

The apparent increase in those kinds of violence
which seem so clearly political in their intention caught
most political scientists by surprise. Gurr summarizes the
preoccupation of political scientists from 1906 to 1968:

> Of 2828 articles that appeared in the American Political
> Science Review from its establishment in 1906 through
> 1968, only twenty-nine appear from their titles to be
> concerned with political disorder or violence. More-
> over, only twelve of the twenty-nine were concerned spe-
> cifically with revolution and fifteen appeared after 1961.
> ....
> By contrast ... about 250 deal with constitutions or

---

[20]Ibid., p. 237.

[21]Ibid., pp. 234, 236.

constitutional issues.[22]

Up until the current deluge of books and articles,[23] social scientists seem to have neglected and perhaps understood poorly the phenomena of political violence. How was this possible? In general, Americans preceived their politics with what now appears to be incredibly myopic vision. Social scientists presented a number of sanguine pictures of the stability, peacefulness, non-violence, and maturity of the American political system. For example, Almond said,

> Both [American and British] systems have been able to manage problems of change and the entry of new groups into politics without resort to violence. And though there have been and still are partisan conflicts, these have rarely led to a fragmentation of society into deeply ideological, closed and antagonistic political groups.[24]

The present deluge of black and student violence has rudely exploded this picture.

What can be the source of such visions? Tentatively there are probably three sources. First, there was the

---

[22]Ted Gurr, Why Men Rebel (Princeton, New Jersey: Princeton University Press, 1970), pp.7, 10.

[23]One bibliography includes over 1,200 items. This writer has consulted over 500. See Douglas Bwy, Social Conflict: A Keyword in Context Bibliography on the Literature of Developing Areas, With Supplementary References from Latin America (Evanston, Illinois: prepared in connection with research supported by the National Science Foundation and the Northwestern University Council for Intersocial Studies, 1966), cited by Gurr, Why..., p. 369. Note the emphasis on "developing" areas and not the United States. On student protests and violence, see Philip G. Altbach, Students, Politics, and Higher Education: A Select Bibliography (Cambridge, Massachusetts: Harvard University Center for International Affairs, 1967).

[24]Gabriel A. Almond and Sidney Verba, The Civic Culture: Political Attitudes and Democracy in Five Nations (Boston: Little, Brown and Co., 1965), p 232. See also Seymour Martin Lipset, Political Man (Garden City: Doubleday and Co., Inc., 1963), pp. 82-83; Nathan Glazer, The Social Basis of American Communism (New York: Harcourt, Brace and World, Inc., 1961), p. 191; and Martin Diamond, "Socialism and the Decline of the American Socialist Party" (unpublished Ph.D. dissertation, Political Science Dept., University of Chicago, 1956), cited by Glazer, p. 191.

assumption of American consensus on important values and myths of authority. Political scientists were often unable to explain political violence, because their understanding of American politics was based on models of peaceful conflict resolution through compromise. Underlying those assumptions of peace was probably a major set of premises that there was a value consensus and/or that there was a single political community or a fairly homogeneous set of interests within the nation.

Second, most American, as opposed to European, political scientists did not take value conflicts very seriously. As just indicated, this lack of concern over value conflicts was due perhaps to the belief that all the "great questions" seemed to have been settled, at least among the ruling elite.[25] Thus, no one paid serious attention to black cries of injustices and student demands for greater political power. This inattention to radical black and student criticism of American society, which should have given prior warning of discontent, left white America and the academic community relatively unprepared for the widespread urban riots and student activism of the late 1960's. Thus, most Americans were not prepared for the current deluge of violence, despite considerable American experience with political violence, such as the American Revolution, the Civil War, vigilantism, nativism, lynching, and labor unrest. Although ideologies sometimes represent only self-serving rhetoric and mere rationalizations, such rhetoric and rationalizations are used precisely because they mobilize political forces for thought and action.

A third possible explanation for American unpreparedness for the present political violence is the difficulty in dealing empirically with values. A few "behavioralists" solved the problem by separating measurable facts from values--throwing the "metaphysical" apples into the barrel for disposal. "Good riddance to bad rubbish." Perhaps we now know what happened to those apples.

Recent discussions of political violence have been more extensive. A number of characteristically descriptive and assertive one-liners on the ubiquity of violence, the race problem, and our idealistic children relfect a new interest in, if not always an understanding of political violence. During the late sixties and early seventies, the

---

[25]See Herbert McClosky, "Consensus and Ideology in American Politics," _American Political Science Review_,Vol. LXIII (June, 1964), pp. 361-382; and H. McClosky, P. Hoffman, and R. O'Hara, "Issue Conflict and Consensus Among Party Leaders and Followers," _American Political Science Review,_ Vol. LIX (1960), pp. 406-427.

pendulum has swung to such characteristic statements as:[26]

> Force and violence are not isolated phenomena to be
> examined as something extraordinary in the life of a
> political community. Their omnipresence suggests a
> vital connection with the contemporary political
> process.

> The race problem in the American South does constitute
> one basic challenge to the legitimacy of the system,
> and at one time did cause a breakdown of the national
> order.

> Violence has always been part of the political process.
> Politics does not merely encompass the actions of legis-
> lative assemblies, political parties, electoral contests
> and other formal trappings of a modern government.

> The thoroughgoing idealistic liberalism of the student
> generation of the 1960's was the ideological beginning
> point of the student movement and of campus unrest as
> they exist today.

Problems of Scope and Method

Despite this new interest in political violence, the
study of political violence involves serious problems of
scope and method which are not easy to resolve. The study
of political violence is broad in scope and thus raises a
number of topics of considerable interest to students of
the social sciences, as well as political science,[27] whatever
their methodological or ideological commitments. Many of

---

[26]The sources are not provided in order to protect
the guilty and not to single out a few for criticism,
especially since some of their work is valuable for understanding parts of the puzzle.

[27]Similarly, this study overlaps with, but may be
distinguished from such broad fields of study as: collective
behavior (see especially Neil J. Smelser, Theory of Collective
Behavior [New York: Free Press, 1963]) and social
movements (see Allan D. Grimshaw, Racial Violence in the
United States [Chicago: Aldine Publishing Co., 1969]: and
Joseph R. Gusfield ed. , Protest, Reforms, and Revolt: A
Reader in Social Movements [New York: John Wiley and Sons,
Inc., 1970]); political socialization (see especially Fred
I. Greenstein, Children and Politics [2nd ed. rev.; New
Haven: Yale University Press, 1969]; and David Easton and
Jack Dennis, Children in the Political System: The Origins
of Political Legitimacy [New York: McGraw-Hill Book Co.,

these topics are extremely difficult to study. One of the
most difficult topics to study is the role of values in
myths of legitimacy. An analysis of values involved in
democratic legitimacy is especially problematic. For
example, in one particular society or political culture,
the United States of America, it is a common place that
equality and liberty are the highest ideals. Few would
disagree on such principles in the abstract, but when one
begins to refine, apply, and operationalize such abstractions
to concrete situations, the agreement on the meaning of
equality and liberty breaks down. Perhaps because of these
difficulties, penetrating empirical studies of the legitimating values of democracy have been limited.

This study will necessarily involve a great deal of
oversimplification of a complex set of interlocking variables and perhaps even intractable questions. Yet oversimplification is involved in all efforts to understand
political phenomena, whatever the methods used--classifi-
cation, generalization, modeling, gaming, simulation, etc.
Most such efforts result in at least some error or partial
failure, but refutation often advances knowledge far more
than the confirmation of hypotheses incapable of refutation.
Having recognized such difficulties and having stated a few
caveats, it is necessary now to plunge into some interesting
hypotheses.

Hypotheses

The following is a list of some of the major
hypotheses of this study. Chapters I-IV provide further
elaborations of these hypotheses. Chapters V-VII are
partial tests of these hypotheses.

One, commonly held opinions and ideas have an
important impact on political behavior. In particular,
ideologically based opinions may lead to political
conflict, some of it violent.

1969]); political socioloty (see expecially Lipset, Political Man); political culture (see Almond and Verba); political integration (Karl W. Deutsch et al., "Political Community and the North Atlantic Area," International Political
Communities [Garden City: Doubleday and Co., Inc., 1966],
pp. 1-91; and Philip E. Jacob and James V. Tasgano, The
Integration of Political Communities [New York: J. P.
Lippincott, Co., 1964]); social class (see Edward C. Banfield, The Unheavenly City: The Nature and Future of Our
Urban Crisis [Boston: Little, Brown and Co., 1968]); and
ideology (see Karl Mannheim, Ideology and Utopia, trans.
Luis Werth and Edward Shils [New York: Harcourt, Brace, and
World, Inc., 1936]).

Two, competing ideas on the proper or just scope
and content of politics may lead to violence. Political
violence is most likely to result from the competition of
ideological partisans over conflicting political goals,
which seem to the participants incapable of peaceful
resolution. Edmund Burke called such competitions
"Great Party conflicts." Harvey Mansfield, Harry Jaffa,
and many others have argued that a political party which
may constitute a legitimate and loyal opposition is
possible only where all major parties agree on the fundamental values of the existing regime. As any human community must be based on some value consensus, many studies
of the American polity have tended to emphasize patterns
of value consensus rather than value conflict. Yet consensus and conflict, integration and disintegration,
stability and change, violence and non-violence may be
integrally related to interacting relations and foundations
of political life which may be understood through a
penetrating analysis of value differences rather than
assuming value consensus.

Three, an explanation of violent political conflict, as opposed to both other political disagreements
or other forms of violence, may lie in large measure in
disagreements over commonly presumed sources of value
consensus and political community. Recognizable social
and economic conditions are most often involved in conflict, because people interpret conditions in the ideological terms of justice and injustice. In America, political justice tends to be defined in terms of democracy.
Democracy is the legitimating ideology of the American
regime. It is the standard of political justice to which
both regime proponents and opponents appeal in American
politics. Yet there may no longer be, if there ever was,
any consensus on the scope or application of democratic
principles.

Four, a key to the understanding of the recent
political violence lies in an appreciation of the great
variety and changing character of American opinions on
political justice, particularly the concepts of equality
and liberty.

Five, an expansion of regime responsibility in the
areas of equality may increase the possibility that
citizens believe the regime itself to be the major source
of injustices in the society.

Six, if citizens believe the regime is responsible
for social injustice, they may also believe that the regime
is illegitimate or no longer worthy of citizens' obedience.

Seven, if various political subcultures have views
of legitimacy which differ greatly from those of the larger
political culture, there may be conflict between the subculture and the larger political culture. This dissertation
hypothesizes and tests provisionally some relationships

between various subcultural values of democratic legitimacy
and black and student violent political behavior of the
1960's and 1970's in America.[28] That is, this dissertation
will test the relationship between various theories of
American democratic legitimacy and violence in America.
The argument presented is that the great variety of meanings
and applications given to American ideals-- such as liberty,
equality, pursuit of happiness, and consent of the governed--
may be not only a source of forensic debate and social conflict, but also a key to understanding some factors which
may contribute to violent political conflict. The current
conflict may be between people who comprehend or define
liberty and equality in different ways.

Two national commissions have made some indication
of the possible existence of these subcultural differences.
The National Advisory Commission on Civil Disorders
reported, "Our nation is moving toward two societies, one
black, one white-- separate and unequal."[29] On campus
unrest, the Scranton Commission reported,

> This shared distinct experience among the young led to
> shared interests and problems which led in turn to the
> development of distinct subcultures. ...The emergence
> of these issues was caused by a change in opinions,
> perceptions, and values-- that is by a change in the
> culture of students.[30]

Others have also noticed subcultural value systems.
Tomlinson has said,

> What produces riots is that most Negro Americans share
> a belief that their lot in life is unacceptable, and a

---

[28]This dissertation also has much in common with
Edmund N. Muller's "A Test of a Partial Theory of Potential
for Political Violence" (State University of New York at
Stony Brook, n.d.). (Mimeographed.) This author arrived at
his formulation quite independently and has some criticisms
to make of Muller's instrument. Muller collected his data
between March and May, 1970.

[29]National Advisory Commission on Civil Disorders,
Report of the National Advisory Commission on Civil Disorders, prepared by a commission directed by Otto Kerner
(New York: Bantam Books, Inc., 1968), p. 1. Cited hereafter as Kerner Commission.

[30]President's Commission on Campus Unrest, Campus
Unrest, prepared by a commission directed by William W.
Scranton (Washington, D. C.: U. S. Government Printing
Office, 1970), p. 61. Cited hereafter as the Scranton
Commission.

significant minority feel that riots are a legitimate and productive mode of protest. The unifying feature is the consensus that Negroes have been misused by whites.[31]

Finally, Aberbach and Walker say,

> We discovered clear indications that a coherent belief system dealing with racial matters has developed in Detroit's black community. This belief system seems well organized and serves as a guide for most of our respondents for formulating their answers to our questions about racial problems.[32]

Eight, those individuals who believe their conditions of life are unjust and wrong by some standard are more likely to believe the regime is illegitimate and to use violence against it than those who accept their conditions of life as normal.

Nine, the intensity of political conflict and violence varies inversely with the intensity of belief in regime legitimacy. High levels of regime support mean low levels of political violence. Declining levels of regime support result in increasing levels of political violence. The degree of changes desired for the regime varies directly with the degree of belief in the regime's illegitimacy. Thus, those seeking reforms have higher levels of support for the regime than those seeking revolution or destruction of the regime. The intensity of political participation also varies directly with the intensity of beliefs. Finally, the intensity of the tactics of political violence varies directly with the intensity of beliefs.

Since these hypotheses are broad in scope, a complete test is not possible here. In Chapter V-VII, an analysis of elite and mass opinions provides a tentative test. A survey of the writings of radical elites quite obviously reveals some of their opinions on regime legitimacy. An analysis of a large number of public opinion surveys of national, black, and student populations helps reveal mass subcultural opinions. Before it is possible

---

[31]T. M. Tomlinson, "Ideological Foundations for Negro Action: Militant and Non-Militant Views," _The Los Angeles Riots: A Socio-Psychological Study_, ed. Nathan E. Cohen (New York: Praeger, 1970), p. 375.

[32]Joel D. Aberbach and Jack L. Walker, "The Meanings of Black Power: A Comparison of White and Black Interpretations of a Political Slogan," _American Political Science Review_, Vol. LXIV, No. 2 (June, 1970), p. 380.

to develop and test these hypotheses, however, it is
necessary to deal with some of the key concepts of political violence.

Definitions and Issues:
Politics, Violence, and
Political Violence

Characteristics of Politics

Politics is not an easily specifiable phenomena, nor
does it have a commonly agreed unity of analysis, such as a
cell or an atom. Rather it is a diverse set of phenomena
which has some broad characteristics and objects of analysis.

Politics as power
According to Weber, "the State is an association
that claims the monopoly of the legitimate use of force, and
cannot be defined in any other manner.[33] Similarly, for
Dahl, politics is found in any relationship "involving to a
significant extent relationships of power, rule, and
authority."[34] Thus, most politics seems to involve human
relations or processes of dominance and submission with the
state or government occupying a central position. Such political realists as Hobbes, Machievelli, and Aristotle
have long recognized that power is the lowest common deno-
minator of politics. This power perspective of politics
emphasizes the coercive, forceful, or violent aspects of
politics.[35] Political scientists as diverse in their

---

[33]Max Weber, cited by Sebastian de Grazia, The Political Community (Chicago: University of Chicago Press,
1948), p. 84.

[34]Robert A. Dahl, Modern Political Analysis (Englewood
Cliffs, New Jersey: Prentice-Hall, Inc., 1963), passim.

[35]For an analysis of wealth and power advantages of
the large commercial republic created by the Constitution of
the United States, see Alexander Hamilton, James Madison,
and John Jay, The Federalist Papers, intro. Clinton Rossiter
(New York: New American Library, 1961). For other power
perspectives, see: Harold D. Lasswell and Daniel Lerner,
World Revolutionary Elites: Studies in Coercive Iedological
Movements (Cambridge: M.I.T. Press, 1965), p.8; Hans J.
Morgenthau, Politics Among Nations: The Struggle for Power
and Peace (New York: Alfred A. Knopf, 1949); and David
Easton, A Systems Analysis of Political Life (New York:
John Wiley and Sons, Inc., 1965).

scholarly interests and methods as Dahl, Lasswell, Morgenthau, and Easton have also tended to place their primary
emphasis on power with some lesser attention given to
another concern of some students of politics-- morality.

Politics as pursuit of morality
          Aristotle saw politics, at least in the polis, as
the purposive seeking of the good life. Similarly, Strauss
says, "All political action has...in itself a directedness
toward knowledge of the good life, or of the good society."[36]
Machiavelli and Hobbes, however, claim this moralistic
perspective obscures the violent side of politics. Yet
even the power perspective also raises the question--
power for what?

Politics as characterized by both power and morality
          Others have occupied a middle or integrating and
synthesizing position on power and morality in politics.
MacIver, among many others,[37] argues that governmental
authority must be distinguished from political power.
According to MacIver, authority is based on the widespread
belief in myths, justifying the dominance or rule of an
elite and the submission or obedience of the mass. Such
moral supports for government reduce the amount of power

---

[36]Leo Strauss, What is Political Philosophy (Glencoe,
Illinois: The Free Press, 1959), p. 10. Jefferson tended
to emphasize the moral virtues and ideals of democracy.
Similarly, Spiro sees power conflicts arising primarily out
of the differing views of the good life for a human commu-
nity (see Herbert J. Spiro, "Politics as a Master Science,"
The Political Experience: Readings in Political Science,
ed. Michael A. Weinstein [New York: St. Martin's Press,
1972], pp. 84-88). See also Michael A. Weinstein (ed.),
The Political Experience: Readings in Political Science
(New York: St. Martin's Press, 1972); H. L. Nieburg,
Political Violence: The Behavioral Process (New York: St.
Martins's Press, 1969); Theodore J. Lowi, The End of
Liberalism (New York: W. W. Norton and Co., Inc., 1969);
and Hamilton, Madison, and Jay, The Federalist....

[37]See E. E. Schattschneider, Two Hundred Million
Americans in Search of a Government (New York: Holt, Rine-
hart, and Winston, Inc., 1969); Walter Buckley Sociology
and Modern Systems Theory (Englewood Cliffs, New Jersey:
Prentice-Hall, Inc., 1967); and Easton, A Systems
Analysis..., pp. 281-282.

required to rule.[38] E. H. Carr points out that politics
involves a curious blending of such seeming opposites as
self-assertion and self-subordination, egotism and
sociability, emnity and good will, conflict and consensus,
coercion and ethics, reality and utopia, real and ideal.[39]
Similarly, Duverger calls politics Janus-faced-- it involves
the interplay of such opposites as integration and conflict,
and thought and action.[40] Schattschneider has made an
eloquent analogy on the softness and harshness of government which helps in understanding the complex nature of
politics:

> From the outside it looks like a security system
> based on a marriage of land and people. From the
> inside it looks like an attempt to create a community.
> Government is like an oyster, hard on the outside and
> soft on the inside. The outside and inside are
> utterly dependent on each other.
> ....
> Thus every government...is torn between the contra-
> dictory demands of the good life and survival.[41]

Every society involves "some degree of desire for cooperation and mutual good will."[42] Thus, as Weinstein says,
politics "involves dialogue and power as well as cooperation

---

[38]Robert M. MacIver, The Web of Government (New
York: The Free Press, 1965), p 87.

[39]E. H. Carr, "Nature of Politics," Readings in
World Politics, ed. Robert Goldwin, revised by Tony Pearce
(2d. ed.; New York: Oxford University Press, 1970), pp
455-460.

[40]Maurice Duverger, "The Two Faces of Janos," The
Political Experience: Readings in Political Science, ed.
Michael A. Weinstein (New York: St. Martin's Press, 1972),
pp. 111-118.

[41]Schattschneider, pp. 24, 28. To prove his point
emphatically, Schattschneider calculates that in the United
States, for example, students outnumber prisoners 200 to 1,
and military forces outnumber police forces by 10 to 1.
See p. 21.

[42]Ibid. See also Robert E. Osgood, Ideals and Self
Interest in America's Foreign Relations (Chicago: University of Chicago Press, 1953).

and conflict."[43] This dissertation takes this synthesizing position and attempts to show the dynamic interaction of such seeming opposites in politics.

Specifically, one cannot separate the cry for black power from the desire for equality. Similarly, one cannot separate student violence in pursuit of a higher morality from a student's desire for power in the regime.[44] Thus, power and morality are inextricably bound together in violent politics.[45] Indeed, the major hypothesis of the dissertation is that perceptions of the morality (legitimacy) of one's goals are closely related to one's willingness to use violence in efforts to achieve the goal, particularly if one perceives violence to be the only effective means to the goal.

This dissertatation will stress such broad characteristics of politics as conflict[46] and ideology. (Of course, one must recognize that most of politics is rather dull and mundane-- involving peaceful cooperation and bureaucratic routinization of conflict.) This dissertation uses a broad definition of politics, much of which is borrowed from the key phrases and concepts of others. Thus, for this paper, politics is individual or collective, authoritative or nonauthoritative efforts, acts, or discussions seeking preservation or change of existing social or economic or governmental relationships of power, authority, influence, or values for the whole or a major part of the society. Such a broad

---

[43]Weinstein, p. 83. Weinstein defines politics as the active reflection "on the human condition or the process of proposing, deciding, executing and evaluating plans for the future public situation."

[44]"The cry for black power and student power, ... and the cry for participation and decentralization constitute political rhetoric because the problems are basically political." (Lowi, p. xiv.)

[45]For persuasive arguments on the connection of moral pursuits and violence, see Edmund Stillman and William Pfoff, The Politics of Hysteria: The Sources of Twentieth Century Conflict (New York: Harper and Row, Pubs., 1964); and Norman Cohn, The Pursuit of the Millennium: Revolutionary Millenarians and Mystical Anarchists of the Middle Ages (New York: Oxford University Press, 1970).

[46]The great attention given to conflict in politics makes sense once one realizes that over half of the 665 "anti words" in the Random House Dictionary are common to a political vocabulary. For this bit of information, see Schattschneider, p. 112.

view of politics seems to encompass many kinds of cooperation or conflict, including socio-economic,
ethnic, or religious spheres as long as they have
community-wide, regime, or political cultural implications. Before undertaking a discussion of political
violence, however, it is necessary to attempt to
define violence.

On the Meaning of Violence

Violence ... is committed by isolated individuals,
by small groups, and by large mobs; it is directed
against individuals and crowds alike; it is under-
taken for a variety of purposes (and at times for
no discernible rational[47] purpose at all), and
in a variety of ways ranging from assassinations
and murders to lynchings, duels, brawls, feuds
and riots; it stems from criminal intent and
from political idealism, from antagonisms that
are entirely personal and from antagonisms of

---

[47]An argument for the "rationality" of political
violence on a variety of grounds took up twenty pages in
an earlier draft. On various criteria of rationality,
see Robert Dahl and Edward Lindbloom, Politics, Economics,
and Welfare (New York: Harper and Row, 1953); Herbert
A. Simon, Administrative Behavior (2d ed.; New York:
MacMillan Co., 1961); Anthony Downs, Inside Bureaucracy
(Boston: Little, Brown and Co., 1966); William C.
Mitchell, Public Choice in America: An Introduction to
American Government (Chicago: Markham Publishing Company,
1971); and Charles E. Lindbloom, The Policy-Making
Process (Englewood Cliffs, New Jersey: Prentice Hall,
Inc., 1968). On various aspects of the rationality of
American citizens, see George S. Blair, "Cumulative
Voting: Patterns of Party Allegiance and Rational Choice
in Illinois State Legislative Contests," American Political
Science Review, Vol. LII (March, 1958), pp. 123-130;
Angus Campbell et al., The American Voter (New York:
John Wiley and Sons, Inc., 1960); V. O. Key, with
the assistance of Milton C. Cummings, Jr., The Responsible
Electorate (New York: Vintage Books, 1968); Richard
M. Merelman, "The Development of Policy Thinking in
Adolescence," American Political Science Review, Vol.
LXV, No. 4 (December, 1971), pp. 1033-1047; Almond and
Verba, Civic Culture...; David E. Repass, "Issue Salience
and Party Choice, " American Political Science Review, Vol.
LXV, No. 2 (June, 1971), pp. 389-400; and William R.
Caspary, "The 'Mood Theory': A Study of Public Opinion
and Foreign Policy," American Political Science Review,
Vol. LXIV (1970), pp. 536-548.

large social consequence. Hence, it has been hard to conceive of violence as a subject at all.[48]

Taken as the harm or death of individuals or the destruction of property, violence is simply a description of a form of behavior, action, or process. Yet it is more than a little interesting because of its impact, effects, and consequences for the life, liberty, property, and happiness of individuals, groups, and the regime. Thus, both the immediate results and political ends of violence lead to its study.

Violation

It might be useful to begin with a good dictionary. Webster's New World Dictionary defines violence as "physical force used so as to injure or damage."[49] Yet when used as a transitive verb, "to do violence to," it is related to the verb "to violate." This is apparently the understanding of some blacks when they call America a violent society:

One of my respondents referred to the problem as being one not of violence, but of "violation." Violence, he said, must be looked at in terms of the violation of the dignity of human beings.[50]

Lincoln also used violence in such broad and humanistic terms, when referring to the effects of both the Kansas Nebraska Act and the Dred Scott Decision on the institution

---

[48]Richard Hofstadter, "Reflections on Violence in the United States," American Violence, ed. Richard Hofstadter and Michael Wallace (New York: Random House, 1971), pp. 3-43.

[49]Webster's New World Dictionary of the American Language (college ed.; New York: World Publishing Co., 1964), p. 1628.

[50]Rodney F. Allen and Charles H. Adair (eds.), Violence and Riots in Urban America (Worthinton, Ohio: Charles A. Jones Publishing Co., 1969), p. 89. See also James S. Campbell, Joseph R. Sahid, and David P. Stang, Law and Order Reconsidered, A Staff Report to the National Commission on the Causes and Prevention of Violence (New York: Bantam Books, 1970), p. 89.

of slavery.[51] Similarly, Madison used the term violence
broadly as a violation of republican standards of political
justice in his Federalist No. 10 discussion of the "violence
of faction." It is not particular forms of behavior torn
out of context which are violent, but rather the subjective
meanings the participants give to such events. One's subjective sense of violation often depends, of course, on the
political interests or ends one seeks to have served,
whether "law and order" or "social change."[52]

It is such a self-interested view which makes a
search for a criteria of distinction between force and
violence so fruitless. Distinctions between force and
violence are difficult or impossible to make, because
political partisans usually define their opponent as
violent, while their own acts are force. Almost everyone
claims his acts are rightful and legitimate means for
seeking the good life, self-defense, or the destruction
of some evil. Yet nearly every writer, whether a social
scientist or a rebel, attempts to make some distinction
between violence and force.[53]

---

[51]"I plainly see you and I would differ about the
Nebraska law. I look upon that enactment not as a law , but
as violence from the beginning. ...I say it was conceived
in violence, because the destruction of the Missouri Compromise, under the circumstances, was nothing less than
violence. It was passed in violence, because it could not
have passed at all but for the votes of many members, in
violent disregard of the known will of their constituents.
It is maintained in violence, because the elections since,
clearly demand its repeal, and this demand is openly dis-
regarded." (Abraham Lincoln, "A Farewell to Whiggery:
Letter to Joshua F. Speed, August 24, 1855," Abraham
Lincoln: A Documentary Portrait Through His Speeches and
Writings, ed. Don E. Fehrenbacher [New York: The New
American Library, 1964], p. 82.) (Italics mine.)

[52]For a contextural and self-interested view held
by Americans of all political persuasions, as indicated by
a national survey, see "Redefining Violence," Time, June 4,
1971, p. 49.

[53]Several grounds for such a distinction are: (1)
degree of harm or destruction, (2) legality of the act,
(3) identity and skill of the prepetrator, and (4) the purposes and justice of the acts. A discussion of the many
possible distinctions made between force and violence
encompassed over thirty pages in an earlier draft. Many
have made this distinction. For rationality as a criteria,
see Vilfredo Pareto, Sociological Writings, ed. Samuel E.
Finer (New York: Praeger, Publishers, Inc., 1966), p. 135.
For success as the Criteria, see Harold I. Lief, "Contempo-

Political motivations or
purposes
        One closely related criterion, which goes some-
what beyond the usual ad hominum distinctions between
force and violence, is that which relies on judgments
of the expressed and inferred motivations or purposes of
the actors. Lief says those distinctions between different
forms of violence based on its purposes and intentions are
not worthwhile, because all forms of violence, aggression,
and force are motivationally the same. This universal
motivation is "the wish to injure, remove or destroy a
threatening object" usually because of rage. Such acts
vary only in degree, a degree which ranges "from kicking
the cat or slamming the door to nuclear war."[54]
        It is likely, however, that in most cases, parti-
cularly political ones, blind rage does not adequately
describe violence. For example, most revolutions are not
founded on blind rage; rather, revolutions are conflicts
over some notion of valued political ends, principles,
or norms.[55] Violence is used as a tool to achieve some

---

rary Forms of Violence," Violence in the Streets, ed.
Shalom Endleman (Chicago: Quadrangle Books, 1968), pp. 49-
51. For degree of harm or destruction as a criteria, see
Hofstadter, "Reflections on Violence," p. 9. For legality
or social conventions as a criteria, see Eugene Victor
Walter, Terror and Resistance: A Study of Political Violence
With Case Studies of Some Primitive African Communities
(New York: Oxford University Press, 1969), p. 23; Andrew
C. Janos, "Authority and Violence: The Political Framework
of Internal War," Internal War: Problems and Approaches,
ed. Harry Eckstein (New York: The Free Press, 1964), pp.
130-141; and Talcott Parsons, "Some Reflections on the
Place of Force on Social Process," Internal War: Problems
and Approaches, ed. Harry Eckstein (New York: The Free
Press, 1964), pp. 38-40.

        [54]Lief, pp. 50-51.

        [55]Carl Leiden and Karl M. Schmitt, The Politics of
Violence: Revolution in the Modern World (Englewood Cliffs,
New Jersey: Prentice-Hall, Inc., 1968), pp. 8-10. Revolution
is "change in social attitudes and values basic to traditional institutional order." (Dale Yoder, "Current Definitions of Revolution," American Journal of Sociology, Vol.
XXXII [November, 1926], p. 441, cited by Leiden and Schmitt,
p. 8). (Italics mine.) In revolution, "basic institutional
values of a social order are rejected and new values
accepted." (Rex O. Hopper, "The Revolutionary Process: A
Frame of Reference for the Study of Revolutionary Movements,"
Social Forces, Vol. XXVII [1950] , p. 271, cited by Leiden
and Schmitt, p. 8.) (Italics mine.) Revolution involves a

perceivable political effect, consequence, goal, or purpose.
Indeed, the fact that the persons, groups, or institutions
attacked or threatened may attempt to block certain acts
indicates that there is at least a moderate understanding
of the effects or ends sought.

Justice and violation

The discussion has come full circle to the statement
of the black man who claimed he was violated every day by
the American regime. What can our ghetto resident mean when
he says he has been violated? His statement deserves
serious attention. He is more than likely to be implicitly
referring to racism, discrimination, poverty, etc. He is
probably expressing his subjective feeling that such conditions of his life are unfair, perhaps even unjust. The
grounds for believing that these things are unjust in the
context of the American political culture (perhaps even
most of the modern world) is quite probably something
approaching the concept of equality. He does not have to
quote the American Declaration of Independence verbatim
for us to infer that equality may be the partial meaning
of statements about his manhood and his interpersonal relations of inferiority with "whitey" or "honkies." Whatever
his standard of justice, he finds his own destructive or
harmful acts legitimately forceful and the acts of the
regime illegitimately violent. Similarly, regime authorities
view such acts as violations of rightful constitutional
authority.

Political Violence

Having given some attention to the concepts of
politics and violence, it is now necessary to deal with
the problem of determining what violence is most political in its nature and its objects. This is a study of
political violence. Not all violence is political, nor
is violence the only means of seeking political ends.
Thus, this study is concerned with the targets of political violence, that violence which may have political ends

---

"fundamental change in the nature of the state, the functions of government, the principles of economic production
and distribution, the relationships of the social classes,
particularly as regards the control of government..."
(William S. Stokes, "The 'Cuban Revolution' and the Presidential Elections of 1948," The Hispanic American Historical Review, February, 1951 , p. 37.) (Italics mine.)
Revolution involves "changing the very system of social
norms," or acts "intending or acquiring a purposive political effect" for a great variety of motives, intentions,
purposes, and values. (Nieburg, Political Violence...,
pp. 14, 136.) (Italics mine.)

or consequencws, and those kinds of political disputes
which are most likely to lead to the use of violence.

As stated above, until recently few American
political scientists have paid any extensive attention to
American political violence, probably because of the dominance in the discipline of an orthodox faith in the validity
of the pluralistic-consensus or conflict resolving model of
peaceful and moderate democratic politics. Interest has
recently heightened in seeking useful terminology to describe or define the subject matter of political violence.
Among the new terms developed to define political violence
is internal war.

Internal War: the targets and objectives of political violence

Eckstein defines internal war as "an attempt to
change by violence or threat of violence, a government's
policies, rules or organization."[56] Janos has defined
internal war perhaps more broadly and usefully as "a violent conflict between parties subject to a common authority
and of such dimensions that its incidence will affect the
exercise or structure of authority in society."[57]
According to Janos, this definition includes small riots
as well as civil war.[58] Unfortunately, Janos neglects
those conflicts, such as ghetto riots, which do not clearly
involve distinct parties, political organizations or
identifiable antagonists. Although ghetto riots in recent
years are not fights between racial groups,[59] one can
easily interpret these riots as attacks expressing, at a
very minimum, conflict with symbols of the white establishment, such as its officials (the police) and its economic

---

[56]Harry Eckstein (ed.), Internal War: Problems and
Approaches (New York: The Free Press, 1964), p. 1; also
Harry Eckstein, "On the Etiology of Internal Wars," History
and Theory, Vol. IV, No. 2 (1965), pp. 135-136.

[57]Janos, "Authority and Violence," p. 130.

[58]Yet it is unlikely that the Boston Tea Party would
be adequately interpreted as a politically significant event
based simply on the magnitude or dimensions of the event: a
minor seaport in an economically underdeveloped part of the
world in the eighteenth century.

[59]On this difference in most riots in the 1960's, see
Allen D. Grimshaw, "Lawlessness and Violence in America and
Their Special Manifestations in Changing Negro-White Rela-
tionships," Racial Violence in the United States, ed. Allen
D. Grimshaw (Chicago: Aldine Publishing Co., 1969), pp. 13-
28.

order (the merchants). Black riots are also extremely
political in their reminders that the blacks have always
represented the most recurring and unresolved problem of
American democracy.[60] Despite this omission by Janos,
internal war is a helpful category in that it draws attention to such traditionally recognized political phenomena
as governmental authority, policies, rules and nongovernmental organizations and groups. Such studies of internal
war broke the ground for empiricists in the field of political violence.

Ted Gurr's articles and his volume Why Men Rebel
are the monumental works on political violence for the
decade of the 1960's.[61] Gurr defines political violence
as "all collective attacks within a political community
against the political regime, its actors-- including
competing political groups, as well as incumbents-- or
its policies." According to Gurr, political violence
threatens the political system by challenging the monopoly
of force and disrupting the normal political processes.[62]
Gurr's discussion clearly implies that almost all violent
disputes, whatever their motivations, purposes, or effects,
become political, because all violence challenges the civil
authority to keep order by using force. Gurr distinguishes
internal wars from turmoil by saying that internal wars
are "designed to overthrow the regime or dissolve the
state."[63]

---

[60]This omnipresent American problem is readily
illustrated in the ambiguity of the Constitution over black
equality, the issue of black slavery in the Civil War (Harry
Jaffa, Crisis of the House Divided: An Interpretation of
the Issues in the Lincoln-Douglas Debates [Garden City:
Doubleday and Co., Inc., 1959]), the radical solution of
the Reconstruction, and the Jim Crow reaction of segregation and disenfranchisement. On the relatively late
development (about 1900) of the Southern racist policy of
Negro exclusion from Southern life-- economically, socially,
as well as politically, see Van C. Woodward, The Strange
Career of Jim Crow (New York: Oxford University Press,
1965).

[61]Gurr's Why Men Rebel was winner of the Woodrow
Wilson Award for the outstanding book in Political Science
for 1970.

[62]Gurr, Why..., p. 4.

[63]Ibid., p. 11.

Objects of political violence

Gurr s writings point out one of the most important aspects to consider when discussing political violence: political violence is directed against something-- usually the state, government, or the regime. Some part or the whole of the regime or political culture is the bone of contention between many moralistic protagonists in American violence. Thus, when considering American political violence, one must center attention on the American regime or political culture. A problem arises as to what is the American regime?

Definition of regime

The regime or political culture includes the overall organization of the institutions of a social order, such as: governmental institutions, structures, and goals; economic production and distribution; and structure and relations of social classes. Underlying the organizational structure of the regime are those myths or values, norms, and rules which justify particular modes of social, economic, or political organization. In short, the regime is the "American way of life," inasmuch as it impinges on governmental authority, political power, governmental operations, and political, social, and economic goals.

The American regime is not, however, a stationary or static phenomenon. Schattschneider has argued that political processes are inherently expansive:

> Political conflict is not like a football game, played on a measured field by a fixed number of players in the presence of an audience scrupulously excluded from the playing field. Politics is much more like the original primitive game of football in which everybody was free to join, a game in which the whole population of one town might play the entire population of another town moving freely back and forth across the countryside.
>
> Many conflicts are narrowly confined by a variety of devices, but the distinctive quality of political conflicts is that the relations between the players and the audience have not been well defined and there is usually nothing to keep the audience from getting into the game.[64]

Recently the American regime has undergone changes which may have increased the saliency of politics among most Americans, but especially among the black and student subcultures. Thus this dissertation will use a broad difinition of politics and

---

[64]E.E. Schattschneider, "The Socialization of Conflict," Introductory Readings in American Government, ed. William C. Mitchell and Robert S. Ross (Chicago: Markham Publishing Co., 1971), p. 137.

regime because of the expansive nature of American political processes and the purposes of the regime.

Regime as target of
political violence

How and why does the regime become the target of political violence? When the meaning of politics expands to include increasingly enlarged aspects of social and economic spheres, government becomes more and more responsible for rectifying the injustices of life in general.

> As long as political leaders see their own power, as well as the very legitimacy of the government itself, as resting upon ability to respond quickly to all hard-pressed demands, there will be pressure toward expansion of government every time society requires adjustment.[65]

This expansion in the meaning of politics also results in more and more disputes becoming based on political objectives or purposes, although these objectives may have been considered previously to be part of private social or economic spheres of life. When government is involved in attempting to alleviate all forms of social and economic inequalities, very little remains which is not involved in political conflict.

Thus, the regime becomes an object of political violence, because it is deemed to be responsible for rectifying or even causing the injustices of life. The recent expansion of the meaning of politics means that government is involved in more areas of life, thus increasing government's responsibilities for injustices. Thus, political violence occurs when a person or group perceives that government has violated them, or they desire to violate it. This violation by government or contending parties is usually in terms of some standard of justice.

Purposes of political violence

Usually, when there has been a perception of violation, the protagonist demands or believes that the political system or its officials should rectify the conditions or relations perceived as unjust. The reaction to perceptions of violation, however, is not always peaceful. The peacefulness or violence of the reaction depends on (1) the degree of violation perceived and (2) the purposes of the person or group perceiving the violation.[66] Thus, if a

---

[65]Theodore J. Lowi (ed.), _Private Life and Public Order_ (New York: W. W. Norton and Co., Inc., 1968), p. viii.

[66]See Chapter IV, below.

citizen perceives the violation to be minor, he may attempt only to enact specific reforms. On the other hand, if the citizen perceives the violation to be beyond redemption, he may seek to overthrow the regime.

Sorel and Fanon are excellent examples of persons seeking to overthrow the regime. In his Reflections on Violence, Sorel states that the term violence should be reserved for those acts which have as their purpose revolt against the existing social order: revolt in which the proletariat seeks to violate and destroy the force of the existing middle class state.[67] Similarly, in his Wretched of the Earth, Fanon indicates that for him violence has as its ultimate purpose the establishment of rule by the people following the destruction of the existing colonial structures.[68] Both Sorel and Fanon, as revolutionaries, boldly assert that they are the ones using violence because the structure deserves violation.

Thus, political violence is directed toward the regime, which some citizens believe has violated them. Based on their perception of violation of the regime values or norms, regime authorities may resist such political violence. The purpose of political violence varies according to the degree of injustice perceived in the violation. Having given some attention to such troublesome terms as violence, politics, regime, and political violence, it is now necessary to move on to a discussion of theories of violence and the most difficult subject of all-- legitimacy, which involves both ideas about political justice and what political forms are most acceptable.

---

[67]George Sorel, Reflections on Violence, trans. T. E. Hulme (London: Collier Books, 1961), p. 195.

[68]Franz Fanon, The Wretched of the Earth, trans. Francois Maspero (New York: Grove Press, Inc., 1968), passim.

CHAPTER II

THEORIES OF VIOLENCE

War, in reality, results from a total situation
involving ultimately almost everything that has
happened to the human race up to the time the
war begins.[1]

Indeed, no factor, political, social, economic or
psychological seems entirely blameless. Incompetence and corruption of elites; cleverness of
conspirators; desertion of intellectuals; social
change, but also social stagnation; poverty, but
also improvement of the social lot; pernicious
ideas and revolutionary ideologies; rising expectations; a sense of injustice, discrimination and
indignation; permissiveness of political regimes,
but also tyranny; too little social mobility, but
also too much of it: all have been cited as lying
at the root of political strife. It is fair to say
that, taken as a whole, current theories and gener-
alizations regarding violence present a confusing
and untidy package.[2]

And the masses of men have in the historical state
submitted to endless sufferings and frustrations
and privations from the quarrelings and follies
and exploitations of those who ruled over them,
for the most part regarding their lot as ordained
by fate or by nature or by God.[3]

---

[1]Quincy Wright, <u>A Study of War</u> (Chicago: University
of Chicago Press, 1942), Vol. I, p. 17.

[2]Ivo K. Feierabend, Review of <u>Why Men Rebel</u>, by
Ted Gurr, <u>American Political Science Review</u>, Vol. LXV,
No. 1 (March, 1971), p. 195.

[3]MacIver, <u>The Web...</u>, p. 75.

Violence and the Social Sciences

Social scientists have identified approximately
four major theories of violence. Although there is overlap of these theories, this discussion analyzes each
separately. These general theories are: (1) instinct,
(2) deprivation-frustration, (3) relative deprivation,
and (4) relative deprivation as perceptions of injustice.

Human Nature and/or Instinct
and Aggression

Many modern political scientists approach violence
as a problem of Hobbesian human nature.[4] For example,
Freud thought man has an instinct for hatred and destruc-
tion-- a death wish. Lorenz claims man has an innate
willingness to fight, which can be controlled only by social
and moral codes.[6] Ardrey argues that a natural aggressiveness arises out of the natural inequality of men.[7] As
Ardrey says in African Genesis, man's aggressiveness is
an evolutionary fact-- the evolutionay father of modern
man was Cain not Abel. Methvin's explanation is:

---

[4]See Konrad Lorenz, On Aggression, trans. Marjorie
Kerr Wilson (New York: Bantam Books, 1967), and "On
Aggression," The Dynamics of Aggression: Individual, Group
and International Analyses, ed. Edwin L Megargee and Jack
E. Hokanson (New York: Harper and Row, 1970), pp. 5-9;
Chicago Press, 1958); J. P. Scott, "The Anatomy of
Violence," Violence in the Streets, ed. Shalom Endleman
(Chicago: Quandrangle Books, 1968), pp. 63-70; J. P.
Scott, Animal Behavior (Garden City: Doubleday and Co.,
Anchor Books, 1963); Desmond Morris, The Human Zoo (New
York: Dell Publishing Co., Inc., 1969): D. Morris, The
Naked Ape (New York: McGraw Hill, 1967); Robert Ardrey,
African Genesis (New York: Dell Publishing Co., Inc.,
1961); R. Ardrey, The Social Contract: A Personal Inquiry
into the Evolutionary Sources of Order and Disorder (New
York: Dell Publishing Co., Inc., 1970); R. Ardery, The
Territorial Imperative (New York: Atheneum, 1966); R.
Ardrey, "The Violent Way," Life, September 11, 1970, pp.
56-65.

[5]Sigmund Freud, Civilization and Its Discontents
(New York: W. W. Norton and Co., Inc., 1961), especially
pp. 65-66.

[6]Lorenz, On Aggression, especially pp. 249-251.

[7]Ardrey, "The Violent Way," p. 62.

Man as we know him has the psychobiology acquired by
living as hunter-predator through some 4,000 generations, as cultivator through some 1,000 generations
and as a creature of civilization for hardly 400
generations.[8]

Man expresses his aggressiveness in several ways
in a social setting. According to Scott, man fights for
dominance and territory, as do almost all animals.[9]
Where there is a well developed social organization, as
for wolves and baboons, the social control provided by
the dominant individuals limits aggressiveness.[10] Conversely, Ardrey points out that social disorganization,
overcrowding, and leisure time provide environmental
stimulants for man's latent aggressiveness. Ardrey
indicates that man has innate social needs for identity,
stimulation, and security. When there is no provision
for these needs, their opposites occur: anominity,
boredom, and anxiety.[11] This instinctive theory of violence
is not based entirely on biological or genetic necessity.
According to Bettleheim, "man and society were born out of
both: violence and gentle cooperation. To neglect either
wellspring of life in our efforts to better human relations
will be fruitless."[12] Nevertheless, such disclaimers of
biological determinism have not silenced the critics of
the instinctive theory. Hannah Arendt says,

In order to know that people will fight for their
homeland, we hardly had to discover instincts of
"group territorialism" in ants, rats and apes; and
in order to learn that overcrowding results in
irritation and aggressiveness, we hardly needed to

---

[8]Eugene H. Methvin, The Riot Makers: The Technology of Social Demolition (New Rochelle, N. Y.: Arlington
House, 1970), p. 118.

[9]Scott, Aggression.

[10]Lorenz, On Aggression.

[11]Ardrey, "The Violent Way," pp. 62-62.

[12]Bruno Bettleheim, "Violence: A Neglected Mode
of Behavior," Violence in the Streets, ed. Shalom Endleman
(Chicago: Quandrangle Books, 1968), p. 36.

experiment with rats. One day spent in the slums
of any big city should have sufficed.[13]

Deprivation-Frustration[14]

Since Marx, the dominant intellectual fashion has
been to find the causes of human behavior in the misery of
existing human conditions. Lately, social scientists have
described this misery as deprivation. This deprivation is
usually most severe among the lower economic classes.[15]
Some, however, have expanded the concept of deprivation to
include practically every human experience and condition
imaginable. Violence and other forms of individual behavior
are supposedly a natural out-growth of the alienation,
frustration, and anomie produced by such deprivation.
Conditions of deprivation lead to frustration and ultimately
to violence, because they present barriers to satisfaction
of inherent human needs and wants.[16] Thus the deprivation-
frustration hypothesis has been expanded to explain violent
interactions between classes and races, expecially between

---

[13]Hannah Arendt, "Reflections on Violence," Journal
of International Affairs, Vol. XXIII, No. 1 (1969), pp. 22-
23. For a discussion of this issue, see also Shalom Endleman (ed.), Violence in the Streets (Chicago: Quandrangle
Books, 1968), pp. 22-23, and 32-33.

[14]The seminal work is John Dollard et al., Frustra-
tion and Aggression (New Haven: Yale University Press,
1957). See also Lewis A. Coser, "Violence and the Social
Structure," Violence in the Streets, ed. Shalom Endleman
(Chicago: Quandrangle Books, 1968), pp. 73-73; Methvin,
The Riot Makers..., pp. 61-63; Richard Meier, "Violence:
The Last Urban Epidemic," Riots and Rebellion, ed. Louis
H. Masotti and Don R. Bowen (Beverly Hills, Calif.: Sage
Publications, Inc., 1968), p. 414; Abraham H. Maslow,
"Deprivation, Threat and Frustration," Psychological Review,
Vol. XLVIII, No. 6 (1941).

[15]Coser, "Violence...," p. 73.

[16]Leonard Berkowitz, "The Study of Urban Violence:
Some Implications of Laboratory Studies of Frustration and
Aggression," American Behavioral Scientist, Vol. 2, No. 4
(March/April, 1968), pp. 14-15. See also Dollard et al.,
Frustration..., p. 3; and Methvin, The Riot Makers...,
p. 59.

blacks and whites.[17]

There are a great variety of forms and sources of the deprivation-frustration-aggression thesis.[18] For example, psychologists have provided a number of hypotheses, explanations, descriptions, and theories as to how frustration arises from deprivation and may reslut in aggression. The most general case is that frustration arises from barriers to goal attainment. Conflicts between two equally desirable or undesirable goals, as well as between a desirable and an undesirable goal, may lead to frustration.[19] The individual organism, whether animal or human, may react to the frustration of a blocked goal by changing either the goal or the means to the goal, or it may resort to withdrawal or aggression. A person frustrated by submission to a stronger group or person may also "scapegoat" or "displace" or "project" his aggression toward a weaker party rather than to the one responsible for his frustration.[20] "Cognitive dissonance" may aggrevate these frustrations further. One form of cognitive dissonance is the gap between the ideal

---

[17]Louis H. Masotti and Dan Bowen (eds.), Riots and Rebellion: Civil Violence in the Urban Community (Beverly Hills, Calif.: Sage Publications, 1968), p. 24. See also Carl Iver Hovland and Robert R. Sears, "Minor Studies of Aggression: Correlations of Lynchings with Economic Indices," Racial Violence in the United States, ed. Allen D. Grimshaw (Chicago: Aldine Publishing Co., 1969), pp. 344-348; and Alexander Mintz, "A Re-Examination of Correlations between Lynchings and Economic Indices," Racial Violence in the United States, ed. Allen D. Grimshaw (Chicago: Aldine Publishing Co., 1969), pp. 349-353.

[18]The most recent work using aggregate data and making ecological inferences to individual psychology is the Feierabends', especially Ivo K. Feierabend, Rosalind L. Feierabend, and Ted Robert Gurr (eds.), Anger, Violence and Politics: Theories and Research (Englewood Cliffs, N. J.: Prentice-Hall, Inc., 1972), which incorporates many of their earlier journal articles and integrates their previous work.

[19]Psychologists call these goal conflicts approach-approach, avoidance-avoidance, and approach-avoidance respectively. For the first conceptualization, see Kurt Lewin, Dynamic Theory of Personality (New York: McGraw-Hill, 1935), especially pp. 229, 313, and 324.

[20]Leonard Berkowitz, Aggression: A Social Psychological Analysis (New York: Mc Graw Hill, 1962), pp. 152-160. See also N. E. Miller and R. Bugelski, "Minor Studies of Aggression: II. The Influence of Frustrations Imposed by the In-group on Attitudes Expressed Toward Out-groups," Journal of Psychology, Vol. XXV (1948), pp. 25, 437-452.

one is taught and the reality one experiences.[21] Such
differences between societal goals and individual needs may
lead to role conflict or a breakdown of consensual norms.
Such a breakdown has been called variously "anomie"[22] or
"alienation."[23] Thus, nearly all organisms, all classes,
and all individuals become frustrated when goals are
blocked. Leiden and Schmitt claim that frustration is
applicable to intellectuals and is a general cause of
revolution. Indeed,

> frustration is one element common to all rebels,
> whatever their aims, political ideas or social
> backgrounds, ...where conditions that create frus-
> trations continue, rebellion is bound to occur.[24]

The absolute deprivation thesis, based essentially
on economic misery, however, is a weak explanation for
intellectual aggression. The evidence against the absolute
deprivation thesis is quite persuasive. George Rudé,
author of The Crowd in History, provides an historical
perspective on economic conditions and violent disturbances. Apparently violent disturbances are more likely
to occur when economic conditions are improving, not when
conditions are very bad:

> Even abysmal, economic conditions were not an auto-
> matic "trigger" to disturbance. In England, strikes
> and trade union activity tended to occur not at
> moments of deepest trade depression and unemployment,

---

[21]Leon Festinger, Theory of Cognitive Dissonance
(Stanford, Calif.: Stanford University Press, 1957).

[22]Emile Durkheim, Suicide: A Study in Sociology,
trans. John A. Spaulding and George Simpson (New York:
The Free Press, 1951); and de Grazia, The Political....

[23]Erich Fromm, Escape from Freedom (New York:
Rinehart, 1941); and Erich Fromm, "Alienation under Capitalism," Man Alone, ed. Eric and Mary Josephson (New York:
Dell Publishing Co., 1962), pp. 57-73. See also Masotti
and Bowen (eds.), Riots and Rebellion..., p. 25.

[24]Leiden and Schmitt, The Politics of Violence...,
p. 84. On intellectuals, see Eric Hoffer, The Ordeal of
Change (first Harper Colophon edition; New York: Harper
and Row, Pubs., Inc., 1964); Eric Hoffer, The Temper of
Our Time (New York: Harper and Row, Pubs, Inc., 1964);
Eric Hoffer, The True Believer (New York: Harper and
Brothers, 1951); and Lewis A. Coser, The Functions of
Social Conflict (New York: The Free Press, 1956).

33

but rather on the upswing of a boom: as in 1792, 1818,
1824, and 1844-46 (the year 1768 appears to have been
an exception). During the French Revolution, we noted,
the most protracted industrial disputes were those of
1791 and 1794 which were years of comparative prosperity; and that when runaway inflation and unemployment set in, as in the winter of 1794-95, strikes
came to an end and food riots took over.[25]

Similarly, Leites and Wolf note that economic conditions
were improving in the Philippines, Kenya, South Vietnam,
and Cuba when rebellions occurred there. Black rioters in
Watts and Detroit had higher employment rates than nonpar-
ticipants and lived in two of the most "prosperous" black
ghettos in the United States.[26] In the Watts riot,
two thirds of the men arrested and convicted were
earning over $300 a month. Forty percent (or over
half of those who had ever been married) were living
with their spouses.... This should alert us to the
fact that rioting is not exclusively a problem of
poverty as currently defined.[27]

The most severe campus disruptions have also occurred
where living and learning conditions were among the best--
Berkeley, Columbia, Wisconsin, Cornell, and Harvard.[28]
Thus, although deprived rats, pigeons, donkeys, and monkeys
may react aggressively to the frustration brought on by
deprivation of one kind or another, such explanations, no
matter how appealing to our materialistic standards of
justice, probably do not account adequately for most
aggressive human behavior.

---

[25]George Rudé, "The Pre-Industrial Crowd," Protest,
Reform, and Revolt: A Reader in Social Movements, ed. Joseph
R. Gusfield (New York: John Wiley and Sons, Inc., 1970), p.
112. See also James C. Davies, "Toward a Theory of Revolution," American Sociological Review, Vol. XXVII (February,
1962), pp. 5-18.

[26]Nathan Leites and Charles Wolf, Jr., Rebellion
and Authority: An Analytical Essay on Insurgent Conflicts
(Chicago: Markham Publishing Co., 1970), pp. 17-18.

[27]Allen and Adair (eds.), Violence and Riots...,
p. 114. On delinquency, see Arthur Miller, "The Bored and
the Violent," Violence in the Streets, ed. Shalom Endleman
(Chicago: Quandrangle Books, 1968), p. 271.

[28]Leites and Wolf, Rebellion and Authority..., p. 18.

Relative Deprivation

The theory which has greatly modified the deprivation theory is the relative deprivation theory. Berkowitz
presents a good summary of the relative deprivation theory:

> Deprivations alone are inadequate....Much greater
> weight must be given to anticipations of the goal than
> merely to the ... deprivation per se. ...Some attention
> [must be given] to hope.... Goal seeking is most
> intense when he is thinking of the goal and anticipa-
> ting the satisfactions. But similarly, his frustration
> is most severe when the anticipated satisfactions are
> not achieved. ...[People are] frustrated only after
> they have begun to hope. ...Rapid change associated
> with great increase in political instability produces
> more hope than can be fulfilled. Hope outstrips
> reality. ...Such [a] process ...may be occurring in
> the case of our present Negro revolution.[29]

Thus, the deprivation felt may be largely dependent on or
relative to the level of anticipations, expectations, and
hopes. The higher the hopes,[30] present or future, the
greater the deprivation likely to be felt and the greater
the potential for violent reactions to such frustrations
of hopes. Leiden and Schmitt point out that

> the actual state of material well being (or ill
> being) of people does not in itself produce revo-
> lutionary fervor, but rather that the attitudes
> of people toward their conditions constitute the
> real source.[31]

Many writers have given a variety of more specific applic-
cations of relative deprivation to explain the participation of women, the young,[32] and the middle class in
revolution.[33]

---

[29]Berkowitz, "The Study...," p. 15.

[30]For examples of violence as a tactic in the pur-
suit of religious and secular heavens on earth, see Cohn,
The Pursuit of the Millennium...; and Stillman And Pfaff,
The Politics of Hysteria... .

[31]Leiden and Schmitt, The Politics of Violence...,
pp. 43-44.

[32]Coser, "Violence and the Social Structure," pp.
82-84.

[33]Leiden and Schmitt, The Politics of Violence...,
p. 45.

Ted Gurr has most extensively postulated, tested, and documented the relative deprivation thesis. He delineates three basic kinds or patterns of relative deprivation or value disequilibrium which subsume many earlier theories of political violence.[34]

> Three distinct patterns of disequilibrium can be specified: decremental deprivation, in which a group's value expectations remain relatively constant but value capabilities are perceived to decline; aspirational deprivation, in which capabilities remain relatively static while expectations increase or intensify; and progressive deprivation, in which there is substantial and simultaneous increase in expectations and decrease in capabilities. All three patterns have been cited as causal or predisposing factors for political violence.[35]

Relative deprivation thus arises chiefly from changes in expectations, which may or may not be stimulated by actual changes in conditions. Gurr says that changes in conditions or expectations, or a combination of both, cause the "perception" of a discrepancy or gap between " values" and conditions.

---

[34] Gurr claims that the relative deprivation theory subsumes many other explanations of political violence and revolution. Aristotole's theory of revolution states that the chief cause of revolution is the discrepancy between differing standards of justice, primarily equality, and actual political conditions of ruling and being ruled. The emphasis in Aristotle is a discrepancy between actual satisfactions and basic needs. For a view that Aristotle's concern is of the separation of economic and political power, see Fred Kort, "The Quantification of Aristotle's Theory of Revolution," American Political Science Review, Vol. LXVI (June, 1952), pp. 486-493. Harold D. Lasswell and Abraham Kaplan find the causative gap in differences between expectations and realizations in Power and Society: A Framework for Political Inquiry (New Haven: Yale University Press, 1956). James Davies postulates differences between expectations and achievements in "Toward a Theory...," pp. 5-18. The Feierabends see the gap between satisfactions and wants (see Feierabend, Feierabend, and Gurr [eds.] , Anger, Violence...). James A. Geschwender finds the discrepancy of status between groups in "Social Structure and the Negro Revolt: An Examination of Some Hypotheses," Social Forces, Vol. XLIII (December, 1964), pp. 248-256. For a summary of these various forms of the theory of relative deprivation, see Gurr, Why..., pp. 37-40.

[35] Gurr, Why..., p. 46.

According to Gurr, discontent and deprivation are not sufficient conditions for political violence to arise. The crucial intervening variable between political discontent and political violence is relative deprivation:

> Discontent arising from the perception of relative deprivation is the basic, instigating condition for participants in collective violence. The linked concepts of discontent and deprivation comprise most of the psychological states implicit or explicit in such theoretical notions about the causes of violence as frustration, alienation, drive and goal conflicts, exigency, and strain.[36]

Thus, Gurr's theory takes account of many psychological explanations-- dissonance, anomie, and social conflict--[37] but especially the frustration-aggression model which "provides the psychological dynamic" for all violence.[38] Gurr says his "approach is not wholly or primarily psychological, however, and it would be a misrepresentation of the arguments and evidence presented here to categorize it so."[39] He claims he uses the psychological variables only as "linkages between and among the societal variables and the dependent political variables."[40]

Relative Deprivation as Perceptions
of Injustice

A better understanding of the meaning of relative deprivation may be possible if one approaches it from the perspective of the political activist's expectations and hopes for justice. Durkheim says that ideas of justice may restrain the appetites or passions.[41] The concern here, however, is more with the high expectations of justice operating as more positive stimulants or motivators of actions. The promise of American life, especially beliefs in total equality and social perfection, may be motivators of black and student political activism.[42] A good number of promises have been made or held out to oppressed blacks and aspiring students. Certainly recent political leaders have promised blacks the almost immediate end of their long

---

[36]Ibid., p. 12.   [37]Ibid., p. 25.   [38]Ibid., p. 23.

[39]Ibid., p. 12.   [40]Ibid.

[41]Durkheim, Suicide..., pp. 145-153.

[42]On black hopes, see Banfield, The Unheavenly City..., p. 206. On perfectibility of democracy, see Tocqueville, Democracy..., Vol. II. pp. 34-35.

suffering, poverty, and discrimination. Similarly, students
and professors have been led to believe that influence and
leading roles in society come from the acquisition of academic degrees and intellectual development. Students are
also taught to seek either value free knowledge or trans-
political truths, both of which may come in conflict with
some regime myths or practices. Surely, most of us consider
a broken promise as wrong and perhaps even unjust. Thus,
when such promises are not fulfilled, blacks and students
can perceive the American system, which made these promises,
as unjust and illegitimate. Certainly, a continuous stream of
broken promises is not likely to foster the trust necessary
for life in any community. Such perceptions of political
injustice provide political motivations for violence. One
can probably understand these motivations only partially
as "psychological dynamics of the frustration-aggression
relationship."[43] A preoccupation with psychological motivations may obscure otherwise quite clear political purposes or aspirations, making the study of political violence
unduly problematic.

It might be helpful here to review Aristotle's
theory of revolution.[44] Aristotle would probably say that
the economic conditions, psychological predispositions and
precipitating incidents discussed by modern social scientists are all factors contributing to revolution. The chief
cause of revolution, however, is differing opinions of what
is justice and injustice. Antedating Madison, Marx, and
others, Aristotle said that the economic interests and
desires of different classes contribute to their differing
understanding of equality as a principle of justice. The
wealthy and/or educated few see their inequality of wealth
and education as entitling them to greater political honors
or offices. Their feeling of injustice is therefore greatest
in a democracy, where their claims to greater political
power, authority, and influence are least likely to be
recognized by the ruling many, who are poor and uneducated.

The poor have a contradictory view of justice. In
their efforts to rectify the injustice of their economic
inequality, the many poor in a democracy are likely to
attempt to expropriate and redistribute the wealth of the
few and to deny the justice of especial political honors
to the few. According to Aristotle, the most likely cause
of revolution in a democracy is the reactions of the many
to their feeling that poverty is unjust. Thus, for Aristotle, the chief cause of revolution in a democracy is the

---

[43]Gurr, Why..., p. 23.

[44]Aristotle Politics ed. and trans. Ernest Barker
(New York: Oxford University Press, 1962), especially Bk. v.

unjustice the poor perceive because of their economic inequality, not simply the economic conditions themelves. In
contrast to Marxian thought, the crucial variable is not
economic conditions, but rather the value interpretations
individuals, groups, and classes place on such conditions.
Thus, the people must believe economic or other conditions
of social life are unjust in relation to some standard or
value before revolution is likely to result indirectly from
economic conditions.

According to Aristotole, the economic misery of
lacking necessities does not cause men to revolt, rather
the seeking of something more than necessities-- superflu-
ities-- may lead men to revolt: "Men are always wanting
something more, and are never contented until they get to
infinity. It is the nature of desire to be infinite."[45]
This point illustrates the crucial junction of economic
interest and desires-- in modern terms, psychological
predispositions. Similarly, the precipitating incidents
merely signal the beginning of a political revolution;
they are not the "root" causes. Particular incidents are
simply the sparks that light the pre-existing and tinderous
build up of combustible material.

The actual source of political conflicts and revolutions is differing opinions, conflicting ideologies, and
contradictory value systems. According to Barker's interpretation of Aristotle, the "general motive [for revolution]
is always a passion for some concept of equality, which is
held to be involved in the very idea of justice."[46] In
Aristotle's own translated words,

> Either side turns to sedition if it does not enjoy the
> share of constitutional rights which accords with the
> concept of justice it happens to entertain.
> ....
> Some take the line that if men are equal in one respect,
> they may consider themselves equal in all: others take
> the line that if they are superior in one respect, they
> may claim superiority all round.[47]

These are the general and most important causes of revolution from which Aristotle moves on to the three contributory
factors: state of mind (the passion for equality), objects
at stake (profit, honor, loss, disgrace), and those initial
incidents which precipitate the revolutionary process.
Aristotle relates psychological predisposition and objectives

---

[45]Ibid., Bk. ii, p. 67.

[46]Ibid., p. 203.

[47]Ibid., Bk. v, pp. 204, 206.

to the concepts of justice of equality and inequality. Thus drastic change is unlikely to occur over small matters or personal quarrels:

> Though sedition springs from small occasions, it does not turn on small issues. The issues involved are large. ...Discord among the notables involve all the state in their consequences ...they [may draw] the whole civic body into their quarrel and divide into factions.[48]

One should not neglect the force and fraud of a few, but to treat them as the whole is to assume that great political conflicts have trivial causes and purposes.

Justice and Contemporary Violence

Following Aristotle's example, this dissertation hypothesizes that perceptions of injustice may be the valued thing deprived which may lead some even to war in politics. Gurr presumptuously says that most analyses of those incidents which precipitated urban riots have resulted in trivial findings and hypotheses. Yet Lieberson and Silverman's study of precipitating events showed that the community's own understanding of events, such as murder, rape, sexual molestation, police brutality, lynching, segregation, and discrimination, was that such events were "wrong," "bad," and "unfair."[49] These events were wrong according to some standard or value. If their analysis is correct, the precipitating events involved violations of "strong social taboos," "strongly held norms," "violation of important mores," and "violation of rights widely accepted as fundamental."[50]

Masotti's analysis of statements by ghetto residents reinforces the hypotheses relating violence to perceptions of injustice with only a few critical exceptions:

> Men engage in civil violence because the current or anticipated distribution of values in their societies is unfair or unjust by some standard. ...It is not

---

[48]Ibid., p. 212.

[49]Stanley Lieberson and Arnold R. Silverman, "The Precipitating and Underlying Conditions of Race Riots," American Sociological Review, Vol. XXX, No. 6 (1965), pp. 887-898.

[50]Ibid.

necessarily the perception of an unequal distribution
of values that moves men to civil violence, but rather
the perception that the inequality in question is also
unjust. And it follows that a perfectly equal distribution of values, if perceived as unfair or unjust,
may be equally a motivating force for violence.[51]

Similarly, frustrations perceived as reasonable or justifiable result in less aggression than those that appear arbi-
trary.[52] That standard of justice may be an absolute principle or the application of some abstract principle in evaluating one's relations with others. There is considerable
European historical evidence for the role of political ideals
in supposedly "anomie" or normless rioting. Rudé says,

> For, both in England and France, the Revolution of 1789,
> by posing sharply in their multiform aspects the new
> concepts of the "rights of man" and the "sovereignty of
> the people" added a new dimension to popular distur-
> bance and gave a new content to the struggle of parties
> and classes.[53]

Political ideals, such as the "rights of man," gained
acceptance among even the formally uneducated peasants and
workers:

> Some historians have doubted the depth of these poli-
> tical ideas among the common people. ...Already in
> August 1789, we find a journeyman gunsmith arrested
> at Versailles for speaking slightingly of General
> LaFayette supporting his claim to a fair hearing with
> an appeal to the "rights of man." ...In 1848...
> Antoine Bisgambilia, an obscure and illiterate mecha-
> nic ...expressed his political convictions as follows:
> "Everybody knows that I don't compromise with my con-
> science and that, as long as I have breath left in my
> body, I shall use it for the triumph of the Democratic
> and Social Republic."[54]

---

[51]Masotti and Bowen, Riots..., p. 22. (Italics mine.)

[52]Nicholas Pastore, "The Role of Arbitrariness in
the Frustration-Aggression Hypothesis," Journal of Abnormal
and Social Psychology, Vol. XLVII (July, 1952), pp. 728-731,
cited by Gurr, Why..., p. 189.

[53]Rudé, "The Pre-Industrial...," p. 114, also p.
112. On the religious value dimensions of popular disturbance in the middle ages, see Cohn, Pursuit....

[54]Rudé, "The Pre-Industrial...," pp. 114-115.

Hannah Arendt

Hannah Arendt argues that modern revolutions parallel the emergence of democratic political thought and particulary the ideas of freedom. Indeed, according to Arendt,[55] war and revolution are the most important realities and characteristics of the modern world. This is true because modern science and technology have made possible, at least in the western world, an almost universal belief in progress, the perfectibility of man, and especially equality of economic conditions.[56] The proclaimed purpose of modern revolutions is a new beginning for man-- freedom for the mass of people. Twentieth century wars, as well as revolutions, also claim justification on the grounds of freedom, whether they are wars of "national liberation" or wars defending freedom against "aggression."

Arendt states that freedom is usually defined in two different senses: (1) liberation from oppression, usually economic, or (2) freedom to institute a political community of self-government-- a constitutional government of laws. According to Arendt, legitimate and successful revolution is founded only on the principle of political freedom.[57] Most modern revolutionaries, however, perceive freedom in the first sense. For example, Marx, Rousseau, and the French People essentially sought freedom from fear, want, necessity, scarcity, and poverty, not the freedom to institute a political community.[58]

Similarly, the widespread American pursuit of happiness, from the beginning, has been a materialistic self-interest. The American way of life to most Americans means a high standard of living. Only if pressed does the average American speak of his political freedoms. This American dream of affluence and consumption has weakened commitment to public objects and has resulted in neglect of the quest for the political purposes of freedom-- political participation and public happiness.[59] Arendt points out, however, that these political purposes have never been completely obscured in America because of the absence, from its early history, of the most wretched conditions of poverty, except for a few. Thus, for Arendt, America qualifies as a democracy only if democracy means government concern for popular

---

[55]See especially Arendt, On Revolution (New York: Viking Press, Inc., 1965).

[56]Ibid., p. 149.

[57]Ibid., p. 8.   [58]Ibid., p. 87.

[59]Ibid., pp. 123-135. On the dangers of an unenlightened self-interest for American politics, see Tocqueville, Democracy..., Vol. II. especially pp. 104-106.

welfare or private happiness. If democracy means freedom
for political participation and sharing of political power,
then the American political system is actually an oli-
garchy.[60]

Alexis de Tocqueville on Relative
Deprivation and Equality

Gusfield and others have credited Tocqueville, a
master theorist, with the original formulation of the relative deprivation theory.[61] Tocqueville was probably the
first modern social scientist to recognize that relative
deprivation is the chief source of political violence. He
did so on the basis of attempting to understand democratic
revolutions along with their key ideal, the quest for
equality. Thus, Tocqueville commented on the growing
acceptance of the idea of equality in France and America
during the eighteenth and nineteenth centuries. His theory
is comprehensive and neglects little of significance. His
theory of revolution encompasses social and economic
conditions, class structure, psychological frustration, and
political ideologies. He based his theories on observations
of contemporary events and conditions. In short, he wit-
nessed and documented the "democratic revolution" of his
age.
     According to Tocqueville, remnant conditions of
economic inequality and exploitation led to the political
disputes of the French Revolution. He found the primary
cause of the crisis and revolution, in his time, to be the
growth of the idea of equality. Contrary to Marx, who saw
class conflict resulting from economic deprivation, Tocqueville argued that unrest and discontent are most likely to
appear when economic and political conditions are actually
improving.[62] For example Tocqueville reported that there
had been great improvements throughout France: much had
improved

---

[60]Arendt, On Revolution, pp. 221, 258-259, and 273.

[61]Gusfield, Protest..., p. 11. Gurr, Why..., however, attributes the first "systematic" attention to relative deprivation to Samuel Stouffer et al., The American
Soldier: Adjustment During Army Life (Princeton: Princeton
University Press, 1949), Vol. I.

[62]For a comparison of Marx and Tocqueville on revolution, see Irving M. Zeitlin, Liberty, Equality and Revolution in Alexis de Tocqueville (Boston: Little, Brown and
Co., 1971). Zeitlin is sympathetic to Marx and perhaps mis-
understands Tocqueville.

the status of the French peasant; he had not merely
ceased to be a serf, he had also become a landowner.
....
[By 1790] in...[the] villages the number of land-
owners was as high as half, often two thirds of the ...
number [later in 1856].
....
Ownership of the soil was vested in innumerable peasant
proprietors; half the cultivatable land was owned by
them.[63]

Moreover, people living in the economically most prosperous
areas of France were the most revolutionary. These improvements made peasants see themselves and their rights in a
light quite different from when the aristocratic and feudal
systems were complete. Under the new conditions, peasants
began to realize more fully that the remaining feudalistic
structures blocked their road to full equality and freedom.

If the peasant had not owned his own land he would
hardly have noticed many of the charges which the
feudal system imposed on all real estate. What could
the tithe matter to a man who had no land of his
own? ... And even restrictions hampering agriculture
mean nothing to an agriculturist who is simply culti-
vating land for the benefit of someone else.
....
The possession of this little plot of earth...fills
him with pride and a sense of independence...part
of the income from his small domain goes to supporting...
[the remaining aristocrats] in the form of charges
which are imprescriptible and irredeemable.[64]

In the meantime, the lords and nobles had, to a
considerable degree, lost their previous political powers
and rights:

Far from controlling the administration of parish
affairs the lord had no say at all in them.
....
The nobles play no part, collectively or individually,
in the administration of public affairs.[65]

---

[63]Alexis de Tocqueville, The Old Regime and the
French Revolution, trans. Stuart Gilbert (Garden City:
Doubleday and Co., Inc., 1955), pp. 23-24.

[64]Ibid., pp. 30-31.

[65]Ibid., pp. 26-27.

Although most nobles had lost political privileges, there remained certain irksome vestiges of that once powerful class: "while ceasing to be the ruling class, they had remained a privileged, closed group, less and less ... an aristocracy and more and more a caste."[66] These signs of inequality seemed unfair and unjust in relation to the new standard of equality:

> If we bear these facts in mind, it is easy to see why the privileges enjoyed by this small section of the community seemed so unwarranted and so odious to the French people and why they developed intense jealousy of the "upper class" which rankles still today.[67]

Thus, when changes in the previous order take place, expectations may rise much faster than achievement. According to Tocqueville, relatively slight retreats or slowing down of the rate of improvement of conditions may cause revolutionary disturbance.[68] During a crisis of changing beliefs, changing habits of obedience and privilege, political socialization (perception of rights and responsibilities) is in an imperfected state. No one knows his place or his role in society,[69] because the values justifying existing social relations are in flux. Positions of class and rank are unclear; social stratification is changing. The lower classes are claiming new rights, and the old masters are resisting.

According to Tocqueville, men of letters and intellectuals gave impetus to the idea of equality then causing economic, psychological, social, and political changes. The development of a new view of equality changes the traditional evaluations of factual conditions of the relations of men. Men alter their behavior according to their new beliefs. The permeation of the idea of equality to all levels of society can thus cause social conflict and perhaps revolution, where privileged classes remain, resist, or fail to get out of the way.

According to Tocqueville, the distribution of privilege is the chief distinguishing feature between democracy and all previous forms of government, which were ruled by an

---

[66]Ibid., p. 204.

[67]Ibid.

[68]For a similar hypothesis, see Davies, "Toward a Theory...," pp. 5-18.

[69]On the role of the marginal, uprooted, and disoriented in millennium movements, see Cohn, Pursuit..., pp. 52, 55, 59-60, 282, 284, and 286.

aristocratic elite. Tocqueville showed that equality of
condition, the decline of social and especially of enduring
hereditary political privilege is the most pervasive characteristic of democratic societies. In a democracy the people
attach decreasing importance to special privileges, even
those based on superior intellect.[70] This equality of
privilege is exemplified in the fact that the overwhelming
obligation of self-government is placed on the shoulders of
the unsophisticated many, for it would not be just to have
special representation by an aristocratic few. Thus,
equality of condition in a democracy is chiefly equality
of political privilege and social status which denies the
validity of political or social distinctions among citizens
based on class, caste, race, family, education, etc.
According to Tocqueville, revolution in American democracy
is most likely to arise out of the inequality of condi-
tions-- social, economic, and educational. During the 1960's
and 1970's in America, the under-privileged blacks and over-
privileged intellectual elite fit this pattern.

On Violence, Privilege,
Power, and Morality

The purpose here is to provide a tentative explanation of why it is that more individuals from some groups
than others seem motivated to participate in political violence. During the 1960's and 1970's in America, young[71]
black urban males of the under-privileged black culture and
young college town males of the over-privileged "counter
culture" have been the most active participants in riots
and violence directed against particular policies and/or
the American regime as a whole. The political significance
of the violence of young black males and of college males
lies in the subjective perception they have of their uncertain status within the regime.[72]

---

[70]See Marvin Zetterbaum, "Alexis de Tocqueville,"
History of Political Philosophy, ed. Leo Strauss and
Joseph Cropsey (5th ed.; Rand McNally and Co., 1969),
pp. 659-660.

[71]The age and sex of these political activists is
not of particular interest politically, since young males
are always the cannon fodder for any kind of conflict or
violent crime. Adolescents and young adults are usually
more energetic and idealistic, and less patient than their
elders. Presumably, the reader is familiar with differences between the sexes.

[72]Again, on socially uprooted or disoriented characteristics of participants in the millennium movements of
the middle ages, see Cohn, Pursuit... .

Privileges

The term privilege best describes the commonly perceived problem of status, place, or position shared by young urban blacks and members of America's college milieu. In this analysis, privilege includes the full range of the advantages and opportunities of society. Thus, privilege involves not only socio-economic status but also opportunities for education, socio-economic status and political power. A privilege is a special claim quite beyond or distinct from any recognized existing right. A privilege is an exceptional and/or extraordinary claim which the established social or political structure has not, as yet, approved. Once the social structure accepts a privilege as legitimate, it may become recognized as an established right.

The term privilege, when modified by the prefixes "under" and "over," points out both the common element (seeking of special claims under existing conditions) and the somewhat differing goals which young blacks and those associated with the college subcultures or communities seek. In terms of the national standards of the "American way of life," many urban blacks have historically been under-privileged economically, educationally, socially, and politically: "He was enslaved, emancipated, disfranchised, segregated and suppressed-- all by violence or the threat of it. ...Church bombings, street murders, Klan floggings and burnings."[73] Blacks can easily perceive such experiences as unjust violations of their natural rights based on their equality as human beings. Thus, some under-privileged blacks seek immediate reparations for their long history of inequality.

On the other hand, students are over-privileged in their educational opportunities, income, and social status. In terms of opportunity, they are not anywhere near being the most deprived of America's population. If anything, American students are an aspiring elite.[74] Thus, some

---

[73]Allen and Adair (eds.), Violence and Riots..., p. 65.

[74]The student case for deprivation is limited to their dissatisfaction with their lower status in the academic community. See Lawrence Veysey, The Emergence of the American University (Chicago: University of Chicago Press, 1965), pp. 295-299; and Lipset, Rebellion..., pp. 18-19, 22-23, and 33-35.

college community residents[75] claim their "right" to preferential treatment, deference to their knowledge, or
respect for their higher morality.

Other than their privileged opportunities for higher
education, how are those radical campus residents who participate in violence over-privileged? There is a good deal of
evidence from sympathetic as well as unsympathetic sources.
On the whole, campus activists tend to be from the prestige
universities and middle or upper-middle class families.
For example, the highest participation in student demonstrations in a 1969 Gallup poll was for students coming
from families with incomes over $15,000; the lowest level
was for students whose family incomes ranged from $10,000
to $14,999.[76] Ardery reports that anywhere from 25% to
81% of students at the eleven colleges he studied reported
family incomes over $15,000 in 1971.[77] College students
are generally economically more privileged than the average
high school student. For example, college students report
twice the spending money per week of high school students
($15.00 versus $7.50). Nearly 66% of college students
report this money is provided by their parents, while only
26% of high school students report parents as a source.[78]
Thus, except for black students, student activists are not
economically under-privileged as a group. Educationally,
most student activism centers at the prestige institutions
as well.

---

[75]Such phrases as college community activists,
young college town males, college community, and academic
milieu all recognize that many political activists are
actually ex-students, perpetual students, and non-students
Yet they are closely associated with or heavily influenced
by those residing in college communities. The phrase also
includes a goodly number of their allies among the intelligentsia.

[76]George Gallup, "Special Report on the Attitudes of
College Students: Student Disorders-- What's Behind Them?
Majority of College Youth Agrees with Goal but not Tactics
of Militants," Gallup Opinion Index, No. 48 (June, 1969),
p. 13. See also Arthur Schlesinger, Crisis of Confidence:
Ideas, Power and Violence in America (Boston: Houghton
Mifflin, 1969).

[77]Philip P. Ardery, "Special Report: Opinion on the
Campus," National Review, Vol. XXIII, No. 23 (June 15,
1971), p. 641. The lowest figures for this income level
of 25%, 43%, and 48% were reported for black Howard University, socially conscious Reed, and rural Indiana University.

[78]"The Un-Radical Young," Life, Vol. LXX, No. 1
(January 8, 1971), p. 25.

According to their educational opportunities, income, class, and family background, these individuals are
members of an elite, although not necessarily qualifying as
upper class members of the establishment. In contrast,
Scammon and Wattenberg describe the middle class American
electoral majority as unyoung, unpoor, and unblack. They
could also have said uncollege, unjewish, uncatholic, un-
eastern, and unpolitical.[79] Perhaps the common practice of
defining class according to wealth may have never been
appropriate. Affluence, when coupled with the educational
requirements of a technological society,[80] may suggest that
education would be a better criteria for designation of
upper class status, particularly in educationally preoccu-
pied America. For example, David Apter bases his categories
of class on educationally based technological criteria.
Apter's classes are the technologically competent, the technologically obsolescent, and the technologically super-
fluous.[81] The technologically competent category includes
the professional-managerial-technical elite closely connected with universities and research centers.[82]

Subcultures[83]

An analysis of the effect of the common experiences
of black and student subcultures may help to explain why
many individuals in these over-privileged and under-
privileged groups are inclined to be at least potentially
receptive to political values divergent from those of the
larger culture. One possible definition of culture is a
system of values, attitudes, orientations, or patterns of

---

[79]See Richard M. Scammon and Ben J. Wattenberg, The
Real Majority (New York: Coward-McCann, Inc., 1970), passim.

[80]Zbigniew Brzezinski, Between Two Ages: America's
Role in the Technetronic Era (New York: The Viking Press,
1970).

[81]David Apter, "Ideology and Discontent," Ideology
and Discontent, ed. David Apter (Glencoe, Ill.: Free Press,
1964), pp. 15-43.

[82]For an attempt to relate these classes to political
party realignments, see Walter Dean Burnham, Critical Elections and the Mainsprings of American Politics (New York:
W. W. Norton and Co., Inc., 1970), pp. 137-139, and 158-159.

[83]For a more extreme theoretical analysis of subcultures and legitimacy, see Alfred W. Penn, "Sociological
Foundations of Legitimation" (unpublished Ph.D. dissertation, Claremont Graduate School, Claremont, Calif., 1967).

behavior fairly commonly held by a social or national group. A subculture may develop where an isolated, homogenous, specialized, and/or deviant[84] group shares a fairly common set of social, ethnic, generational, economic, linguistic, and occupational interests and psychological experiences.[85] Thus, a subculture develops out of a shared psychological, social, and economic environment, milieu, or situation which form a matrix of experiences forming[86] a cohesive pattern of expectations and group identifications more or less unique within the larger culture.

These interests, experiences, and values are of great variety and diversity. They may tend to accumulate and reinforce a developing common sense of identity[87]

---

[84]See Penn, pp. 136-138; Lester W. Milbrath, Political Participation: How and Why Do People Get Involved in Politics? (Chicago: Rand McNally and Co., 1965), pp. 119, 131; James W. Clarke and E. Lester Levine, "Marijuana Use, Social Discontent, and Political Alienation: A Study of High School Youth," American Political Science Review, Vol. LXV, No. 1 (March, 1971), p. 121; and Leon Festinger, "A Theory of Social Comparison Processes," Human Relations, Vol. VII (May, 1954), pp. 117-140.

[85]Some criminological literature gives extensive attention to subcultures of violent behavior. See Marvin E. Wolfgang and Ferracuti Franco, The Subculture of Violence: Toward an Integrated Theory in Criminology (London: Tavistock, 1967); Gurr, Why..., pp. 160-168; Lewis Yablonsky, The Violent Gang (Baltimore, Maryland: Penguin Books, 1966); Michel McCall, "Some Ecological Aspects of Negro Slum Riots," Protest, Reform, and Revolt: A Reader in Social Movements, ed. Joseph R. Gusfield (New York: John Wiley and Sons, Inc., 1970), p. 358; and Shalom Endleman, "Introduction," Violence in the Streets, ed. Shalom Endleman (Chicago: Quandrangle Books, 1968), p. 25. This study has attempted to indicate that violence is only a form of behavior like walking or running which cannot be adequately explained or understood by mere description. Violent acts may be "caused" or explained by a wide variety of psychological predispositions and/or motivations, social and economic interests and political purposes.

[86]On "cross cutting" and cumulative interests and cohesion, see David B. Truman, The Governmental Process: Political Interests and Political Opinions (New York: Alfred A. Knopf, Inc., 1951), especially pp. 315 ff.

[87]Abdul A. Said, "Introduction," Protagonists of Change: Subcultures in Development and Revolution, ed. Abdul A. Said (Englewood Cliffs: Prentice-Hall, Inc., 1971) p. 7. See also Lasswell and Lerner, World... .

separate from that of the larger political culture. Such
common objective experiences lend themselves to a common
set of subjective explanations or definitions of the
broader political culture or situation.[88]   If these shared
experiences and the values which may develop out of them
are sufficiently stereotyped, differentiated, or "strange,"
then members or agents of both the subcultural "in" group
and the larger cultural "out" group may sometimes perceive
the other party as a severe threat to their respective life
styles and values. "In" group and "out" group ideological
and violent conflict may arise from such perceived differences. The role of social experience in forming and pro-
ducing a receptivity to differing ideologies and social conflicts is a key element in Mannheim's theory of the sociology of knowledge.[89]   Mannheim's thesis is that some groups
experience a special existence which enables them to
develop their peculiar political orientations. The experiences of those living in two American subcultures, the
black community and the student-intellectual community, may
perhaps present milieus uniquely receptive to or supportive
of radical rejections and/or reinterpretations of the ideas
of the dominant political culture.[90]

It is necessary to recognize not only potentially
conflictual interactions but also the cooperative interde-
pendence of subcultures and the American political culture.
That is, all subcultures are themselves an integral part of
the wider American political culture.[91]   In America in 1972,
the areas of agreement and cooperation between subcultures
and the larger culture are probably greater than the
differences. For example, most blacks probably want simply
social equality and a bigger slice of the materialistic
American version of the good life. Similarly, many student
radicals desire simply to realize in practice the ideals
of American democracy. The intrinsic integration, as well
as differentiation, of the ideas of the American political
culture and of a subculture is also evident in the fact
that, while most blacks are concerned about improvement
of their race, such as elimination of prejudice and discrimination, they do not all belong to the same class even

---

[88]See Jean Blondel, An Introduction to Comparative
Government (New York: Praeger Publishers, 1969), p. 488.

[89]See Mannheim, Ideology and Utopia.

[90]See Penn, pp. 189-190; Everett Rogers, Diffusion
of Innovations (New York: Free Press, 1966), pp. 169-170;
and Joseph Cropsey, "Radicalism and Its Roots," Public
Policy, Vol. XVIII, No. 3 (April, 1970), pp. 301-319.

[91]An exception might be new immigrant groups.

within the central city.[92]
    Simply put, not all blacks or students are deter-
ministically destined to be violent or even dissenting
political activists merely because of where they tend to
live, what they experience, and what they tend to believe.
Conversely, there are many others who are not blacks or
students, but who are, nevertheless, under-privileged or
over-privileged in terms of the existing regime's distribution of benefits. Some of these people may also participate in political violence. Yet blacks and students are
probably most active, because each of their experiences
come to have a common meaning within the context of their
two under-privileged and over-privileged subcultures within the American political culture. What general kinds of
experiences, then, are peculiar to these two under-
privileged and over-privileged groups which may cause them
to develop into distinctive subcultures apart from the
American political culture?

Isolation
    First, both communities are somewhat isolated from
the social whole. Large numbers of blacks live in segregated Northern urban centers, some by choice, but most
involuntarily. This isolation is more than geographic:
it is also social and economic. The lower class and
cultural status of most blacks is in sharp contrast to
the middle class affluence and life styles of the middle
class majority. Most blacks also share common social and
economic experiences of discrimination, poverty, social[93]
and political disorganization. These experiences may tend
to alienate a large percentage of blacks from a society
supposedly dedicated to equality. Within this subcultural
milieu, a significant minority of blacks may be committed

---

[92]St. Clair Drake and Horace R. Cayton, Black
Metropolis: A Study of Negro Life in a Northern City
(2 vols.; New York: Harper and Row Publishers, Inc.,
1952). This analysis of the "Black Metropolis" found
roughly the usual classes-- lower, middle, and upper. All
three classes were cross-cut by the church goers and the
underworld "shadies." For an exception based on the caste
position of blacks in the rural South before World War II,
see John Dollard, Caste and Class in a Southern Town (New
Haven: Yale University Press, 1937).

[93]See Lee Rainwater and William L. Yancey, The
Moynihan Report and the Politics of Controversy (Cambridge:
M.I.T. Press, 1968); U. S. Dept. of Labor, Office of Policy
Planning and Research, The Negro Family: The Case for a
Nation, prepared by Daniel Moynihan (Washington, D.C.:
Government Printing Office, 1965), cited hereafter as the
Moynihan Report; and Scott, "The Anatomy...," pp. 63-70.

to a different set of values because of perceived disparity
between reality in the community and the values of equality
espoused by the larger culture. In short, black experience
with life may teach a significant minority of blacks a
different set of ideas.

Similarly, student isolation from the general
public also teaches them ideas which may be inharmonious
with those of the larger culture. Most college campuses
are relatively isolated physically and perhaps ideologically from the outside community.[94] College communities,
particularly the prestigeous ones, tend to be sanctified
places where discussions include consideration of anti-
regime ideas, along with others, in order to arrive at
such academic goals as trans-political truths and value
free analyses. The college campus may be the first place
many young, impressionable, and immature students have
their values vigorously attacked or reinforced. The
physical isolation from the outside world and the crowding
into a relatively small area of college campuses make face
to face communication easier and facilitate common agreement on political ideologies, organization, and action.
The geographic concentration of both blacks and students
gives them territory to defend from outsiders, whether
from police or other groups perceived as agents of the
larger political culture. That defense, however, is
characteristically founded on a kind of "scorched earth"
policy.[95]

Mass media

The mass media accentuates and advertizes the news
worthy problems and similarities of these subcultures and
their differences from the larger culture. For example,
in magazines, movies, and on television, blacks see
idealized versions of middle class affluence, which they
may feel is unjustly denied them. As Tocqueville might
suggest, the media also makes blacks aware that they
share their under-privileged position with millions of
other blacks living outside of their own immediate community. The mass media and underground press also communicate ready-made and easily understood ideologies, doctrines
and tactics for blacks, intellectuals, and students.
Although there is little unity in such ideoloties, a great

---

[94]See Commission on Isla Vista, Report of the Commission on Isla Vista, prepared by a commission directed by
Martin Trow (Santa Barbara, Calif.: University of California, October 9, 1970), especially pp. 12-26.

[95]On territoriality in ghettos, see Richard E.
Rubenstein, Rebels in Eden: Mass Political Violence in the
United States (Boston: Little, Brown and Co., 1970).

number of them in recent years have been extremely critical
of American society, culture and politics.

Youth as a counter culture--
"The Generation Gap"
Many people have suggested that the black and
student communities also share common demographic characteristics which may make them more receptive to counter
cultural ideas. The most important common demographic
characteristic is that black urban communities and colleges
are overwhelmingly inhabited by young people. At first
glance, age seems to be the most characteristic attribute
of both political disruption and political subcultures.
Yet family background, education, and socio-economic
class variables seem to be more explanatory or determina-
tive of different political attitudes than mere age alone.
One explanation for recent student discontent has
been the "generation gap"[96] or the existence of a youth
culture.[97] To be sure, the young have always provided the
energy and idealism for a great number of disruptive
activities and peaceful social movements of all kinds.
Walter Miller reports youthful street gangs existed as
early as 1800 in America.[98] Lipset shows that American
student protest movements also have a long history.[99]
Closer to the interests of this paper, Berger reports the
young have always been one source of recruits for "counter
culture" movements or deviant groups. He reports "bohemian-
like or hippy-like behavior" going back at least to 1850 in

---

[96]See Lewis S. Feuer, The Conflict of Generations:
The Character and Significance of Social Movements (New
York: Basic Books, Inc., 1969).

[97]See Scranton Commission.

[98]Walter Miller, "White Gangs," The Anti-American
Generation, ed. Edgar Z. Friedenberg (New York: Transaction
Books, distributed by Aldine Publishing Co., 1971), pp.
177-216.

[99]On student protests over the Korean War and sup-
port for socialism during the depression, see Lipset,
Rebellion..., especially pp. 49, 184, 189, and chaps. iv-v.
On earlier European student movements, see Edith H.
Altbach, "Vanguard of Revolt: Students and Politics in
Central Europe, 1815-1848," Students in Revolt, ed. Seymour
Martin Lipset and Philip G. Altbach (Boston: Beacon Press,
1970), pp. 451-474.

America.[100]

The young also seem to be more predisposed to participate in violent behavior than other age groups. They
are also higher participants in crimes. Indeed, Easton and
Dennis report that the adolescent has less respect for
political authority and higher police contact than grammar
school children or those over thirty.[101] Their responses
to perceived injustices are also more likely to be energetic. For example, a national Harris poll of whites found
that 33% of the age group thirty-five and under would be
"mad, resentful and fight back" if discriminated against;
the national sample average was only 26%.[102] The Campbell
violence commission study of fifteen cities reported that
teenagers, both white (21%) and black (19.5%), were more
predisposed toward violence than any other group.[103]
Similarly, arrestees in black riots were more likely to be
young.[104] In Tomlinson's study, 30% of the militants were

---

[100]Bennett M. Berger, "Hippie Morality-- More Old
Than New," The Anti-American Generation, ed. Edgar Z.
Friedenberg (New York: Transaction Books, distributed by
Aldine Publishing Co., 1971), pp. 82-83, citing Malxolm
Cowly, Exile's Return: A Literary Odyssey of the 1920's
(New York: The Viking Press, 1964), and Henry Murger,
Scenes of Bohemian Life (n.p.: n.d.).

[101]Easton and Dennis, Children in the Political
System..., pp. 298-300.

[102]Hazel Erskine, "The Polls: Demonstrations and
Race Riots," Public Opinion Quarterly, Vol. XXXI, No. 4
(Winter, 1967-1968), p. 667.

[103]Angus Campbell and Howard Schuman, "Racial Attitudes in Fifteen American Cities." Supplemental Studies for
the National Advisory Commission on Civil Disorders (Washington, D. C.: U. S. Government Printing Office, July,
1968), p. 58.

[104]Robert M. Fogelson and Robert B. Hill, "Who
Riots? A Study of Participation in the 1967 Riots,"
Supplemental Studies for the National Advisory Commission on
Civil Disorders (Washington, D. C.: U. S. Government Printing
Office, July, 1968), p. 235. See also Nathan E. Cohen (ed.),
The Los Angeles Riots: A Socio-Psychological Study (New
York: Praeger, 1970); and the Kerner Commission. The
oversupply of the young may help to explain in absolute
numbers greater political activity during the late 1960's
and early 1970's (see Hugh Folk, "Oversupply of the Young,"
The Anti-American Generation, ed. Edgar Z. Friedenberg [New
York: Transaction Books, distributed by Aldine Publishing
Co., 1971], pp. 161-176; and Frances Weismiller, "Youth and
Revolution," Claremont Courier [Claremont, Calif.], November
14, 1970, pp. 12-14). The greatest increases in the supply
has been on campus.

male youths.[105]

Many suggest that this "generation gap" is more important than a mere difference in age would suggest. Blacks and teenagers together make up a full 38% of the population.[106] Thus, if blacks and the young make a coalition with the poor and intellectuals, they may constitute a potential realignment of political parties and thus provide a large block of votes for mobilizing social reform. This seemed to be Senator McGovern's strategy in the race for the presidency, at least until his nomination by the Democratic Party. This possibility is already evident in the fact that in 1971-1972 young voters eighteen to twenty-five were registering 60%-75% (depending upon the source) with the Democratic Party rather than with the Republican Party. A 1969 Harris poll also suggests the possibility of a black/youth coalition. This study shows that teenagers and blacks take nearly the same position on the unfairness of the draft (65% of blacks and 65% of teenagers in agreement). The same study also shows that 60% of blacks and 59% of teenagers agreed with the statement: "People running the country don't want to listen to young people." Similarly, 46% of blacks and 45% of teenagers expressed belief in the hypocrisy of parents.[107]

Despite these shared discontents, the young blacks and whites do not present a new phenomenon, as the term generation gap suggests. Most studies reveal that young people generally reflect the views and values of their parents.[108] Indeed, Douglas points out that most campus

---

[105]See Chapter VII, and T. M. Tomlinson, "The Development of a Riot Ideology Among Urban Negroes," American Behavioral Scientist, Vol. XI (March/April, 1968), pp. 27-31.

[106]Louis Harris, "A Young People's Alliance of Whites, Blacks, Growing," Long Island Press, September 11, 1969.

[107]Ibid. On disillusionment and fading images of benevolence of political authority in pre-adolescence and adolescence, see Greenstein, Children..., pp. 51-52.

[108]See "The Un-Radical Young," p. 24; Samuel Lubell, "That Generation Gap," The Public Interest, Vol. XIII (Fall, 1968), pp. 52-60; and Seymour Martin Lipset and Sheldon S. Wolin (eds.), The Berkeley Student Revolt: Facts and Interpretations (Garden City, N. J.: Doubleday-Anchor Books, 1965). The one exception seems to be those in the drug culture. Yet they tend to be withdrawn radicals or nonpolitical. See Clarke and Levine, pp. 120-130; and Geoffrey Simon and Grafton Trout, "Hippies in College," The Anti-American Generation, ed. Edgar Z. Friedenberg (New York: Transaction Books, distributed by Aldine Publishing Co., 1971), pp. 19-27.

activists come from liberal or radical families.[109] Lubell
and Lipset also found that radical students are the sons
and daughters of leftist parents.[110] These findings are
fairly universal among most young people. One national
poll found that at least 37% of young people accept or agree
with their parent's values and ideals.[111] This is true of
black youngsters as well as of white youth.[112]

It is also interesting to note that nationally the
young were <u>not</u> the group most likely to oppose the war in
Vietnam. Lipset has said,

> Opinion surverys dealing with the relationship of age
> as such to opinion towards the Vietnam war indicate
> that from 1965 to 1971, those in the lowest adult age
> group, twenty-one to twenty-nine years old, were con-
> sistently <u>less likely</u> to oppose the war than their
> elders though the gap narrowed in recent years.
> . . . .
> As a matter of fact, those fifty and over remained
> the most anti-war age group through to 1971.[113]

Although the young provided a substantial portion of the
1968 anti-war McCarthy campaign, they also made up a large
portion of the supporters for George Wallace in 1968 and
for conservative James Buckley in his 1970 senatorial
campaign in New York. Moreover, McCarthy's young suppor-

---

[109]William O. Douglas, <u>Points of Rebellion</u> (New
York: Random House, Vintage Books, 1970), p. 29.

[110]Lubell, "That Generation Gap"; and Lipset and
Wolin, <u>The Berkeley...</u> .

[111]"The Un-Radical Young," p. 24.

[112]Raymond J. Murphy and James W. Watson, "The
Structure of Discontent: The Relationship Between Social
Structure, Grievances, and Riot Support," <u>The Los Angeles
Riots: A Socio-Psychological Study</u>, ed. Nathan E. Cohen
(New York: Praeger, 1970), p. 194.

[113]Lipset, <u>Rebellion...</u>, pp. 38-39. "This
'generation gap' that one would have expected wherein the
young oppose the war and the old support it, simply failed
to appear." (Philip E. Converse and Howard Schuman,
"'Silent Majorities' and the Vietnam War," <u>Scientific
American</u>, Vol. CCXXII [June, 1970], p. 22). See also
Milton J. Rosenberg, Sidney Verba, and Philip E. Converse,
<u>Vietnam and the Silent Majority</u> (New York: Harper and Row,
1970), pp. 65-73.

ters were anti-war, but they were not anti-establishment.[114]

A study of young combat soldiers in Vietnam also indicates a predominance of pro-establishment views among some youths. In this study, the young soldiers expressed antipathy to anti-war protesters, whom they said were an over-privileged social group. But most important, they were motivated to fight obviously by desire to stay alive but also by a desire to defend the American way of life. Their belief in the legitimacy of American institutions was, to be sure, quite apolitical and only latently ideological as a set of shared sentiments and salient values. Most (over half) specifically connected the war with defending America on "stop communism" grounds. When asked to "tell me in your words, what makes America different from other countries," These soldiers responded generally in answers involving the creature comforts of the American standard of living.[115] A typical comment referred to the United States materialistically as the " land of the big PX."[116]

An analysis of the opinions of young union members may be useful to emphasize the marginal usefulness of the term generation gap as an explanation for the widespread existence of any youthful counter culture. Although union members under twenty-five rank somewhat higher in their concern for "civil rights" as the most pressing issue (7.21% versus 4.4% for total union membership) and lower in their concern for "law and order" as the most pressing issue (6.25% versus 14.2%), these younger union men, along with the more senior union members, also place inflation (27.88%) and high taxes (18.26%) in positions of the highest priority. The younger union members are half as likely to identify with the Democratic Party (27.35% versus 70.0% for those over fifty-five), and they are more likely to identify themselves as independent (29.71% versus 6.7% for union membership as a whole).[117] These young

---

[114]Melvin Kahn, "Students for McCarthy-- What Unites Them," The Anti-American Generation, ed. Edgar Z. Friedenberg (New York: Transaction Books, distributed by Aldine Publishing Co., 1971), pp. 49-52.

[115]Interestingly, only one black out of nine in the combat unit called America racist.

[116]Charles C. Moskos, Jr., "Vietnam: Why Men Fight," The Anti-American Generation, ed. Edgar Z. Friedenberg (New York: Transaction Books, distributed by Aldine Publishing Co., 1979), pp. 217-238.

[117]United Rubber Workers, Research Dept., Membership Attitudes and Opinion, A Report to the United Rubber, Cork, Linoleum, and Plastic Workers of America (1970).

58

union members may be leaning, however, not to the left but
toward George Wallace, as did 20% to 25% of the young in
a national poll in March, 1971.[118] In 1968, a good part of
the Wallace support may have been in the South, as only 13%
of the young under thirty outside of the South voted for
Wallace in 1968. Nevertheless, this figure for the political affiliation of the young compares with the national
vote in 1968 as a whole: it is not very different.

The facts just surveyed indicate that a youth counter culture antithetical to American values is not as omnipresent as some would suggest.[119] Indeed, one national
study reveals that most young people do not advocate the
counter cultural values of hedonism, anti-puritanism, and
anti-materialism. Sixty-one percent agreed that "hard work
leads to success"; 66% agreed that wealth is "the kind of
success worth striving for"; 57% stated that premarital
sexual relations are not "all right," even if you are planning to marry;[120] and 62% believe marijuana smoking leads
to hard drug addiction.[121] Similarly, marijuana usage is
most likely to be frequent among those students from
families with incomes over $25,000. The highest figure
for non-usage (56%) was for those with income backgrounds
of $10,000 or less.[122]

This review indicates that youth is probably likely
to be only somewhat more discontented than their elders.
Moreover, the young generally do not share similar ideologies of discontent. The young probably do not constitute
anything near a ready-made subculture or political constituency with similar feelings of discontent. Thus, if the
definition of subculture, in terms of predominant values
within a substrata of the political culture, is adequate,
this study must reject age itself as more than a small
contributory factor in the development of subcultural

---

[118]See Lipset, Rebellion..., pp. 12, and 121. See
also Seymour Martin Lipset and Earl Raab, The Politics of
Unreason: Right-Wing Extremism in America, 1790-1970 (New
York: Harper and Row, 1970).

[119]See Charles A. Reich, The Greening of America
(New York: Bantam Books, Random House, 1971); Jean-
Francois Revel, Without Marx or Jesus: The New American
Revolution Has Begun, trans. Jack Bernard (New York:
Doubleday and Co., Inc., 1971); and Scranton Commission.

[120]Seventy-eight percent no for sexual intercourse
if dating; 69% no if going steady.

[121]"The Un-Radical Young."

[122]"Playboy's Student Survey," Playboy, Vol.XVII,
No. 9 (September, 1970), p. 236.

values. The young have in common only their energy and perhaps idealism. The directions in which such energy and
idealism may go are multiple, from supporting a Maoist revolution, voting for George Wallace, to stopping communism.

The consequences of subcultures for the political system: imperfect socialization

Both the black ghetto and the college community may
be two distinctive subcultures in that their members, generally young people, do perhaps share common values. The
development of these political subcultures has been through
cumulative and reinforcing interactions of behavior and
values within a given time and space. This continual
interaction may result in a process of political deso-
cialization or "deauthorization."[123] The result of the
differential experiences of the black and student subcultures may be a "disjunctive socialization process,"[124]
or "differential socialization."[125] Under this condition,
there is imperfect learning or acculturation of some of
the ideas or myths of the larger political culture-- that
is, the subculture is not fully integrated into the value
system of the larger political culture.[126] The evidence
would indicate that whatever regime efforts there are to
indoctrinate or to socialize have little effect on either
blacks, who cannot believe what is said in the light of
social reality, or on academicians, who have a professional
interest in doubting the conventional wisdom, myths of

---

[123]Luiz Simmons, "Students as a Subculture: Look
Out Nation-State, 'Cause Youth is 'Gonna Get Your Momma,"
Protagonists of Change: Subcultures in Development and
Revolution, ed. Abdul A. Said (Englewood Cliffs, N. J.:
Prentice-Hall, Inc., 1971), p. 29.

[124]Henry Bienen, Violence and Social Change
(Chicago: University of Chicago Press, 1968), p. 48.

[125]Coser, "Violence and the Social Sturcture,"
pp. 71-84.

[126]For literature on political integration, see
Jacob and Toscano, The Integration...; and Deutsch et al.,
"Political Community...," pp. 1-91. On political develop-
ment, see Lucian W. Pye, Aspects of Political Development
(Boston: Little, Brown and Co., 1966); and Gabriel A.
Almond and G. Bingham Powell, Jr., Comparative Politics:
A Developmental Approach (Boston: Little, Brown and Co.,
1966).

the regime and idealized images of political authority presented by well-meaning parents[127] and perhaps high school civics teachers.[128]

Thus, life in certain subcultures may result in a high receptivity to alternative political ideas, at least by a significant portion of the subcultural population. The specific content of such ideas may vary considerably within the same community. Similarly, there will be differential perception of the legitimacy of the values of the wider culture, giving rise to alternative objectives that may or may not be sought through political violence. Some of these objectives are: radical reform, anarchy, and revolution.

The Meaning of Subcultural Experiences
and Values: The Injustice of the
Relative Deprivation
of Privilege

When there is a great discrepancy between one's expectations of privilege, social status, or political power, and the actual distribution of power and status within the regime (as selectively perceived in one's subculture), a form of relative deprivation of privilege may occur. Many political activists have implicitly justified their violent political acts in terms of the injustices of the relative deprivation of their rightful privileges. Those who attack the regime are those who experience relative deprivation of the privilege to which they aspire or expect. Thus, those who attack the regime are those who believe the regime has denied them privileges which they perceive as rights. Yet larger percentages of individuals in some groups than in other groups may experience this relative deprivation of privilege.

Deprivation of black activists

For example, Negroes are clearly under-privileged, because they believe they lack the full rights and privileges of citizenship as a result of their socio-economic inequality, exemplified by poverty, discrimination, and segregation. Such racially engendered deprivation is real, but it is not absolute. Black deprivation is relative in terms of perceived progress in relation to white middle

---

[127]Greenstein, Children..., pp. 39-40, 45-46. See also Robert D. Hess and David Easton, "The Child's Changing Image of the President," Public Opinion Quarterly, Vol. XXIV (1960), pp. 632-644.

[128]"The Negro American-- What Must Be Done," Newsweek, November 20, 1967, pp. 33-42, 46-48, 51-54, 57-60, and 65.

class affluence judged in the light of the egalitarian
norms of the political culture. Thus, although 45% to 60%
(depending on the subject) of blacks nationally believed
they had progressed in schools, restaurants, jobs, voting,
pay, and housing,[129] many of the most severe riots took
place in Watts and Detroit, areas in which living conditions
were better or progressing more rapidly than in many other
black communities around the nation.

How deprived were those who actually participated
in ghetto riots? Campbell's study shows that those who planned
to join a riot were fairly dissatisfied with housing (59%),
reported no personal experience with job discrimination
(51%), and had white friends (63%).[130] Not everyone was
completely dissatisfied by their deprivation. In Watts, the
employed felt higher levels of discrimination than the unemployed (49.2% versus 38.1%).[131] Murphy and Watson suggest
this may mean greater actual contact with discrimination.[132]
Brink and Harris report that those most likely to say they
would join a riot are the lower-middle, middle, and upper
income Negroes, but not the lower income Negroes.[133] Sears
and MacConahay report that intermediate economic status

---

[129]Louis Harris, "Report from Black America: A Newsweek Poll," Newsweek, June 30, 1969, pp. 17-26, 31-35.

[130]See Campbell and Schuman, "Racial Attitudes...,"
p. 58. Tomlinson says that levels of unemployment were
quite similar for militants, the uncommitted, and conserva-
tives: about 70% in each group were employed. See T. M.
Tomlinson, "Ideological Foundations for Negro Action: A
Comparative Analysis of Militant and Non-militant Views of
the Los Angeles Riot," Journal of Social Issues, Vol. XXVI,
No. 1 (1970), pp. 96-98. See also Nathan S. Caplan and
Jeffery M. Paige, "A Study of Ghetto Rioters," Scientific
American, Vol. CCXIX (August, 1968), pp. 15-21; and
Nathan S. Caplan and Jeffery M. Paige, "Data on Newark and
Detroit Negro Residents," Report of the National Advisory
Commission on Civil Disorders, National Advisory Commission
on Civil Disorders (Washington, D. C.: U. S. Printing
Office, 1968), pp. 171-178.

[131]Murphy and Watson, "The Structure of Discontent...,"
p. 206.

[132]For evidence, see below, Chapter VII.

[133]William Brink and Louis Harris, Black and White:
A Study of U.S. Racial Attitudes Today (New York: Simon
and Schuster, 1966), p. 266.

levels were the most participative in the Watts riot.[134]
Hometown people, rather than recent immigrants from the
South, contributed most to the Watts rioting, as they did
in other riots as well.[135]
    Thus, the active were not objectively worse off than
the inactive. Yet the active tended to feel greater subjective dissatisfaction. Tomlinson reported that larger percentages of his militants identified themselves as lower
class (20% versus 11% conservatives and 14% uncommitted);
and lower percentages of militants reported middle class
status (28% versus 37% conservatives and 35% uncommitted).[136]
Militants were also more likely to find social contacts with
whites distasteful, even though they voluntarily had more
such contacts.[137] Most important, the militants had higher
aspirations:

> The consciousness of repression leads to discontent only
> when it is felt unnecessary. This is the reason why a
> rising class, which is actually becoming constantly
> better off objectively, generally rebels most readily,
> and why the most severe repression has so often failed
> to cause a revolution.[138]

Tomlinson says that the rioters are distinguished, not by
their objective employment level, but by their subjective
dissatisfaction with their present jobs.[139] The militants
had higher aspirations probably based on their somewhat
higher levels of education: 63% completed high school compared with 57% of the conservatives and 53% of the uncommitted. Similarly, twice as many of the militants had a
college degree (7% versus 3%).[140] Militants had higher

---

[134]David O. Sears and John B. MacConahay, "The Politics of Discontent," The Los Angeles Riots: A Socio-Psychological Study, ed. Nathan E. Cohen (New York: Praeger,
1970), p. 467.

[135]Murphy and Watson, "The Structure of Discontent...," p. 198. See also Kerner Commission.

[136]Tomlinson, "Ideological...," JSI, p. 97.

[137]Ibid., p. 103.

[138]George Sawyer Pettee, The Process of Revolution
("Studies in Systematic Political Science and Comparative
Government," Vol. V; New York: Harper and Bros., 1938),
cited by Murphy and Watson, "The Structure of Discontent...," p. 208.

[139]Tomlinson, "Ideological...," JSI, pp. 99-100.

[140]Ibid., p. 96.

levels of self-esteem and political efficacy. They were
less likely (74% versus 82% conservative and 80% uncommitted) to say "voting is the only way people like me can
have a say about how the government runs things." In
Newark, rioters were more dissatisfied than the non-involved
with present job status (70% versus 55.6%), job opportunities (67.6% versus 56.1%), and obstacles (69% versus
50%).[141]

    Apparently, riot participation for blacks may be
closely related to their deprivation in terms of their perception that they deserve, but have been denied, social and
economic equality commensurate with that of other races,
groups, or individuals. Thus, the fact of deprivation alone
does not lead blacks to violence. Only those who perceive
this deprivation to be a state of under-privilege in relation to other groups (probably based on the idea of
equality) resort to violence.

Student deprivation

    Similarly, not all those so privileged with respect
to education are radicals or even violent. The intervening
variable for students, as with blacks, is their subjective
perception of a deprivation-- in this case, probably the
deprivation of power and influence. Access to the privileges of education and socio-economic status over and above
the average opportunities may, perhaps, lead some students
to believe their education qualifies them for greater political power based on their "competence," "merit," and
"virtue."[142] In "The Revolt of the Thinking Class," Rein
Taagepera says,

> The services of these new groups are indispensible to
> society's new mode of functioning. The new groups know
> it themselves, and so do others. But there is no empty
> niche waiting for them in society's privilege structure,
> the new class has to struggle to gain a share of power
> commensurate with its share of services.
> ....
> [They may] feel they are entitled to more than a con-
> sultive role.[143]

---

[141]Kerner Commission, p. 175.

[142]This writer agrees with Henry Fielding, who made
Tom Jones say, "It is just as easy for a man not to go to
school and know something as it is for a man to go to school
and know nothing." This profound insight is not meant to be
applied to this writer or any reader. The source is the
movie, "Tom Jones."

[143]Rein Taagepera, "The Revolt of the Thinking
Class," Queens Quarterly, Vol. LXXVIII, No. 1 (Spring,
1971), pp. 19, 25.

Thus, some members of the academic community may feel
deprived of their rightful claim to lead or at least to
have special influence within the American political system.
    According to Aristotle, there are two sources for
discontent among the educated: having both property and
office equal to other citizens.

> Men of education become revolutionary when the distri-
> bution of office is equal. ... If there is equality of
> property , men of education would be aggrieved by the
> system, feeling that they deserve something more than
> mere equality; indeed as a matter of actual observation,
> they often rise in revolt and cause civic discord for
> this very reason.[144]

The great injustice which intellectuals face is that few
recognize or appreciate their educationally based enlightenment. The educated probably seek both power and morality
in politics. Thus, one should not see student and intellectual dissent and violence purely as a grab for power
devoid of purpose. For example, many intellectuals argue
that the present leadership, in permitting (perhaps even
supporting) the gross injustices of poverty, racism, and
imperialism, is morally incompetent to rule.
    Similarly, Schlesinger believes that one reason for
the characteristic inclination of the intellectual toward
change is their social and economic position: "as outsiders, with power and status below what they consider
their deserts, they tend to succumb to envy and resentment."[145] They often consider themselves guardians of
reason and seekers of reform, change, and social justice.[146]
Similarly, Ward Elliot describes the basically liberal
establishment created by the Roosevelt revolution as the
guardians. They are "the sophisticated reformist intellectuals" in and out of government and power:

> They shared their own version of the Platonic dream of
> an educated elite .. possessed of the inward convic-
> tion that they must always do what they believe to be
> best for the commonwealth.[147]

---

[144]Aristotle Politics Bk ii, pp. 65, 67.

[145]Schlesinger, Crisis..., p. 69.

[146]Arthur M. Schlesinger, Jr., Violence: America
in the Sixties (New York: Signet Books, 1968), pp. 63, 86.

[147]Ward Elliot, "The Guardian Ethic," Praxis
(Claremont, California), May, 1971, p. 14.

Elliot's references are to a well-established liberal elite now generally sharing power with business, military, and other elites. Yet his term the "guardians" is also reflective of the best intentions of the over-privileged socio-economically who are now out of power but aspire to it.

Privilege in Transition: "Revolution
of Rising Expectations"

If such deprivations of privilege are timeless, why is it then that this problem of the relative deprivation of privilege is coming to a crisis at this time in America? The social science literature on ghetto riots is replete with explanations of the psychological frustration created by socio-economic deprivation. As indicated above, the most sophisticated of these analyses focuses more precisely on relative deprivation rather than on absolute deprivation.[148] One useful cliche to describe this contemporary phenomena is the "revolution of rising expectations."[149] In this revolution of rising expectations, the fundamental source of frustration is not merely those actual conditions which have always existed for most American blacks and all poor people everywhere. Relative deprivation depends on the subjective meaning given to these conditions. Relative deprivation among blacks is their belief that they are now rightfully and justly entitled to socio-economic status and privilege equal to those of the white working and middle classes who dominate the American polity. Today blacks expect fulfillment of the American creed of equality of political privilege to manifest itself in social and economic equality, as it does for the middle class.

---

[148]Some analyses focus on a sudden increase in the gap. Empirically, probably the most drastic changes have occurred in changes in expectations. With Sputnik, the academic community suddenly achieved a status hitherto denied in American history. A return to normality has dashed these hopes. Similarly, the irresponsible promise of an end to poverty roused black hopes beyond any possibility of the immediate fulfillment promised. Changes in ideas have always been more dangerous than changes in conditions which are less rapid. Ideas are easy. Actual change is much more difficult.

[149]Aristotle's solution may be the only one, but it does not coincide with the democratic aspirations of contemporary thought. "It is more necessary to equalize men's desires than their properties: and that is a result which cannot be achieved unless men are adequately trained by the influence of laws." (Aristotle *Politics* Bk ii, p. 64.)

The modern understanding of that creed of equality,
however, is possibly an expansion or intensification of the
American dream of "equality of opportunity," originally
applied essentially to political conditions. As Tocqueville
suggested, social and technological improvements make
possible the thought of perfecting equality by showing means
of expanding its application:

> In proportion as castes disappear and the classes of
> society approximate-- as manners, customs, and laws
> vary, from the tumultuous intercourse of men-- as
> new facts arise-- as new truths are brought to light--
> as ancient opinions are dissipated and others take
> their place-- the image of an ideal perfection, forever
> on the wing, presents itself to the human mind.[150]

The intellectuals are likely to play key roles in this
expansion of the application of equality. For example,
Tocqueville attributes noble and thorough-going objectives
to intellectuals in the French Revolution:

> The guidance of public opinion, when its first stir-
> rings made themselves felt, came entirely into the
> hands of the philosophers, that is to say the intel-
> lectuals, it was only to be expected that the direc-
> tives of the Revolution should take the form of ab-
> stract principles, highly generalized theories, and
> that political realities would be largely overlooked.
> Thus, instead of attacking only such laws as seemed
> objectionable, the idea developed that all laws indis-
> criminately must be abolished and a wholly new system
> of government, sponsored by these writers, should
> replace the ancient French constitution.[151]

Political equality is easily attainable, at least
in legislation, due to its application to a limited set of
formal institutions and activities, such as voting. In
contrast, an expansion of equality into economic spheres
requires more thorough-going and fundamental changes in
society. These fundamental changes may inevitably pit
the rich against the poor, whites against blacks, and the
highly educated against those less educated. Such class
politics may tend to break down the Madisonian system of
the multiplicity of interests which has hitherto reduced

[150]Alexis de Tocqueville, "Democracy in America,"
The Enduring Questions of Politics, ed. Werner Feld, Alan
T. Leonard, and Walter W. Torey, Jr. (Englewood Cliffs,
N. J.: Prentice-Hall Inc., 1969), p. 155.

[151]Tocqueville, The Old Regime..., p. 205.

class conflict.[152] Large percentages of blacks and aca-
demics use inequality as their justification and/or ration-
alization for the use of violence to redress their particular lack of privileges. Both claim they do not have
enough privilege.

Potential For Violence

If those seeking these privileges begin to constitute a significantly active minority within these generally
under-privileged and over-privileged communities, the
general public may resist their efforts. The result may be
violence between the agents of both those seeking change
because of their belief in their unfair share of regime
privileges and those desiring preservation of the existing
social, economic, and political order. In American democracy, Tocqueville predicted not only racial conflict but
also resistence by the American middle class to those with
great poverty, opulence, or education:

> Between these two extremes ... of democratic communi-
> ties stands an innumerable multitude of men almost
> alike ... possess[ing] sufficient property to desire
> the maintenance of order. ... Such men are the natural
> enemies of violent commotions. ... [This keeps] others
> still and secures the balance of the fabric of
> society.[153]

The intellectual condemnation of the middle class
culture may contribute to the uneasiness of the American
majority. Intellectuals often believe they can rise above
the often vulgar materialism inexorably unleashed in the
American society of the Madisonian design-- a large
commercial republic. Note that, with little modification,

---

[152]In 1830, Tocqueville said the following about
America: "America has already lost the great parties which
once divided the nation; and if her Happiness is considerably increased, her morality has suffered by their extinction ... in the absence of great parties; the United States
abound with lesser controversies; and public opinion is
divided into a thousand minute shades of difference upon
questions of very little moment." (Toqueville, _Demo-
cracy..._, Vol. I, p. 111.)

[153]_Ibid._, Vol. II, p. 266. Similarly, Aristotle
said that the middle class lends stability to the regime by
counter-balancing the over-strong, over-noble, and over-
wealthy, and by restraining the over-poor, over-weak, and
the ignoble. See also Aristotle _Politics_ Bks iv-v, pp.
181-214.

Zetterbaum's paraphrase of Tocqueville's description of
aristocratic conditions could describe the intellectual
state of mind:

> An aristocratic state of society ... is a certain
> elevation of mind and scorn of worldly advantages,
> strong convictions and honorable devotedness, refined
> habits and embellished manners, the cultivation of the
> arts and of theoretical sciences, a love of poetry,
> beauty, and glory, the capacity to carry on great
> enterprises of enduring worth.[154]

This new aristoi condemns and demeans the sickness of the
middle class[155] and its apparent support or complicacy in
racism, police brutality, repression and imperialism. To
some intellectuals, the middle class regime is symbolized
and typified by low tastes, immoral politics, and the
ideas of Richard Nixon, J. Edgar Hoover, Billy Graham,
Ronald Reagan, Spiro Agnew, and Walter Reuther.
    This aristocratic vision stands in marked contrast
to the stultifying conformity, materialism, and intellectual
mediocrity that Tocqueville predicted for American democracy. Tocqueville saw these as the inherent consequences
of breaking the aristocratic bonds which had hitherto kept
selfish individualism in check. Such fragmentation of
social bonds institutes mass public opinion as the major
force in politics, at the expense of an exclusive reliance
on either philosophers, intellectuals, statesmen, or
aristocrats. If the masses believe certain behavior to be

---

[154]Zetterbaum, "Alexis de Tocqueville," p. 660.

[155]A recent example is found in a review of a novel
by F. D. Reive, where the reviewer says, "This ... novel ...
portrays all the ugliness of the American middle class."
(Quoted in "Age of the Bomb," p. 629.) Intellectual hate
for the middle class was discussed in a lecture by Howard
Elison, "Why It Is Terrible to Hate the American People,"
lecture presented at Claremont, Calif., November 19, 1969.
Seymour Martin Lipset, in a lecture, "Politics of the
Intellectual," at Claremont, California on December 18,
1969, discussed both liberal and conservative criticism
of mass mediocrity and the low tastes of businessmen.
Intellectual estrangement from American society is also
more sympathetically discussed by Schlesinger, Crisis...,
pp. 59-60, 86, 239-240; and by Hofstadter, "Reflections...," p. 11. Wildavsky sees our age essentially as
an elitist "revolt against the masses." (See Aaron Wildavsky, The Revolt Against the Masses: And Other Essays on
Politics and Public Policy [New York: Basic Books, Inc.,
Publishers, 1971], especially chap i, pp. 20-51.) See
also Reich, Greening... .

immoral and improper, they may unjustly harass the few who
behave in the unapproved manner, whether they are the poor
or the uneducated. The ruling middle class is not likely
to give immediate support to what they may perceive as a
radical and immediate effort to redistribute material
opportunities or political power. Of course, those blacks
seeking economic and social equality and those intellectuals seeking the right to rule morally believe their
causes are just. Thus, when the high stakes of blacks
and some intellectuals confront the "backlash" resistance
of the "silent" and "forgotten" white middle and white
lower classes, the consequences might easily be violence.
According to some in the over-privileged and under-
privileged groups, violence might be the only means to
achieve immediate change in the application of the principle of equality.

Thus, the argument of this dissertation is that
some significant minority, perhaps a majority of members
of the black community and the academic milieu may hold
ideas contrary to those more commonly held in the nation.
These ideas are formed partially by common experiences in
a shared environment. This thesis has identified those
conditions as the existence of under-privileged and over-
privileged subcultures. Some portion of individuals within
these communities or subcultures may resort to violence.[156]
Thus, there may be intimate connections between subculture,
privilege, privilege and equality, equality and justice,
and ultimately injustice and violence. Yet all members of
any group do not hold the exact same opinions, nor do they
all resort to violence, nor do they all have the same immediate political purposes or alternatives. That is, some
may seek reform, others may advocate revolution, still
others see anarchy as a solution.

---

[156]For peripheral comments on subcultures and vio-
lence, see the following articles in the Harry Eckstein
edited volume, Internal War...: Marion J. Levy, Jr., "A
Revision of the Gemeinschaft-Gesellschaft Categories and
Some Aspects of the Interdependencies of Minority and Host
Systems," pp. 251-259; Arnold S. Feldman, "Violence and
Volatility: The Likelihood of Revolution," especially pp.
112-128; and Seymour Martin Lipset, "Democracy and the
Social System," especially pp. 267-312.

CHAPTER III

TOWARD AN UNDERSTANDING OF LEGITIMACY:
PROBLEMS OF ANALYSIS, MYTHS OF
AUTHORITY, AND OBJECTS   OF
DEMOCRATIC LEGITIMACY

Might not legitimacy be a forbidden subject, one
of those deep mysteries that men are not permitted
to touch? Had I any right to meddle with it?[1]

Acceptance of, and even devotion to, authority is
a pervasive phenomenon which we take for granted;
it has an atmosphere of ubiquity, ever-present yet
inconspicuous.[2]

This chapter discusses the problematic study of
legitimacy, competing regime myths, democratic legitimacy,
objects of democratic legitimacy, the change of legitimacy
myths, and the relationship of changing myths and values
to political violence in America. The value of a study of
legitimacy may lie in deriving an improved understanding
of such general political objectives and problems as stability and change, conflict and concensus, obedience and
disobedience. Yet there are considerable difficulties to
such a study.

Problems in the Study of Legitimacy

Easton says,

It is important for us to explore some of the reasons
why the whole idea of legitimacy has played so central
a part in reflections on political life (especially on
problems of political obligation) even though in em-

---

[1]Guglielmo Ferrero, The Principles of Power: The
Great Political Crises of History, trans. Theodore Jaechel
(New York: G. P. Putnam's Sons, 1945), p. 277.

[2]Greenstein, Children..., p. 53.

pirically oriented perspectives it has received sur-
prisingly little attention.[3]

In fact, the subject is so little explored that practically
anything and everything has been said about legitimacy.
There does not seem to be any way of avoiding the thicket
into which this discussion now plunges.

Sources of Legitimacy

Studies of political socialization have found
ubiquitious sources of legitimacy beliefs, ranging from
the womb to the United Nations. For example, Weber's
sources are rational, legal, traditional, and charismatic.[4]
Easton's sources are ideological, structural, and personal.[5] Most sources of legitimacy lie either in the
social nature of man[6] and/or in his fear of anarchy and
war.[7] Freud saw legitimacy beliefs arising out of a fear
of punishment by authority figures.[8] Recently, most social
scientists see legitimacy beliefs arising out of certain
dynamic processes of bargaining[9] or learning. What is
learned or how it is learned varies considerably from writer
to writer. Merelman says people rationalize rewards from
authority into a belief in the legitimacy of that authority.
Greenstein concentrates on the process of political socialization by a variety of agents: parents, teachers, neigh-
bors, peers, media, and leaders.[10] According to Weber and
MacIver, people learn traditions, customs, and mores.[11]
Dahl notes that psychological predispositions affect political leaders.[12] Others have discussed many personality

---

[3]Easton, A Systems Analysis..., pp. 278-279.

[4]Max Wever, Theory of Social and Economic Organization, trans. A. M. Henderson and Talcott Parsons (New York:
Oxford University Press, 1947), pp. 124-130, 334-339.

[5]Easton, A Systems Analysis..., p. 287.

[6]MacIver, Web..., pp. 16-17.

[7]Ferrero, The Principles..., pp. 32-33. Also see
MacIver, Web....

[8]Freud, Civilization..., pp. 112-112.

[9]Nieburg, Political Violence..., pp. 70-71.

[10]Greenstein, Children..., p. 2. See Easton,
A Systems Analysis..., p. 280.

[11]Weber, Theory of Social ..., pp. 114-115; MacIver,
Web..., p. 47.

syndromes or types which affect individual political beha- [13]
vior. Some of these personality types are: authoritarian, [13]
democratic, [14] cabalistic, [15] punitive, [16] and anomic. [17]
Theories of integration of political values also attempt
to explain the origin of legitimacy beliefs. [18] The
great variety of theories and the controversy concerning
them suggests that theories of the origin, sources, and
causes of legitimacy beliefs may be premature. A more
useful step may be to attempt to partially clarify the
elusive concept of legitimacy in the particular context
of American democracy.

Mystery of Legitimacy

With such a wide variety of causes or sources, it
is not surprising that the subject of legitimacy has an
aura of mystery. In fact, anthropologists approach primitive legitimacy through a study of magic. Ferrero calls
legitimacy the "Genie of the city." Sometimes students of
political philosophy are accused of useless metaphysical
speculations on the subject. Thus legitimacy seems to have
an essentially ephemeral character, even if one approaches
it in terms of a concrete set of attitudes, as do most
empiricists. There are considerable difficulties, no matter
what one's approach may be. The difficulties of conceptual
clarity and the passionate character of the values involved
best demonstrate the problematic character of studying
and understanding legitimacy.

---

[12] Robert A. Dahl, A Preface to Democratic Theory
(Chicago: University of Chicago Press, 1956).

[13] T. W. Adorno et al., Authoritarian Personality
(New York: Harper, 1950), passim.

[14] Harold D. Lasswell, Power and Personality (New
York: Viking Press, Inc., 1962), pp. 148 ff. See also
Robert E. Lane, Political Ideology: Why the American Common
Man Believes What He Does (New York: The Free Press, 1962).

[15] Lane, Political Ideology....

[16] S. Rosenzweig, "The Picture Association Method
and Its Application in a Study of Reaction to Frustration,"
Journal of Personality, Vol. XIV (1945), pp. 3-23.

[17] Durkheim, Suicide...; and de Grazia, Political
Community.

[18] See Karl W. Deutsch, Nerves of Government (New
York: The Free Press, 1963), pp. 151-154, 209; Parsons, "Some
Reflections..."; and Jacob and Toscano, The Integration....

Conceptual Clarity

Legitimacy is a relatively new concept in modern political analysis. Even though students of political philosophy, expecially those interested in justifications of political obligations for citizens, have discussed related concepts, Weber was the first twentieth century social scientist to give major attention to the problem of legitimacy.[19] Weber's concern was why men obeyed authority. His description or definition of government authority as "monopolization of violence"[20] has had considerable influence, but most, including Weber, have stressed that coercion and force are not adequate explanations of obedience to government.[21] At least some part of obedience seems to involve voluntary acceptance of or consent to authority. It is such voluntary aspects of obedience that

---

[19]The concept was then more or less promptly forgotten until the 1950's. The term legitimacy does not appear in The Social Science and Humanities Index from 1907 to 1950. Of course, a few political philosophers had used the term earlier. Rousseau makes the source of all legitimacy the general will or popular sovereignty. Burke, less persuaded by democracy, found the sources of legitimacy in the constitutions of civil societies. (See Allan Bloom, "Jean-Jacque Rousseau," and Francis Canavan, "Edmund Burke," both in History of Political Philosophy, ed. Leo Strauss and Joseph Cropsey [5th ed.; Chicago: Rand McNally and Co., 1969], pp. 524-528, and 608-609). A recent (1968) edition of International Encyclopedia of the Social Sciences had over thirty major entries on legitimacy, encompassing practically every discipline in the social sciences.
Some related concepts are : political community (see de Grazia, Political Community); political myth (see Lasswell and Kaplan, Power and Society, pp. 116-125); diffuse support (see Easton, A Systems Analysis..., p. 163, et passim); authoritativeness (see Young C. Kim, "Authority: Some Conceptual and Empirical Notes," Western Political Quarterly, Vol. XIX [June, 1966], p. 233); political trust (see William A. Gamson, Power and Discontent [Homewood, Ill.: Dorsey Press, 1968], chap. iii); system affect (see Almond and Verba, Civic Culture, chap. iv); political allegiance (see Lane Political Ideology, chap. x); and value consensus (see McClosky, "Consensus and Ideology...").

[20]H. H. Gerth and C. Wright Mills (eds.), From Max Weber: Essays in Sociology (New York: Oxford University Press, 1946), pp. 78, 334-336.

[21]Easton, A Systems Analysis..., pp. 301-302, and Ferrero, The Principles..., p. 40.

seem so intractable to social scientists. "Neither the
myths of authority nor the situations can be reduced
to be exactly definable elements postulated by science."[22]
Weber saw the noncoercive sources of obedience in such
vaguely defined phenomena as traditions, customs, and
charisma.[23]

Even though the term legitimacy is troublesome in
terms of conceptual clarity, it is probably no more imprecise than some other related concepts used by social
scientists. The most directly empirical attempts to analyze
the legitimacy of the American political system have been
various survey questions statistically clustered into
scales measuring political attitudes about various aspects
of the American political life, such as its structures,
principles, patterns of behavior, procedures, rules, values,
or norms. Some of these scales tap somewhat indirectly
some aspects of the legitimacy dimension of American political life. More specifically, these scales attempt to
measure such political attitudes as political alienation,[24]
government responsiveness, cabalism,[25] nationalism, a sense
of civil obligation,[26] political output affect,[27] political

---

[22]MacIver, Web..., p. 6.

[23]Weber, Theory of Social...; pp. 124-130, 324-329.

[24]Since "early" Marx, political alienation has been
a favorite concept. See Fromm, "Alienation..."; Nettler,
"Alienation," Sociological Measurement, ed. Bonjean et al.
(San Francisco; Chandler, 1967); A. Davids, "Alienation,
Social Apperception, and Ego Structure," Journal of Consul-
ting Psychology, Vol. XIX (1955), pp. 21-27; Kenneth
Keniston, The Uncommitted: Alienated Youth in American
Society (New York: Harcourt, Brace and World, Inc., 1965);
Joel D. Aberbach, "Alienation and Political Behavior,"
American Political Science Review, Vol. LXIII, No. 1 (March,
1969), pp. 86-99; Marvin Olsen, "Two Categories of Poli-
tical Alienation," Social Forces, Vol. XLVII (1969), pp.
288-299; and J. Clark, "Measuring Alienation Within a
Social System," American Sociological Review, Vol. XXIV,
No. 6 (1959), pp. 849-852.

[25]Lane, Political Ideology; and Kenneth Sherrill,
"Mass Attitudes Toward Power and Legitimacy in the Urban
Conflict," Paper presented before the American Political
Science Association meeting, Los Angeles, California,
September, 1970.

[26]Almond and Verba, Civic Culture....

[27]Ibid.

trust,[28] political distrust,[29] discontent, political
cynicism,[30] political disengagement and disaffection,[31]
political efficacy,[32] attitude toward government,[33]
sense of citizen duty,[34] patriotism,[35] powerlessness,[36]
nationalism,[37] and authoritarianism.[38] From the
perspectives of ideology, conflict, and violence, such

---

[28]John P. Robinson, Jerrold G. Rusk, and Kendra B.
Head, Measures of Political Attitudes (Ann Arbor, Mich.:
Survey Research Center, Institute of Social Research Uni-
versity of Michigan, 1968).

[29]Donald Stokes, "Popular Evaluations of Government:
An Empirical Assessment," Ethics and Bigness: Scientific,
Academic, Religious, Political, and Military, ed. Harlan
Cleveland and Harold Lasswell (New York: Harper and Baltic,
1962), pp. 61-72.

[30]See McClosky, "Consensus..."; Lane, Political
Ideology..; And Sherrill, "Mass Attitudes..."

[31]Richard C. Hofstetter, "Political Disengagement
and the Death of Martin Luther King," Public Opinion
Quarterly, Summer, 1969, pp. 174-170.

[32]Campbell et al., American Voter.

[33]Ibid.

[34]Angus Campbell et al., The Voter Decides (Chicago:
Row Peterson and Co., 1954).

[35]B. Christiansen, Attitudes Toward Foreign Affairs
as a Function of Personality (Oslo, Norway: Oslo University
Press, 1959).

[36]See A. Neal and M. Seeman, "Organizations and
Powerlessness: A Test of the Mediation Hypothesis,"
American Sociological Review, Vol. XXIV (1964), pp. 216-
225; and Kerner Commission.

[37]L. W. Ferguson, "The Isolation and Measurement of
Nationalism," Journal of Social Psychology, Vol. XVI (1942),
pp. 215-228.

[38]Adorno et al., Authoritarian...; and R. N. San-
ford, "The Genesis of Authoritarianism," Attitudes: Selected Readings, ed. Marie Jahoda and Neil Warren (Baltimore,
Maryland: Penguin Books, Inc., 1966), pp. 109-115.

diverse concepts as alienation,[39] political output
affect,[40] (general) attitudes toward govenment,[41] political distrust,[42] and patriotism[43] may perhaps be especially useful for discovering whatever relationships
there may be between feelings about regime legitimacy and
political violence.

Some of the concepts developed for scaling are
partially compatible with the concern in this thesis for
perceptions of the legitimacy (rightfulness, desirability,
trustworthiness) of the most general ideologies, purposes,
structures, authorities, and policies of the regime--
political, social, economic, and cultural.[44] Legitimacy
items need to tap the passionately moralistic feelings
of self-proclaimed radicals, whether they are privileged
whites or the under-privileged blacks. Such a concept of
legitimacy, tied to ideological feelings and attitudes
of acceptance or rejection, may explain politically motivated violence more adequately than strictly ad hominem

---

[39]The concept of alienation is, however, peculiarly
vague. On this conceptual problem, see especially Eugene
J. Meehan, Contemporary Political Thought: A Critical
Study (Homewood, Ill. : The Dorsey Press, 1967), especially
pp. 394-406 on Eric Fromm and Robert Nisbet. The items in
the alienation scales and studies indicate a number of definitions for even such a familiar concept as alienation.
For example, alienation may be "the subjective feeling of
estrangement from the society and the culture it carries"
(Measuring Middle Class Discontent, Nettler, "Alienation"
[italics mine]); "Loss or absence of a previous or desired
relationship" (Measuring Radical Young, Keniston, The
Uncommitted...); "incapacity and discontent" (Measuring
Uppermiddle Class and Lower Class Alienation, Olsen, "Two
Categories..." [italics mine]); a combination of "egocen-
tricity, distrust, pessimism, anxiety, and resentment"
(Measuring Intellectual Discontent, Davids, "Alienation...");
"the degree to which a man feels powerless to achieve the
role he has determined to be rightfully his in specific
situations" (Clark, "Measuring..." [italics mine]); or "the
discrepancy between the power a man has and what he believes
he should have"(Clark, "Measuring..." [italics mine]).

[40]Almond and Verba, Civic Culture....

[41]Robinson, Rusk, and Head, Measures of Political....

[42]Stokes, "Popular...."

[43]Christiansen, Attitudes....

[44]See discussion of regime, pp. 33-36 , above.

and deterministic reliance on the demographic characteristics of individuals, groups, or subcultures. For
example, the socio-economically based notion of authoritarianism[45] and its cousins-- cabalism, cynicism, and
futility-- fail to explain political discontent among
the upper middle class.[46] Similarly, the procedural
views of democracy, as expressed in the notion of political efficacy, may fail to adequately explain the general
role of passionately and deeply held beliefs in political
conflict. The ideological perspective on legitimacy used
here attempts to avoid such psychological reductionist
traps as explaining political conflict in terms of either
psychopathology or psychological predispositions. Abnormal
psychology is better left to such experts as criminolo-
gists, social workers, psychiatrists, psychologists,
sociologists, and social psychologists. Psychological
determinism is probably as questionable as economic determinism.

The rather direct attitudinal approach to legitimacy suggested here is not without certain difficulties
of its own. Few social scientists have given much guidance
on the subject. Many social scientists have used the term
legitimacy (parenthetically and rhetorically) in relation
to the current wave of violence. Nevertheless, few have
given systematic attention to the relation of actual
attitudes or feelings on political legitimacy to violent
politics.[47]

The Passionate Content of Legitimacy[48]

"One ought both to be feared and loved." (Machiavelli)

The hypothetical linkage between legitimacy and
violence is understandable only within the context of the
intense sentiments, passions, and feelings which a few may
express about conditions of political life. It is precisely

---

[45]See Lipset, _Political Man_, especially chap iv,
"Working-class Authoritarianism," pp. 87-126.

[46]On this problem, see Robinson, Rusk, and Head,
Measures Political...; and Olsen, "Two Categories...."

[47]For the only exception with which I am now familiar, see Müller, "A Test...," whose work I received late,
but which, nevertheless, I have incorporated into this
dissertation.

[48]An earlier draft included a twenty page section
on the ideologically loaded language of legitimacy.

the "irrational," subjective, ephemeral, evaluative,
"noncognitive," and affective character of legitimacy myths
that give them such great potential as motivations for
extremist political behavior. Thus, connotatively free
terms--such as preference, identification, integration,
support,[49] confidence, acceptance,[50] compliance,[51] and
perhaps even consensus and appropriateness-- are not
appropriate to convey, let alone explain, or lead to an
understanding of the passionate feeling some may have
about the conditions of political life. Dispassionate
and indifferent terms may be appropriate to describe
minor acts of civil disobedience, disagreement, or
dissent-- such as an impulsive act of jaywalking, a dispassionate Oxford debate, and ritualized union picketing--
but they hardly describe killing or arson. A term such
as preference to explain values seems like a paper tiger:
it is hardly capable of communicating the fundamental
issues raised by radical ideologies and violent political
acts. Few men are likely to fight to the death to defend
any of their "preferences." Terms like justice, right,
wrong, equality, liberty, patriotism, traitor, conspirator,
love, hate, loyal, disloyal, and affection-- these terms
do convey the passionate side of politics. Where the
subject warrants such terms, they should be used.[52]

Problems of Values in the Study of Legitimacy

Besides the problems of conceptual clarity and the
central role of irrational, passionate, or metaphysical
language and values in understanding the mystifying concept

---

[49]Easton, A Systems Analysis...; and Deutsch, Nerves....

[50]Dahl, Modern...; and Janos, "Authority...."

[51]Peter M. Blau, Exchange and Power in Social Life
(New York: John Wiley and Sons, Inc., 1964); Deutsch,
Nerves...: and Amitai Etzioni, A Comparative Analysis of
Complex Organizations (New York: Free Press of Glencoe,
Inc., 1961), pp. 14 ff.

[52]On the importance of language in presenting
alternative world views outside of the dominant culture,
see Herbert Marcuse, One-Dimensional Man: Studies in the
Ideology of Advanced Industrial Society (Boston: Beacon
Press, 1969).

of legitimacy, there has also been the more general problem of developing a scientific understanding of the values
involved in legitimacy myths. In attempting to operationalize values into measurable facts or instrumental values
or means,[53] social scientists have variously defined
values[54] as: (1) unorganized or potential political
interests;[55] (2) habits or expectations; (3) desired
sociological conditions, such as economic class, power,
and status; (4) definable basic human physiological and
psychological needs,[56] or (5) valued things, objects, and
events;[57] (6) customs;[58] and (7) specifiable welfare,
power, and interpersonal values.[59] Such operational defi-

---

[53]See Arnold Brecht, Political Theory: The
Foundations of Twentieth Century Political Thought (Prince-
ton, N. J.: Princeton University Press, 1967); and Felix
E. Oppenheim, Moral Principles in Political Philosophy
(New York: Random House, 1968).

[54]Truman, Governmental Process..., see especially
pp. 159, 512-513, 516-518; and Harold D. Lasswell,
Psychopathology and Politics (New York: Viking Press,
1960), p. 12.

[55]Truman, Governmental Process....

[56]Maslow has suggested that a hierarchy of needs
exists in which the satisfaction of each level of needs must
be met before the next level of needs can motivate behavior.
These levels of needs are: physical, safety, love, esteem,
and self-actualization (see Abraham H. Maslow, "A Theory of
Human Motivations," Psychological Review, Vol. L [1943],
pp. 370-396; and James C. Davies, Human Nature in Politics
[New York: John Wiley and Sons, 1963], especially pp. 8-
63). Murry delineated twelve viscerogeneric needs and
twenty-four psychogeneric needs (see Henry A. Murry et al.,
Explorations in Personality [New York: Oxford, 1938]; and,
for a quick summary of Murry's theory, see Calvin S. Hall
and Gardner Lindsey, Theories of Personality [New York:
John Wiley and Sons, Inc., 1957], chap. v, "Murry's Person-
ology," especially pp. 172-184).

[57]Lasswell and Kaplan, Power and Society..., pp.
55-56.

[58]Bronislaw Malinowski, Crime and Custom in Savage
Society (Totowa, N. J.: Littlefield, Adams, and Co.,
1967), pp. 36-49.

[59]Gurr, Why..., pp. 25-26.

nitions of values may diminish, demean, or debunk[60] the
potential power of passionately held ideological values.
To operationalize values in such concrete, material, and
mundane terms may possibly mean defining them out of
methodological existence.

The difficulty of knowing what ultimate or absolute
vaules are true[61] or universal[62] may have led some social
scientists to attempt to escape from, ignore, or neglect
this apparent morass in the study and discussion of values.
To many social scientists, philosophical discussions have
been far too fruitless, solutionless, and unending. Thus,
political scientists have sought to penetrate the smoke
screen of reason or the "good," because some classical
political philosophers may have perhaps obscured the role
of the dimly understood human physiological and psychological needs and passions in human behavior. Yet deep
penetration into the darkness of the human psyche may
not be any more fruitful than discussions of the Platonic
"forms."

With respect to the role of values in political
conflict, Lasswell and others may have neglected the
potential role of obscurely understood democratic values
in motivating some to engage in political conflict. Lasswell speaks of the "valued outcomes" of personal sentiments
or preferences for power, enlightenment, wealth, well-being,
skill, affection, respect, and rectitude.[63] Though a
democratic socialist by his own personal preferences, Lasswell admits that he cannot, in his role as a social scientist, judge whether a valued political thing can be described as "democratic" or undemocratic." When Lasswell
attempts to construct a paradigm for a democratic personality, as opposed to an authoritarian personality, Almond
suggests that

> Lasswell's democratic qualities of humaneness,
> sharing, multivalues, trust, and nonanxiety ... are
> not specifically political attitudes and feelings

---

[60]Martin Diamond, "Democracy and The Federalist;
A Reconsideration of the Framers' Intent," American Political Science Review, Vol. LIII (1959), passim.

[61]Oppenheim, Moral Principles....

[62]Brecht, Political Theory....

[63]Lasswell and Lerner, World Revolutionary..., p. 8.
See also Lasswell and Kaplan, Power and Society....

and they may actually be encountered in great fre-
quency in societies that are not democratic in
structure.[64]

Building on Lasswell's values by adding two more
(spontaneity and security) and integrating those values
with Parsonian functions[65] of the social system by
adding two other functions (goal change and self transformation), Karl Deutsch found that the Soviet Union and
the United States were "strikingly close together" on a
number of value scales.[66] Deutsch's findings coincide
with the economic and technological determinism of the
convergence theory.[67] Whatever the truth of such similarities or dissimilarities, it is unlikely that most
citizens and officials of either country share Deutsch's
particular perceptions. They certainly behave as if there
were important regime differences. The social scientist,
by seeking an understanding of values on his own rational
and objective criteria may perhaps fail to perceive values
on the same passionate terms as most political activists.
Gurr's treatment of legitimacy and the role of
values in political violence is also peripheral and presumptive. Gurr criticizes others for not developing value
hierarchies: this failure results in seeing only the
singular and absolute values reflected in ideologies.[68]
Thus Gurr shortchanges such "absolutist" values as justice,

---

[64]Almond and Verba, Civic Culture..., p. 10,
commenting on and citing Lasswell, Power and Personality,
p. 94.

[65]Goal attainment, adaptation, pattern maintenance,
and integration.

[66]Karl Deutsch, A speech given before the Western
Political Science Association, Sacramento, California,
April, 1970.

[67]For critiques of the convergence theories, prima-
rily those of Sorokin and John Kenneth Galbraith, see
Bertram D. Wolfe, An Ideology in Power: Reflections on the
Russian Revolution (New York: Stein and Day Pubs., 1969);
and Zbigniew Brzezinski and Samuel P. Huntington, Political
Power: USA/USSR (New York: Viking Press, 1964). See also
Pitikin Sorokin, Russia and the United States (London,
1950); and John Kenneth Galbraith, Interview with Anthony
Louis, New York Times, Magazine Section, December 18,
1968.

[68]Gurr, Why..., p. 67.

good, equality, and liberty.[69] Gurr does admit that such
values may motivate some human behavior, but he deals only
cursorily with such "oughts." Unlike MacIver and Ferrero,
Gurr is probably mystified by the operation of such super-
stitions and myths. In one place, he indicates that
relative deprivation is "the term used ... to denote the
tension that develops from a descrepancy between the
'ought' and the 'is' of collective value satisfaction."[70]
Yet, for Gurr, these values or "oughts" are synonomous with
"goods and conditions of life," which men seek. Values
seem all of the same cloth. On this scale, bales of hay
or liberty tend to be both valued and commensurable. For
example, Gurr does not see the possibility that values,
such as common notions of justice, are independent variables capable of generating political violence on their
own. Values are always secondary and post hoc rationalizations for political behavior. In short, Gurr simply
assumes that "normative and utilitarian justifications"
for violence are subordinate, secondary, and derivative
for social determinants and intervening psychological
variables.[71] "Beliefs ... can motivate men to organize
and participate in political violence only if they are
already discontented."[72]

The key question here must be-- discontented with
what? The usual meaning of political discontent is that
people interpret or believe some condition to be undesirable, perhaps even wrong, according to some standard of
the good, whether absolute or relative. Such beliefs
about political justice may possibly be independent
variables motivating political action. Of course, one
should not expect such values to be the only motivators
of all violent action. Yet, by seeking strictly material
explanations for all violence, one may overlook potential
causes of uniquely political violence. Gurr's subject,
however, as well as that of this dissertation, is
precisely political violence, not all forms of aggression

---

[69] Gurr gives over 120 pages to values, 54 to ideologies, and 45 to coercion. He makes occasional offhand
comments on such political ideals as equality, liberty,
etc., but his topical index has absolutely no listings for
equality, inequality, liberty, freedom, justice, civil
rights, natural rights, Declaration, Constitution, law,
liberalism, conservatism-- in a word, no references to
those political ideals and values which may be potential
sources of public debate and perhaps even violence in
politics.

[70] Gurr, Why..., p. 23.

[71] Ibid., p. 326.

[72] Ibid., p. 319. (Italics mine).

in response to all forms or perceptions of deprivation. Some obvious distinguishing features of political violence are that (1) it has political objects as its targets, and (2) having political targets, it might even have political purposes. Thus, the "politicization of discontent" should be at the center of Gurr's study of political violence.[73] The value loaded expectations so central to Gurr's relative deprivation thesis require that considerable attention be given to values. Yet Gurr makes little attempt to test the hypothesis that values may be independent variables causing political violence. His total position is clear under the concept of relative deprivation. For Gurr, values and expectations are subordinate to the psychological dynamics of the frustration-aggression relationship.[74]

Stolz, a radical political scientist, recognizes the importance of democratic values and principles in American politics in his intemperate attack on those he calls the pluralists:

[The] vision [of American liberalism] deflates American politics. Rather than dealing with the dynamic tension established between aspiration and reality, the workers of the liberal paradigm direct academic attention to the "folklore of populism," comment upon the "myth of participation," and demonstrate empirically that where "factual information is required, the theory of populistic democracy provides us with no knowledge about the real world." Yet Aristotle, Machiavelli, de Tocqueville, Michels and many others observe, to the contrary, that in a democracy the principle of equality is one of the foundations out of which political action arises. It is very much part of the real world of politics. To dismiss this aspiration as a myth leaves us with a diminished perception of the American political tradition.[75]

Strauss and his students make a similar kind of critique by accusing behavioralists of having nihilistic tendencies. Behavioralists approach "a state of indifference

---

[73]Ibid., p. 12.

[74]Ibid., p. 23.

[75]Matthew F. Stolz, "The Liberal Paradigm and the Rediscovery of Violence in America," Paper presented at the Western Political Science Association convention, Sacramento, California, April 1-4, 1970, p. 31, quoting Dahl, A Preface..., p. 59. Note that for MacIver, Web..., the term myth is meant to encompass both the true and false values which give order to society.

to any goal or aimlessness and drift,"[76] They judge
"every preference, however evil, base, or insane ... as
legitimate as any other preference."[77] In turn, Bluhm
makes this criticism of the "Straussians."

Strauss goes on to add a word of praise for the
"judicious collections and analyses" of the behavioralists. "The useful work done by the men called
political scientists is independent of any aspirations
toward 'scientific' political science," he writes, ie.,
independent of any aspirations toward an exclusive
right to explain politics. Unfortunately, however,
Professor Strauss does not go on to show how the political philosopher, the seeker after the good order, can
use the "judicious collections" of the naturalistic
student of the empirical order. He himself makes no
use of them whatever.[78]

The approaches of Lasswell, Gurr, and others are thus
inadequate for the discussion of a topic laden with see-
mingly "authoritarian" or "absolutist values-- legitimacy.
Similarly, "Straussians" have given little guidance in
clarifying our understanding of legitimacy.

Toward an Understanding of Legitimacy

In the course of attempting to find a useful explanation of legitimacy, this discussion has reviewed a large
number of diverse approaches. Taking clues from Easton and
Almond and needing a beginning, the hypothesis of this
paper is that when someone deems a system to be legitimate,
then that person either passively accepts or actively
supports the general political system or political culture.
That is, all regimes depend at least partially on some
measure of social contract.[79] Yet the possible justifi-

---

[76]Strauss, What..., p. 19.

[77]Leo Strauss, Natural Right and History (Chicago:
The University of Chicago Press, 1953), pp. 40-45.

[78]William T. Bluhm, Theories of the Political
System (Englewood Cliffs, N.J.: Prentice-Hall, Inc.,
1965), p. 108. See Strauss, What..., p. 13; and Leo
Strauss, "An Epilogue," Essays on the Scientific Study of
Politics, ed. Herbert J. Storing (New York: Holt, Rine-
hart and Winston, Inc., 1962), pp. 307-327.

[79]See Jean-Jacques Rousseau, Social Contract (various
editions); Schattschneider, Two Hundred Million...; and
MacIver, Web....

cations or terms of obligation for each regime's social
contract varies. Webster s New Collegiate Dictionary
definition of the adjective legitimate illustrates such
diverse justifications for acceptance of authority.
Webster's definition of legitimacy includes:

1. Lawfully begotten; born in wedlock. 2. Real;
genuine. 3. Accordant with law; lawful; hence,
existing or ruling by hereditary right; as a
legitimate monarch. 4. Conforming to recognized
principles or accepted standards; as, legitimate
reasoning. Syn. See LAWFUL. v. t. ... to give
legal force to. Hence, to authorize or justify.[80]

According to Webster, what is legitimate, right, or proper
may be whatever the law, the king, reason, religion, or
philosophy says, authorizes, or justifies. Such an all
encompassing definition indicates the variety of competing
myths of legitimacy.
     All regimes have characteristic myths justifying
their particular kind of authority over the social whole.
Even though these myths do have a mysterious or sanctified
character, it is still possible to identify at least the
central principles or values which justify the authority
of particular kinds of regimes-- whether democratic, monarchial, or oligarchic. In general, "a government is legitimate if the power is conferred and exercised according
to principles and rules accepted without discussion by
those who must obey."[81] Besides fear, people obey on the
basis of some belief that a given system of authority is
superior to any alternative system. The belief in the
superiority of the system usually relies on some grounds
of the justice or goodness of the particular form of
political authority. Some divine, supernatural, absolute,
or "natural" principle, myth, folklore, law, or right
claims to justify the existing or some future structure
of authority.

Myths of Authority

     According to MacIver and Weber, the usual basis
for uninstitutionalized, primitive, or charismatic forms
of authority lies in some respect for the age, ancestry,

---

     [80]Webster's New Collegiate Dictionary (Springfield,
Mass.: C. and C. Merriam Co., Publishers, 1961), pp. 952-
953. (Italics mine.)

     [81]Ferrero, The Principles..., p. 135.

wisdom, skill, or powers of a particular person.[82]
Primitive forms of legitimating myths usually lie in a
culture's magic, taboos, and religion. Ferrero's
analysis is very good for a beginning in identifying the
key modern myths or principles of legitimacy for differing
regimes:

> In Western Civilization they are reduced to only four
> altogether: the elective principle, the hereditary
> principle, the aristo-monarchic principle, and the
> democratic principle. From these four principles a
> certain number of rules were drawn, which must be
> strictly observed in the conferment and exercise of
> power if the government is to be legitimate. A
> power is legitimate when the methods used, first to
> establish it and then to exercise it, are conform-
> able to these principles and to the rules drawn
> from them.[83]

It is further possible to reduce these four principles into
two categories based on the hereditary and elective criteria.
Though not always, most monarchial and aristocratic regimes
tend toward hereditary forms of selection or succession of
the ruling authority, while most democratic regimes confer
or pass on authority through some form of election.

Monarchial and aristocratic myths of authority

Justification for the authority of a king or monarch usually lies on some grounds of the ruling individual's
superiority. The philosopher king has a natural right to
rule based on his natural superiority of intellect, wisdom, or goodness. Some kings have also claimed to represent the higher sanctity of existing community customs or
traditions. Hitler claimed both to be superior (der Fuhrer)
and to represent that mystical blend of blood and soil,
the spirit of a chosen people (the German volk). Earlier
absolutist monarchs had claimed to have a "divine" right
to rule. They also may have claimed to represent the sovereign community or nation state. Finally, most monarchs
claimed to be able to pass their superiority on to their
heirs. Extreme forms of kingship include tyranny, abso-
lutism, dictatorship, and totalitarianism.

Justification for rule by the aristocratic few
lies in some claims of the superior (aristocratic or noble)
qualities of a class, rather than of a single person. As

---

[82]Weber, _Theory of Social..._, p. 328.

[83]Ferrero, p. 135, see also p. 22. See MacIver,
Web..., pp. 31, 33, 37, 48, 75, and 89; Blondel, _An Introduction..._, pp. 252-253; and Dahl, _Modern..._, p. 49.

in monarchy, this superior right to rule is usually deemed
to be hereditary. In practice, the "best" class usually
means some privileged class of wealth and/or education.
Extreme justifications of class rule are the caste systems,
found in Hinduism and racism, and the rule by an elite
which claims exclusive knowledge of the truth, such as
the Communist Party or a priestly class. In the twentieth
century, bureaucratic, military, communist, or technocratic
elites have claimed the right to rule based on "scientific"
or secular superiority, rather than on a divine justification.

The problematic character of democratic legitimacy

The basis of both monarchy and aristocracy lies in
the notion of superiority-- the inequality of men, usually
claimed to be genetically transferable to offspring. On the
other hand, democratic legitimacy is based, at the very
least, on the belief in the political or human equality of
all men. Since all men are equal, the true grounds for
making political authority legitimate lie simultaneously
in the often conflicting doctrines of majority rule and
minority rights. Thus, since all citizens are equal, all
majorities and all minorities, at least theoretically,
consent voluntarily to governmental authority.[84] Though
supposedly "government of, for, and by the people,"
democracy also implies some obligations to obey authority.
Yet the mere assertion of a peoples' right to rule individuals, true or untrue, is not enough to make authority
acceptable and thus to secure obedience. The people must
believe that they have actively and voluntarily consented
to be ruled. If the authority of a democratic government
is to be reasonably secure, the people must believe the
legitimizing myths of peoples' rule to be empirically true.
Thus, democratic myths of authority are the most tenuous
and problematic of all. The notion of rule by a government,
especially through representation, conflicts with the notion
that people actually rule themselves. That is, the citizen's obligation to participate in the rule of himself may
conflict with the idea that he has any obligation to obey
others.

Thus, in a democracy, there is a conflict between
the dual roles of obedient subject and consenting participant. Respect for the authority of government is weakened
by the notion that, being equal, everyone should have the
freedom to rule himself. Thus, the citizen's dual role,[85]

---

[84]Joseph Tussman, Obligation and the Body Politic
(New York: Oxford University Press, 1960), pp. 23-31.

[85]Almond and Verba, Civic Culture..., pp. 35-36,
168-169, 178-182, 338-343, and 346-351.

as participant and subject with rights and obligations,
is always in tenuous balance. More concretely, majority
rule may result in the violation of the minority rights
of some groups, both privileged and under-privileged.
Some have argued that in democratic practice only a passive
or acquiescent majority would permit minority groups to
protect themselves through a passionate and energetic veto
over an inactive majority.[86] Assuming that the most
intense minorities would probably be the privileged, many
have condemned this view as a theory of democratic
elitism.[87]

Legitimacy in the Context
of the American Regime

American principles of legitimacy are <u>not</u> based
simply on the continually reinterpreted positive law of
the land-- the Constitution. American legitimacy also
lies in the absolute natural law of the Declaration. The
Declaration claims to present a universal and true standard of justice-- natural rights. If citizens perceive
conflict to exist between the Constitution and the Declaration, the regime's legitimacy becomes questionable. As
Lincoln recognized, natural rights is a maxim of perfection. Such ideals of perfection have created problems of
order, as well as hopes:

> It is not to be supposed, because of America's dedica-
> tion to the political creed set forth in the preamble
> of the Declaration of Independence, that conflicts as
> to national purpose were thereby to be avoided. Not
> only did equality as a principle hold out great prom-
> ises of moral and material improvements; it also
> made demands. ... Lincoln often compared it to the
> Gospel injunction, "Be ye perfect as your Father in
> heaven is perfect." It held up a standard that was,

---

[86]See Robert A. Dahl, <u>Who Governs? Democracy and
Power in an American City</u> (New Haven: Yale University
Press, 1961), p. 318; James W. Prothro and Charles M.
Griggs, "Fundamental Principles of Democracy: Bases of
Agreement and Disagreement," <u>Journal of Politics</u>, Vol. XXII
(May, 1960), pp. 276-294; McClosky, Hoffman, and O'Hara,
"Issue Conflict...," pp. 406-427; Peter Bachrach, <u>The
Theory of Democratic Elitism: A Critique</u> (Boston: Little,
Brown, 1967); and Jack L. Walker, "A Critique of the
Elitist Theory in Democracy," <u>American Political Science
Review</u>, Vol. LX (June, 1966), pp. 285-295.

[87]Bachrach, <u>The Theory...</u>; and Walker, "A
Critique...."

in a sense, beyond attainment. In inviting men to aspire to what they could never wholly attain, it engendered frustrations which could not but embitter political life. Like the Gospel, in the name of peace it brought not peace but a sword.[88]

Such beliefs in perfection have perhaps encouraged a great variety of interpretations of the meaning of equality, liberty, and happiness.

One problem which democracies face is that most men are not satisfied with political equality alone, because human needs involve more than merely the equal freedom of citizenship. As Arendt argues, most citizens seek freedom from economic deprivation as well. Perhaps a majority since Franklin D. Roosevelt have accepted the promise of economic equality as a public goal to be provided by the modern American welfare state. In addition, recent civil rights legislation and movements have held out the promise of social equality, as well as economic and political equality. Currently, American Negroes, student radicals, and some white intellectuals may be seeking to accelerate this trend toward social and economic equality, not just the fulfillment of such aspects of political equality as the vote. Similarly, seeing themselves as the purveyors of important new ideas, doctrines, and ideologies, some intellectuals are seeking greater political power and honors in order to achieve their higher goals for American democracy. Stolz sees the contemporary crisis as a conflict of democratic principles with students and blacks representing the true principles of democracy:

As Michels observes, any society, and particularly a democratic society, continuously passes away from or toward its integrating principle. In the contest of American politics the actions of its citizens are pertinent to the nation's democratic foundations. Their actions extend, restore or attack equality and political liberty. And if Aristotle is correct, the virtuous citizen is he whose actions defend, at least in the American situation, the democratic possibility. An act of violence, accordingly, may be judged legitimate or illegitimate in so far as it enlarges or diminishes democracy.[89]

Though many may be frustrated, angered, and enraged by conditions, only a few may actually resort to violence. The key is that people must believe that those conditions

---

[88]Harry V. Jaffa, Equality and Liberty (New York: Oxford University Press, 1965), pp. 46-47.

[89]Stolz, "The Liberal...," pp. 16-17.

violate some standard of justice, however vaguely or
narrowly applied. Moreover, in order for the government
to remain, citizens must believe it has upheld such a
standard of justice. A discussion of the objects of
democratic legitimacy may lead to a greater understanding
of this rather abstract interpretation of the possible
relation between democratic legitimacy and violence.

Objects of Democratic Legitimacy

Several aspects of a regime may be acceptable to
its citizens. Generally, legitimacy is rather diffuse
support for the regime. Several objects of this diffuse
support are both analytically distinct and perhaps even
empirically separate. These objects are the ideologies,
rules, institutions, authorities, policies, and efficiency
of the regime.

Legitimating Ideologies

When speaking of a legitimate or an illegitimate
political system, one must eventually become interested
in those political ideas or myths which constitute or make
up the written and/or living constitution of a nation or
a country. If citizens believe those principles are acceptable standards of political justice, then those principles
constitute a standard for judging the operation of the
country's institutions. Almost everyone would say that
the most advertised general principles and ideals of the
American democratic regime, equality and liberty, are
desirable and just.[90] Most radicals would judge the operational system in light of these expressed democratic
standards of justice. Thus, discontented people may find
the system fails, falls short, or is wanting according
to its own standards. They may deem the system worthy of
destruction or radical transformation also according to
its own standards.

The legitimating ideology of the American nation is
that of liberal democracy. If there is wide agreement as
to the meaning of that ideology in practice,[92] then that
regime is integrated,[91] has value consensus,[92] has an
authoritative ideology,[93] has a sense of political

---

[90]For empirical evidence of agreement on at least
these abstractions, see Prothro and Griggs, "Fundamental...;" and Kirkham, Levy, and Crotty, Assassination....

[91]Deutsch et al., "Political Community...."

[92]McClosky, "Consensus and Ideology...."

[93]Miller and Bugelski, "Minor Studies...," p. 25.

community and has a public philosophy:[94] there is
widespread conviction in the moral validity of the
regime's ideology.[95] Such an ideology states the regime's
goals, principles,[96] ideals,[97] and standards of justice.
If the people believe these principles are actually being
applied to or implemented in the regime's operating procedures, rules,[98] norms,[99] institutions,[100] inputs, and
outputs[101] then most citizens will have some widespread
affection or diffuse support for the political system.
On the other hand, if there is conflict between the
ideology of an elite or some partisan group and the dominant ideology or patterns of beliefs of the community,
then there may be a weakening of support for the system.
In such conditions of low support, the treatment of
dissenting and partisan minorities may be severe, as regime
authorities seek coercively to enforce support. Yet diffuse
support is <u>not</u> all of a single ideological piece.[102] Though
ideology may be the most important object of citizen support
for the regime, there must also be support for the institutions, structures, authorities, personalities, policies,
and efficacy of the regime.

Gamson has argued that there is a hierarchy of
importance for these objects of regime support. That is,
there are different levels of political trust. Within
these levels, there may be a dynamic interaction among
various regime components in the political life of people.
For example, support for incumbents may generalize into
trust at the next higher level of political institutions,
up through public philosophy, political community, and
finally the regime.[103] Similarly, an increase or a decline
in the legitimacy of one part of the political system may
spill over into a higher or lower level. Any substantial
change in a major institutional, personal, or policy com-
ponent may force a redefinition of regime principles,

---

[94]Gamson, <u>Power...</u>, pp. 39-52; and Easton, <u>A Systems Analysis...</u>.

[95]Easton, <u>A Systems Analysis...</u>, p. 287.

[96]<u>Ibid</u>.

[97]Prothro and Griggs, "Fundamental...."

[98]Easton, <u>A Systems Analysis...</u>.

[99]Gamson, <u>Power...</u>.   [100]Lipset, <u>Political Man</u>.

[101]Almond and Verba, <u>Civic Culture...</u>.

[102]Muller, "A Test...," p. 21.

[103]Gamson, <u>Power...</u>, pp. 39-52.

values, or norms, which could ultimately delegitimize the
regime's ideology or institutions. Whatever the direction
of generalized political trust or whether there is indeed a
neat hierarchy is not of critical importance. What is
crucial for understanding the legitimacy of the regime is
that such support must be fairly comprehensive, including
a wide range of regime objects.

Norms and Rules of the Game
and Ideology

One close relationship of great importance is the
application of abstract regime ideologies to practical
procedures, rules of the game,[104] and norms. A legitimating ideology can sanctify or ritualize various instru-
ments, tools, or procedures for its application to empirical conditions or situations. When widely accepted, these
formal procedures and processes[105] become relatively
recurring and stable habits, patterns, structures, and
institutions. For example, one can argue that the
Constitution of the United States was an effort to set up
operating legal and political institutions to implement
certain abstract principles, implied or explicit, in the
Declaration of Independence.[106]
The Constitution of the United States may have
become so sanctified[107] as to replace the Declaration as
the key standard for political justice in America. The
Constitution either established or provided a framework
for the development of particular rules and norms for
political activity. Some deplore and others praise
these procedures. For example, some citizens may attack
some rules of the game-- such as the qualifications for
voting, the seniority system, the electoral college, political conventions procedures, legislative apportionment,
or court procedures-- precisely because they perceive
these procedures as failing to coincide with the higher
principles of either the Declaration or the Constitution.
On the other hand, affection for constitutional procedures
or rules of the game may result, at least for a time, in
support for the system in the actual absence of widespread
acceptance of abstract democratic principles, such as
minority rights or the right to peaceful dissent. Ideologies, myths, rules, and techniques are constantly interacting, thus modifying tnd elaborating themselves. For
example, citizens and the Supreme Court may amend or rein-

---

[104]Truman, Governmental Process....

[105]Nieburg, Political Violence..., p. 69.

[106]Ferrero, The Principles..., p. 42.

[107]Easton, A Systems Analysis..., p. 300.

terpret the Constitution in an effort to reflect more
accurately such abstract principles as equality and "one
man one vote."

Institutions

Certain institutional features-- such as the
separation of powers, bicameralism, and federalism-- may also
be sanctified or desanctified in reference to abstract ideological principles. For example, some critics have perceived increases in presidential and judicial power as being
undemocratic. Similarly, some believe the intervention
of the national government in the states and in the economy
to be a threat to individual liberty. Others see such
interventions as necessary for the protection of equality
and liberty. The debate over court ordered or "forced"
school busing to seek racially integrated schools is a
more specific example. Both sides of the busing issue
say individual liberties or opportunities are at stake.

Authorities

At the next level, formal institutions, as well as
beliefs in the validity of the regime ideologies, may lend
legitimate authority to incumbent officials. Some social
scientists have made attempts to measure levels of contemporary popular approval of officials or politicians in
general, as well as for particular incumbents. Of course,
public support for and opinions about incumbents nationally
vary considerably from year to year and from issue to issue.
The Survey Research Center (University of Michigan) scales
of political trust may provide a partial measure of a
sense of legitimacy. Several social scientists have used
these scales to measure the degree to which people believe
government officials in general wield power justly,
honestly, and benevolently. Several of these studies have
found that the politically unsophisticated,[108] or those
with low self esteem,[109] have less trust for politicians
than the general population. White children[110] have
higher levels of political trust for political authorities

---

[108]MacIver, Web..., p. 39.

[109]Morris J. Rosenberg, "Misanthropy and Political
Ideology," American Sociological Review, Vol. XXI (December,
1956), pp. 690-695; and Lane, Political Ideology....

[110]See Edward S. Greenberg, "Children and Govern-
ment: A Comparison Across Racial Lines," Midwest Journal of
Political Science, May, 1970; and "Black Children and the
Political System," Public Opinion Quarterly, Fall, 1970.

than do white adults[111] or black children.[112]   Other
studies reveal that American adults generally have had
relatively high levels of political cynicism and scepticism about politicians.[113]
     There are problems, however, with such measures
of political trust. The concern in this study of political
violence is the support or lack of support for the diffuse
objects or symbols of the American regime, not the temporary
or changing public relations problems of grand or petty
officials, or the ordinary citizen's perhaps very healthy
scepticism about politicians. Certainly, one commonly
shared experience is confrontation with the petty bureau-
crat who regularly slights and annoys so many citizens.
Yet few would confuse the acts of petty officials with the
justness of the regime. One usually recognizes an obsti-
nate clerk for what he is-- an arrogant aberration.[114]
It is also unlikely, for example, that an intense dislike
for the noncharismatic personality of President Nixon will
mobilize sufficient collective discontent to violently
bring down the American regime. Though an absence of
popularity, along with other factors, such as discontent
with particualr policies, may prevent the re-election of
such an incumbent,[115] that would hardly constitute a change
in the regime.
     Perhaps it would be useful to take an even more
explicit example which bears on contemporary violence.
Some have said that the widespread black hatred of policemen or some police practices, as reflected in numerous

---

[111]Hess and Easton, "The Child's ...," pp. 632-639.

[112]Dean Jaros, Herbert Hirsch, and Frederick J.
Fleron, Jr., "The Malevolent Leader: Political Socializa-
tion in an American Subculture," American Political Science
Review, Vol. LXII, No. 2 (1968), pp. 564-575.

[113]Campbell et al., Voter Decides, pp. 187-194;
Robert E. Agger, Marshall N. Marshal, and Stanley A. Pearl,
"Political Cynicism: Measurement and Meaning," Journal of
Politics, Vol. XXIII (1961), pp. 477-501; and Edgar Litt,
"Political Cynicism and Political Futility," Journal of
Politics, Vol. XXV (1963), pp. 312-323. The generally pre-
jorative connotations of the term politicians may elicit
such responses, while the term statesman might elicit more
favorable responses.

[114]Lane, Political Ideology..., found support for
bureaucracy in general among his Eastport group of "common
men."

[115]Dahl, Modern..., p. 31; and MacIver, Web...,
p. 36.

studies and polls after urban riots, is a reflection of the
waning belief in the legitimacy of the American regime
among blacks in general. Certainly, policemen are very
important symbols of the coercive enforcement of regime
values. Yet it seems unlikely and unreasonable that any
community with extensive and potentially more benevolent
contacts with other agencies of government could possibly
identify the police as the regime itself. Bond elections
in Los Angeles during 1971 also suggest that blacks do not
view the police as the regime or even as essentially unjust.
The black community of South Central Los Angeles voted
overwhelmingly for greater police protection. Similarly,
in 1972 in San Francisco, blacks have protested in mass
demonstrations against the closing down of police sub-
stations in some black areas. Obviously, most members of
the black community seem to be distinguishing between
police malpractice, such as brutality[116] and those unjust
actions which would be more representative of the whole
regime. Of course, those black radicals who believe the
regime is inherently racist do see the police as one of
the most significant tools of that injustice. Similarly,
some New Left anarchists do believe petty bureaucrats and
all other forms of authority or kinds of regime are illegitimate. Thus, if distrust of a particular leader fits into
a widely perceived pattern of unfair or unjust acts of
agencies or officials, then discontent or alienation may be
more general, as it is for some militant black groups and
some groups associated with colleges or intellectual castes.
The legitimacy of the system as a whole may indeed be in
question for these groups.
    Often what holds up an unpopular, inept, or foolish
leader is the belief that his position symbolically represents rightful authority. The source of this legitimate
authority of officials may rely on belief in legitimating
ideologies, myths of sovereignty, and representational or
constitutional authority.[117] For example, most Americans
support most officials of the political system, because
they are symbols of higher political positions and roles.[118]
Thus, the distrust of some particular authority figure is
seldom transferable to the whole political system. Positions of authority, if not the incumbents, tend to be

---

[116]It should be noted that the definition of
brutality used by many black radicals and social scientists
includes social and psychological abuses and not just physical harm. The Cohen edited volume, Los Angeles Riots...,
includes frisks, search, and insulting language within the
definition of police brutality.

[117]MacIver, Web..., p. 36.

[118]Greenstein, Children..., p. 29; and Hess and
Easton, "The Child's...," pp. 632-639.

96

idealized symbols of the legitimate political institutions
or ideologies.[119]
    Thus, individuals, groups, or factions support or
do not support what the regime stands for. Such regime
standards are found in legitimating ideologies and constitutions. Citizens perceive these standards in regime
actions as "living constitutions." In summary, it is
necessary to emphasize that the ultimate objects of support are the political ideals of the regime. These
ideologies may insulate the regime from its inept officials
and unsuccessful policies. The crucial link in the web
that legitimates authority is the diffuse belief in the
system.

Policies and Efficacy as Objects
of Legitimacy

    The ineffectiveness of government activities,[120]
policies, and outputs;[121] the inability to resolve political issues,[122] to manage crises,[123] to respond to citizens' needs,[124] to provide citizen participation[125] and
security,[126] and to reflect contemporary consensus[127]--
according to many social scientists, all these may result
in diminishing degrees of legitimacy. Conversely,
others[128] claim that legitimacy may be won by meeting
citizens' expectations, interests, and consensual

---

[119]Easton, A Systems Analysis..., pp. 289-291.

[120]Penn, "Sociological...."

[121]Almond and Verba, Civic Culture..., p. 186.

[122]Lipset, Political Man..., pp. 64-65; and
Seymour Martin Lipset, The First New Nation: The United
States in Historical and Comparative Perspective (New York:
Anchor Books, 1967), pp. 45-54, and 59-60.

[123]Joseph R. Gusfield, "Mass Society and Extremist
Politics," American Sociological Review, Vol. XXVII (February, 1962), pp. 19-30, cited by Gurr, Why..., p. 188.

[124]Campbell, Sahid, and Stang, Law..., p. xxxi.

[125]Ibid.; and Almond and Verba, Civic Culture...,
pp. 203-204.

[126]Gamson, Power....

[127]Nieburg, Political Violence..., p. 53.

[128]Dahl, Modern..., pp. 31-32; Easton, A Systems
Analysis..., p. 285.

values[129] through rewards, satisfaction, and punishment.
Such a rationale or trade off of the costs and the benefits
of citizenship is an appealing explanation, especially
among those who humanistically wish to see a one to one
relationship between reforms and political stability.[130]
Yet legitimacy is a more subjective, noncognitive, and
diffuse sense of affection than most such supra-rational
analyses suggest. Diffuse affection for the regime may
in fact be such a "rain and shine" attachment as to
enable a political system to weather all kinds of crises
of ineffectiveness.[131]

Regime legitimacy and government efficacy are
related, but they are probably separate dimensions.[132] If
loyalty to regime ideologies and symbols is indeed only
learned, indoctrinated, or inculcated, then such myths
certainly may be "irrationally" separated from objective
levels of government efficacy.[133] Moreover, the potentially
most efficient regimes, totalitarian ones, are usually
only tenuously legitimate, if by legitimacy one means
at least some large measure of voluntary acceptance or
consent relatively independent of coercion.[134]

A key question to consider is: government should
be effective for what purposes, goals, or values?[135] As
different regimes have different ideologies or myths
legitimizing them, it is obvious that their citizens
probably judge them by differing criteria of effectiveness

---

[129]Nieburg, Political Violence..., p. 53.

[130]Later in this paper, there is a presentation of
the argument that rapidly rising expectations of governmental reforms or policies may actually serve to delegitimize a regime, if its capabilities are not up to its promises. See Ferrero, The Principles..., p. 143; and
Blondel, An Introduction....

[131]Almond and Verba, Civic Culture..., p. 192;
Easton, A Systems Analysis..., pp. 278, 283; Ferrero,
The Principles..., pp. 143-144; and Blondel, An Intro-
duction..., p. 250.

[132]Almond and Verba, Civic Culture..., p. 186;
and Hamilton, Madison, and Jay, Federalist..., No. 37.

[133]Jacob and Toscano, The Integration....

[134]Ferrero, The Principles..., p. 134.

[135]Morton J. Frisch and Richard G. Stevens (eds.),
American Political Thought: The Philosophic Dimensions of
American Statesmanship (New York: Charles Scribner's Sons,
1971), pp. 5-6.

as well.[136] That is, citizens may see a bad policy as
being inconsistent with the regime's own images of itself.[137] Thus, many American social scientists consciously
refer to democratic standards of effectiveness as including
citizen participation,[183] consent,[139] consensus,[140] and
equal treatment.[141] Many go one step further by assuming
an almost automatic legitimacy for democratic regimes.[142]
Generally, the use of coercion or force of any kind, by
lacking voluntary consent, gives an undemocratic and/or
an ineffective character to the regime.[143]

It still appears that the clearest understanding
of legitimacy lies in terms of legitimating ideologies,
standards, and myths. Such elusive metaphysical concepts,
principles, and values are indeed, as Ferrero said, the
Genie of the City. The belief in relatively absolute
values, however, is not a static condition, for values
change. Sometimes changes in values are incredibly rapid.
Such almost inevitable mutability of values makes the
legitimacy of any regime very fragile.

---

[136]Ferrero, The Principles..., pp. 22-23; and
Blondel, An Introduction..., p. 251.

[137]Gurr, Why..., p. 186.

[138]Almond and Verba, Civic Culture..., pp. 157,
203-204; and S. N. Eisenstadt, "Communication Systems and
Social Structure: An Exploratory Comparative Study,"
Public Opinion Quarterly, Vol XIX, p. 151.

[139]Blondel, An Introduction..., p. 463.

[140]Nieburg, Political Violence..., p. 53.

[141]Almond and Verba, Civic Culture... .

[142]Lipset, Political Man..., pp. 67-68, and 70;
Almond and Verba, Civic Culture..., p. 203.

[143]Blondel, An Introduction..., p. 463; Richard A.
Schermerhorn, Society and Power (New York: Random House,
1965), passim; and Gurr, Why..., passim.

CHAPTER IV

TYPOLOGY OF POLITICAL VIOLENCE

Toward a Typology of Purposes
and Tactics of Violence

This first section of Chapter IV begins by placing
this study within the general context of previous social
scientific work related to the purposes of political violence.

Violence and Sociology: Collective
Behavior and Social Movements

Smelser on the purposes of
social movements
According to Smelser, all collective behavior is
"mobilization on the basis of a belief."[1] Social mobilization takes two forms: the collective outburst and the
collective movement. Collective outbursts are spontaneous
actions, such as panics crazes, and hostile outbursts,
typically in response to immediately threatening situations.
Some collective outbursts are both politically motivated
and violent. Smelser also discusses two types of collective
movements, perhaps of greater interest to political scientists. These movements are the norm-orientied movement and
the value-oriented movement. Norm-oriented movements
are directed toward the change or the preservation of
"regulatory standards of interaction."[2] As such, norm-
oriented movements are exemplified by social reform movements or protest movements.[3] Norm-oriented movements
may seek the change of every conceivable kind of social,
economic, educational, religious, or political norm,
rule, or regulation, but they are usually limited to
either a narrow area of rule change or a specific policy
area.

---

[1]Smelser, Theory..., p. 8.

[2]Ibid., p. 9.   [3]Ibid., p. 270.

Certainly, not every disagreement or act of
opposition passionately questions the right of the
present government to rule. In our contemporary context,
one must take care not to claim that all protests or
demonstrations, or even all violence, represent a desire
for a different political order. Only some dissent is
treason or conspiracy. Generally, political actors
express vigorous disagreement only with rather specific
regime policies, practices, and some minor rules of the
game. If a number of citizens believe a government to
be truly illegitimate, its rule will be "insufferable,"
at least for that portion of the population. An expression of illegitimacy typically involves certain
individuals acting collectively as members of a subculture or faction to radically oppose and/or change
existing regime principles[4] rather than to reform a few
norms or policies.

Although overtly involving mere changes in minor
rules of the political game, many political conflicts, if
ideologically defined or articulated, may actually involve
more fundamental principles. Nevertheless, even though
desires for changes in rules may result in significant
political conflict, few are likely to lead to political
violence. An example of one significant conflict over
norms is the direct popular election of the American
president, which first appears to be a mere change of
procedure. Actually, institution of the direct popular
election of the president may involve an effort to realize
a more direct or participatroy form of democracy, exemplified by the solgan "one man, one vote." Similarly,
liberal efforts to reform the seniority system or fili-
buster rules in Congress ultimately seek to weaken the
political power of southern politicans "going slow" on
civil rights. Finally, a progressive income tax schedule

---

[4]Hobsbawn makes the distinction between reform and
revolution on pages 10-11 of his *Primitive Rebels* (New York:
W. W. Norton, 1965):
"The principle is quite clear. Reformists accept the
general framework of an institutional or social arrangement, but consider it capable of improvement, or, where
abuses have crept in, reform; revolutionaries insist
that it must be fundamentally transformed or replaced.
Reformists seek to improve and alter the monarchy, or
to reform the House of Lords; revolutionaries believe
that nothing useful is to be done with either institution except to abolish them. Reformists wish to
create a society in which policemen will not be arbi-
trary and judges at the mercy of landlords and merchants; revolutionaries, though also in sympathy with
these aims, a society in which there will be no policemen and judges in the present sense, let alone landlords
and merchants."

constitutes an effort (often circumvented) to redistribute
wealth founded on a value preference for economic equality.
Smelser claims norm-oriented movements do not involve
questions of legitimacy, as do value-oriented movements
which battle over the "general sources of legitimacy."[5]
Yet, as just indicated, changes in some values or norms
may ultimately imply or lead incrementally to changes in
more fundamental values. Thus, the distinction between
norms and values may often be more analytical than
empirical.

Smelser says value-oriented movements, which
involve the change in "general sources of legitimacy,"
include political revolutions, sect formations, nationalistic movements, nativist movements, messianic movements,
millenarian movements, utopian movements and charismatic
movements. Secular or political ideologies involved in
value-oriented collective movements include nationalism,
communism, socialism, anarchism, and syndicalism. There
may, of course, be religious and political combinations,
such as Christian Socialism or Islamic Nationalism.
Some of these value-oriented movements may lead to widespread questioning or conflict over the legitimacy of the
existing regime and to political violence. In summary,
collective movements, whether norm-oriented or value-
oriented, may change crucial roles or fundamental
principles by attempting to radicalize, intensify, and
redefine the regime's organizations or institutions of
authority, power, or influence. These attempts to change
norms and values may be associated with a high potential
for political violence. Even though potentially violent,
norm-oriented movements are less likely than value-
oriented movements to actually seek the violent imposi-
tion of new regime myths of authority.

Smelser excludes "institutional mobilization of
action," public opinion, and propaganda from the study of
collective behavior. Organizations, public opinion, and
propaganda are, however, certainly crucial aspects of
politics, if not of collective behavior. Smelser also
makes some exclusions and distinctions which are valid
for this study. Like others, he makes the distinction
between the criminal and reformist purposes with respect
to the norms and/or the values of collectivities. Criminal
activity seeks to subvert rather than change rules, while
reformers break laws or regulations in order to substitute
or create new rules.[6] With the important exceptions of
law breaking, probably encouraged by prohibitions of
alcohol and marijuana, the American experience has been
that criminals are unlikely to pose real threats to either

---

[5]Smelser, _Theory..._, p. 9.

[6]_Ibid._, p. 177.

the basic modes of operations and/or standards of conduct
within the existing regime. On the other hand, radical
reform activity may involve important changes in the political order. Some regime supporters may perceive such
reform activities as substantial threats to the existing
political order, as they did the feminist, trade union,
and universal suffrage movements.

Smelser says that individual deviation represents
no clear effort to change existing "components of action"
for the whole system of social action.[7] Yet supporters of
and activists in the "counter culture" movement, while
claiming little or no formal social organization or leadership, do indeed often see their behavioral norms on leisure,
marijuana, long hair, and sex as politically significant
efforts to bring down peacefully a puritanical social
order, the capitalist economic system, and "fascist" political systems through a "cultural revolution."[8] The
American counter cultures may have great political implications. This is especially true for the Yippie movement,
which has indicated that cultural revolution has as its
ultimate intentions a fundamental change in American
values leading eventually, either peacefully or violently,
to a radical political alteration of the American regime.[9]
In summary, Smelser provides a few important insights and
concepts: (1) the crucial role of beliefs is in mobilizing collective behavior, including collective political
behavior; and (2) there are two kinds of collective
movements-- norm-oriented and value-oriented. The protest,
reformist, deviant, and revolutionary movements covered in
the study of collective behavior may have political purposes and/or impacts.

Gusfield

Gusfield's chief interest is social movements. He
defines social movements as "socially shared activities
and beliefs directed toward change in some aspect of the
social order."[10] Gusfield's examples of social movements
include civil rights activities, nationalistic movements,
utopian settlements, ghetto riots, and student movements.
Generally, Gusfield excludes, with key exceptions, a major

---

[7]Ibid., p. 78.

[8]Reich, Greening...; and Abbie Hoffman, Revolution for the Hell of It (New York: Pocket Books, 1970).

[9]See Hoffman, Revolution...; Jerry Rubin, Do It
(New York: Simon and Schuster, 1970); James Simon Kunen
The Strawberry Statement: Notes of a College Revolutionary
(New York: Avon Books, 1970); and Reich, Greening... .

[10]Joseph R. Gusfield, "Introduction: A Definition
of the Subject," Protest..., p. 2.

portion of Smelser's field of study, such as crowds, mobs, riots, panics, fads, and fashions. Gusfield's interests and those of this paper are the more purposive kinds of human behavior seeking changes in the social order. Under his general category of social movements, Gusfield includes only those crowds, mobs, and riots which have social and political purposes. For example, ghetto riots are reflexive, rather than cognitive, expressions of a purposive phenomenon-- the civil rights movement. These riots may also involve the development of new norms and values.[11] In summary, Gusfield's social movements include those structures and those beliefs which are contrary to dominant practices or beliefs.[12] The fact that Gusfield excludes social trends, public opinion, and voluntary associations from the study of social movements does not mean they should be excluded from politics; certainly, many voluntary associations are involved in political activities.

Gusfield and others tend to neglect or pass over those individuals, movements or institutions which resist social change. No civil rights activist, however, would neglect the Ku Klux Klan, white citizens' councils, or some police departments, or George Wallace (segregationist Governor of Alabama). Certainly, conservative, traditional, preservative, or reactionary movements may also give rise to conflict and violence. Without resistance, social movements would merely provide impatient but peaceful participants a vehicle for social change in a nonviolent context of evolutionary and consensual change. Thus, resistance may lead to violent conflict. Although limited to those groups and ideas working potentially against the existing political order, this study does not deny the political or social significance of the "hard hat"[13] or "backlash"[14] phenomenon. For reasons of both mere interest and convenience, this study is limited to the political violence of the left. The main interest here is the relation between anti-regime opinions and anti-regime behavior, not pro-regime opinions and the violent behavior of supporters of the regime. Perhaps political scientists can provide a more specific and better understanding of such anti-regime opinions and behavior than these sociologists have.

---

[11]Ibid., pp. 4, 7, and 8.

[12]Ibid., p. 8.

[13]New York construction workers who clashed violently with anti-war demonstrators in 1968.

[14]Angry white reactions to militant civil rights groups.

The Political Scientist on the Purposes
of Political Violence

Edward Banfield

Edward Banfield claims urban lower class riots,
whether black or white, have always had four motives or
purposes. These motives are: rampage, pillage (fun and
profit), righteous indignation, and demonstration.[15] Two
of these purposes are most significant politically. These
are: (1) righteous indignation, expressing a minority
belief in the injustice of public authorities and/or of
the regime, and (2) political demonstrations over specific
policies or rules, which may end in violence. Granted, fun
and profit may also be significant black motives, yet it
seems clear that one can hardly attribute the large number
of ghetto riots in recent years entirely to those motives
which have always been present for all poor men at all
times-- pillage and rampage (fun and profit). Fun and
profit are probably secondary intentions or benefits.
Yet Banfield, like others, seems to be saying that before
one can impute political motives to the black participants
in urban riots, these participants must make explicit
reference to Plato's Republic, the Declaration of Independence, the Gospel, or contemporary ideological ortho-
doxy.

Eckstein

Eckstein's definition of internal war subsumes the
many possible purposes of radical political violence--
reform, protest, and revolution-- as well as the potential
modes and tactics of political violence-- riots, coups,
revolutions, and wars of independence.[16] Eckstein also
includes social deviation within the category of internal
war. This inclusion may obscure any effort to distinguish
criminal or other forms of violence from political violence.
Yet one form of social deviance, the "counter culture," may
have political purposes or impacts. Within his discussion of
internal war, Eckstein excludes some violent activity,
such as ghetto riots. Like Banfield, Eckstein seems to
believe political participants must have an explicitly
articulated ideology. Yet if highly articulated, sophisticated, and ideological judgments about politics were
necessary to designate political purposes, then political
participation would be confined to the political philosophers, which is only possible in an imaginary city, as
Plato himself recognized, and no student or citizen of
democracy would accept.

---

[15] Banfield, Unheavenly..., pp. 187-192.

[16] Eckstein, "On the Etiology...," pp. 135-136.

Janos[17]

Janos usefully excludes crime, pathological aggression, and individual attacks from his discussion of political violence.[18] Like Eckstein, Janos also excludes ghetto riots from political violence. Yet it seems an unrealistic and narrow definition of political violence to include only those political actions which are clearly and explicitly executed, planned, and directed toward immediately specifiable or instrumental goals. Given the limited sense of political efficacy or political power of blacks, much of black political action is essentially expressive and may not be directly instrumental in achieving black political power, let alone much more specific purposes. Involuntary segregation, disenfranchisement, and discrimination have almost insured that much of black ghetto political action is relatively unorganized and inarticulate.[19] Thus, Janos' exclusion of "small scale" political violence makes his discussion rather useless, expecially in light of contemporary urban violence.

Gurr

Gurr's analysis of political violence is more useful in terms of the purposes of this paper. According to Gurr, political violence includes many magnitudes and tactics, such as revolution, guerrilla war, coups d'etat, rebellions, and riots.[20] Gurr collects and tabulates the number of violent events by country and, through factor analysis, derives three statistical clusters. He calls these clusters the three "dimensions" of the universal phenomenon of political violence. These three clusters are: turmoil, conspiracy, and internal war.

---

[17]Janos, "Authority...," pp. 130-141.

[18]Janos says they are "too small" to affect authority, which is probably an inadequate criteria for exclusion. All politically significant movements or ideologies have small beginnings.

[19]The political purposes of the inarticulate are discussed in Rudé's study of pre-industrial crowds. See George Rudé, The Crowd in History: A Study of Popular Distrubances in France and England, 1730-1848 (New York: John Wiley and Sons, Inc., 1964). See also Hobsbawn's study of pre-democratic protest, primitive rebels, and social banditry in Hobsbawn, Primitive....

[20]Gurr, Why..., p. 4. Like Janos, Gurr distinguishes riots and revolutions only by their magnitude, not purposes, which may in fact vary. For an example, see Gurr, Why..., p. 5.

Gurr says turmoil is characteristically spontaneous and unorganized and includes such events as riots and
demonstrations. He says turmoil is "quite distinct both
statistically and substantially" from what can be called
a "revolutionary dimension, characterized by more organized
and intensified strife."[21] The two revolutionary categories, which Gurr distinguishes from turmoil are: (1)
internal war-- civil war, guerrilla war, and some coups--
and (2) conspiracy-- plots, mutinies, and most coups.
Conspiracies are simply small scale internal wars; they
have limited participation, are accompanied by small
scale terrorism, and include primarily small scale
guerrilla wars and coups. Internal wars are "designed
to overthrow the regime or dissolve the state."[22]

Though Gurr does not deal adequately with the
particular purposes and political, rather than psychological, motives of violent political participants, his
terms have political, as well as statistical significance.
They indicate that political purposes are related to
change in the political regime, its actors, and its
policies. Gurr's generally non-quantitative distinctions
indicate that the most useful way politically to categorize
violent political events may be according to their political purposes, ends, and goals. The typology of political
violence which follows uses a similar set of qualitative
distinctions of political purposes.

A Typology of Violence: Legitimacy
and Purposes of Political Violence[23]

Henderson has reportedly said that "any classifica-
tion is better than no classification-- provided you don't

---

[21]Ibid., p. 10 (italics mine).

[22]Ibid., p. 11.

[23]See also August Meier, "Who Are the 'True
Believers'? A Tentative Typology of the Motivations of
Civil Rights Activists," Protest, Reform, and Revolt: A
Reader in Social Movements, ed. Joseph R. Gusfield (New
York: John Wiley and Sons, Inc., 1970), p. 482; Arnold
S. Kaufman, The Radical Liberal: The New Politics; Theory
and Practice (New York: Simon and Schuster, A Clarion
Book, 1970), pp. xii-xiv; Joseph R. Gusfield, "The Struc-
tural Sources of Protest, Reform, and Revolt," Protest...,
p. 192; Jack Newfield, A Prophetic Minority (New York:
New American Library, 1967), pp. 15-16, and 24; William
S. Stokes, Latin American Politics (New York: Thomas Y.
Crowell Co., 1959), pp. 235-236; Cropsey, "Radicalism...";
Richard E. Peterson, "The Student Left in American Higher
Education," Students in Revolt, ed. Seymour Martin Lipset
and Philip G. Altbach (Boston: Beacon Press, 1970), p. 212;

take it too seriously."[24] As noted above, some social scientists have made a number of useful distinctions between the differing purposes of violence. It would be useful here to construct a typology of violence which will incorporate both political and other purposes of violence. The master hypothesis of this thesis is that one may be able to derive an understanding of most of the political purposes of political violence by analyzing differing attitudes about the legitimacy of the regime. In other words, it may be possible to show that nearly all violent political behavior is uniquely related or unrelated to the concept of legitimacy. A certain amount of violence accompanies most social changes, yet the scale of violence probably increases the more severe the ideological conflicts over regime myths.

There are approximately eight purposes of violence corresponding more or less with several types of groups or political orientations with varying degrees of attachment to the regime, ranging from total acceptance to total rejection.[25] These types are summarized in Chart 1. The types are analytical or ideal models. As analytical constructs, they will overlap with the usually mixed purposes of individuals and subgroups within any mass of diverse participants in any one political event, whether a caucus, convention, rally, or riot, whatever the official or designated purpose of the organizers. Diverse outcomes or. purposes result from leadership, interests, and skills, aw well as from the dynamics of any rapidly emerging and changing situation. Ambivalent or mixed purposes are more

---

Burton R. Clark and Martin Trow, "The Organizational Context," College Peer Groups, ed. Theodore Newcomb and Everett Wilson (Chicago: Chicago University Press, 1966); Muller, "A Test...," p. 14; Gamson, Power..., chap. iii; Lane, Political Ideology..., chap. x; and Almond and Verba, Civic Culture..., p. 101.

[24]A. L. Kroeber and Clyde Kluchkhohn, Culture: A Critical Review of Concepts and Definitions (New York: Random House, 1963), p. 77, quoting Henderson.

[25]Other social scientists have used similar criteria of acceptance or rejection of predominant value systems for constructing typologies. On types of religious sects-- conversionist, adventist, introversionist, and agnostic-- see Bryan R. Wilson, "An Analysis of Sect Development," American Sociological Review, Vol. XXIV (February, 1959), pp. 3-15. On psychological modes of individual adaptation-- retreatist, revolutionist, rebellious, innovative, conformist, and ritualist -- see Robert K. Merton, "Social Structure and Anomie," Social Theory and Social Structure (Glencoe, Ill.: Free Press, 1957), pp. 131 ff.

CHART 1

LEGITIMACY CONTINUUM: DEGREE OF REGIME REJECTION/ACCEPTANCE

Subcultural Categories	Rejection			
	Anarch-ists	Revolution-aries	Radicals	Reformers
Students	Hippies Yippies	Rev. Youth Mov't II ("Weather-men") Tom Hayden Trotskyites Maoists Progressive Labor P.	Left ac-tivists S.D.S. Rev. Youth Mov't I	Pacifists Intellec-tuals Democra-tic so-cialists Pot smokers
Blacks	Muslims	Cleaver Panthers Communists	M. L. King Black Liber-ation Army	NAACP M. L. King
White Middle Class	K.K.K. Catho-lic Rev.	Radical Chic	Radical liberal Norman Thomas Eugene Debs Kaufman	Populists Upton Sinclair Progres-sives Northern Calif. N. East A. Schle-singer "Progres-sive Center" SILENT MIDDLE

Notes:

Sources making similar distinctions or typological analyses: Peterson, "Student...," p. 212. (This writer discovered Peterson's continuum way into the development of this typology but has modified and adapted his typology.) Note especially the student categories. For student sub-cultures, see Clark and Trow, "Organizational...." For a

CHART 1--Continued

Establishment	Traditionalists	Deviants	Acceptance
			Super-Patriots
Profession-al Academics Collegiates	Conservatives Vocationalists		Y. A. F.
Uncle Tom	S. Baptists	"Shadies" Numbers racket	
AFL-CIO	Southern California	Mafia Homo-sexuals Femi-nists	Reactionaries John Birch George Wallace
MAJORITY AMERICA			

discussion of "degrees" of challenge to the political
regime, see Muller, "A Test...," p. 14. See also Gamson,
Power..., chap. iii; Lane, Political Ideology..., chap.
x; Almond and Verba, Civic Culture..., p. 101; and Drake
and Cayton, Black Metropolis...

likely than clear intentions, especially in the case of
highly visible and public issues, such as war, civil
rights, or student power.[26] In other words, anarchists,
revolutionaries, radicals, reformers, establishment
people, traditionalists, deviants, and super-patriots may
all be present and active in any given occurrence of
violence. Again, these categories of purposes are analytical, ideal, and abstract.

The Anarchists and Non-Conformers: Apoliticos or Withdrawn Radicals

The first group includes those who find essentially
no existing regime as legitimate. This group of individuals may be characterized variously as anarchists, chili-
astics, anarcho-syndicalists,[27] communalists, utopians,
nihilists,[28] sect formers, withdrawn radicals,[29] the self
indulgent,[30] or counter culturalists. Their purpose is to
destroy or stop the regime from functioning, or, at the
very least, to refuse to participate in any regime or
social institution. Most within this group would agree
that institutions ought to be absolutely voluntary and
relatively free of restraints on the individual. According
to members of this group, the individual has a right of
liberation from almost any restraining authority. These
men do not accept citizenship in any organized, structured,
or institutionalized political community, other than the
most primitive and voluntary. This general category
might include such contemporary groupings (or states of
mind) as the Yippies: the Haight-Ashbury, Sunset Strip,
and East Village drug cultures; hippies; and ninteenth
century American communes.[31] Most of the philosophical
anarchists are probably withdrawn radicals or aesthetics,

---

[26]Peterson, "Student...."

[27]Stokes, Latin American....

[28]Strauss, Natural Right....

[29]Cropsey, "Radicalism...."

[30]Kaufman, Radical....

[31]Most early American communes were unrestricted
only in theory. In fact, they often had quite authoritarian leadership by a charismatic one or few. If individual
behavior is unrestrained or undirected, the life span of
these communities has often been short in practice, because
the acquisition of necessities of life often require work
or social organization.

if not merely people indifferent to political action.[32]
Thus, not all anarchists resort to violence, although many
may do so if they perceive a threat to their independent
existence from the dominant political culture and/or socio-
economic system. If their alienation from the regime is
almost total and quite thorough-going, then the potential
for violence may be high.

The range of tactics is quite broad for anarchist
like groupings. These tactics may include confrontation
creating situations, such as passive resistance, sit-ins,
and mass demonstrations, or may involve mildly violent
acts, such as take-over of buildings or even the storm
trooper tactics of using or stockpiling weapons or bombs.
The acts of the desperately individualistic few-- assassination, mass murder, indiscriminant violence-- may best
be categorized as terrorist. The underground "Weatherman"
faction of the S.D.S. perhaps falls within this terrorist
category. Again, most of those involved in counter
cultural movements or deviant groups simply drop out, or
at most, attempt to change or to "corrupt" existing
standards of conduct, both social and political.

It is important here to emphasize the distinction
between the counter cultural aspects of anarchism and
social deviation. Where deviation is limited to single
or narrow areas of cultural mores or norms, it is not a
genuine counter cultural movement denying the whole organization of the society. Such non-anarchistic and limited
forms of deviation might include homosexuality, wife
swapping, feminist or women's liberation movements, marijuana smoking, hitch-hiking, "bumming," and welfare rights
advocates. These individual forms of social deviation do
not constitute a genuine counter cultural movement, unless
these partial rejections are cumulative and reinforcing.
Nevertheless, if aggregated throughout the larger culture,
widespread incremental and partial deviance may reflect a
more thoroughgoing change, breakdown, or assault on cultural values. Such changes are unlikely to be particularly
violent, unless articulated and aggregated into an organized class, social, or ideological movement, interest
group, or political party, such as politically motivated
counter cultural anarchists. In this paper, the term
deviants refers to unaggregated and limited purpose
groupings, some of which fall within the criminal category of violent purposes.

In order to demonstrate this category of anarchists, it might be useful to outline the beliefs of one
such counter cultural anarchist-- Abbie Hoffman. Abbie

---

[32]On the difficulty of campus political activities
enlisting soldiers from the drug culture, see Simon,
"Hippies...."

Hoffman believes the means to achieve his particular view
of liberty and equality include both violent revolution
and cultural revolution. His approach to revolution is
violent in that he advocates action over discussion.
According to Hoffman, discussion does not convince anyone
and tends only to delay action and to obscure issues and
purposes.[33] He says, "Don't listen to words," act, for
"action is the only means to reality... [and] morality."[34]
In order to emphasize the ineffectiveness of debate, Hoffman describes several occasions in which he "acts"-- while
others discuss the advisability of various actions, Hoffman
smashes a display case and blocks a public doorway.[35] He
says further that "conflict develops when one feels himself
to be in the right and runs into opposition."[36] Thus, he
predicted the violence at the 1968 Democratic convention--
people "will fight and die" for their beliefs there.[37]
Hoffman's revolution is also cultural in that it is an
assault on the regime's values on drugs, sex, money, and
the family. His tactics in discrediting these values are
drama, comedy, and ridicule.[38] According to Hoffman,
"the poet revolutionaries are the most dangerous of all."[39]
One must "create art and destroy property."[40]

Revolutionaries: Marxists-Leninists-Maoists-Castroites

The second group includes the revolutionaries.
One may further subdivide this category into an anomic or
alienated group and into an activist group.[41] Revolutionaries see the existing regime as beyond redemption.
Thus, they describe the regime in such terms as corrupt,
repressive, imperialistic, and racist-- for them the regime
is illegitimate. The purpose of the revolutionary is the
planned or unplanned, organized or unorganized use of
violence to overthrow or secede from the regime. As they
seek the realization of alternative political structures,

---

[33]Hoffman, Revolution..., pp. 14-16.

[34]Ibid., p. 13.   [35]Ibid., pp. 23-24.

[36]Ibid., p. 203.   [37]Ibid., p. 174.

[38]Ibid., p. 107.   [39]Ibid., p. 183.

[40]Ibid., p. 161.

[41]Kenneth Keniston, "The Sources of Student
Dissent," Journal of Social Issues, Vol. XXIII, No. 3
(1967), pp. 100-115.

programs, or ideals, revolutionaries tend most often to use tactics planned to create fear and terror.

The revolutionaries of today include the Communists, Trotskyites, the Black Liberation Army (the Cleaver faction of the Black Panthers), the Youth Revolutionary Movement II (the Weatherman faction of the S.D.S.), and the Soledad Brothers. The range of revolutionaries is broad, including elitists, Leninists, participatory democrats, counter culturalists, and withdrawn radicals.[42] Movements of nationalist, class "warfare," messianic, millenarian, or utopian character tend to be revolutionary in that they seek to radically transform the existing regime. Their purpose is the destruction of the existing regime and its replacement with another. The new regime might be Marxist-Leninist, Maoist, or Castroite-- a people's republic of some character. In many respects, the regime form advocated may be unspecified, but it always involves a major transformation of the existing relations of authority. For example, the early S.D.S.'s Port Huron Statement sought a participatory democracy or hippie apoliticos. If the movement is leftist, its declared intention, either immediate or ultimate, is usually avowed to be democratic. On the other hand, if the anti-regime movement is rightist, fascist, or racist, such as the American Nazi Party or the Klu Klux Klan, it is avowedly opposed to liberal democracy. Extreme rightist purposes are beyond the scope of this study, yet they may symbolically represent the whole of American society for some leftists.

The targets of revolutionary attacks are quite diverse, including key public utilities, officials, and buildings. Similarly, the tactics of revolutionaries may be quite diverse, consisting of nearly the total range of both peaceful and violent activities. For example, revolutionaries may take advantage of the sporadic violence of others, which may be merely expressive of anti-regime norms. They may also use the terrorist tactics of some anarchists, both because of the capacity of such tactics to destroy and because of the common interest of revolutionaries and anarchists in the destruction of the existing political order. On the other hand, some who reject the regime-- such as the religious Muslims, or counter culture hippies, or bohemians-- seek separation by passive resistance or withdrawal from politics and political culture.

Hayden: white revolutionary

Tom Hayden is of particular interest in the revolutionary category, because his Port Huron Statement is reflective of widespread political sentiments among academic populations. Hayden's conversion from romantic

---

[42] Reich, Revel, Hoffman, Kunen, Marcuse, and Rubin see the dropout and/or artist bohemian as a revolutionary, whether violent or not, as did Adolph Hitler.

idealism to revolutionary violence is especially interesting. Since his romantic and idealistic founding of the Students for a Democratic Society and his writing of the Port Huron Statement of 1962,[43] Hayden's thought has undergone considerable transformation. The two continuing elements in his thought are alienation and participatory democracy. His concern over these two elements might mark him essentically as an anarchist, yet his continuing discussion of a better regime indicates he still has some faith in at least some system. He sees the need for some as yet unspecified political structures. Hayden's ultimate goal is destruction of the old system and creation of a more just regime, probably by revolution.

According to Hayden, "all great movements have a vanguard," even his ostensibly leaderless and nonelite movement. Yet, "this vanguard must not get too far ahead of the people."[44] Therefore, before revolution is possible, the American people must be diverted from their apathetic acceptance of the repression of the system. The way to awaken the people to the fact of repression is to confront them with the inequalities and injustices of the regime and thus to intensify their latent alienation. According to Hayden, the events of the 1968 Democratic Convention in Chicago are an excellent example of the success of this confrontation tactic. The events in Chicago provided a stage on which to dramatize the injustices of the political system.[45] Hayden plans to begin his movement with the more overtly alienated individuals-- the poor (both black and white), radical liberals, students. Eventually, he

---

[43]Students for a Democratic Society, Port Huron Statement (New York: Student Department of the Leauge for Industrial Democracy, 1964). Reprinted: Tom Hayden, "Port Huron Statement," How Democratic is America?, ed. Robert A. Goldwin (Chicago: Rand McNally Inc., 1971), pp. 1-16; and Tom Hayden, "Port Huron Statement, " American Radical Thought: The Libertarian Tradition, ed. Henry J. Silverman (Lexington, Mass.: D. C. Heath and Co., 1970), pp. 357-379.

[44]Tom Hayden, "Post Chicago Interview," Telling It Like It Was: The Chicago Riots, ed. Walter Schneir (New York: New American Library, 1969), pp. 119-133.

[45]For a Violence Commission report which largely agrees with Hayden's assessment of those events, see Daniel Walker, Rights in Conflict: The Violent Confrontation of Demonstrators and Police in the Parks and Streets of Chicago During the Week of the Democratic National Convention of 1968, A report submitted by Daniel Wlaker, Director of the Chicago Study Team of the National Commission on the Causes and Prevention of Violence (New York: New American Library, 1968)

hopes to enlist the aid of white collar workers and intellectuals in his subversion.[46]   The success of his revolutionary aims depends ultimately on the radical alienation
of the majority.
      Apparently, the use of confrontation tactics has
not been as rapidly successful as Hayden would like.
According to Newfield, Hayden has grown more bitter and
revolutionary each year. For example, in 1962, Hayden
had condemned the use of violence in the Port Huron Statement, becuase "it depersonalized the targets of hate."
Today Hayden seems to think that violent revolution appears
to be the only effective alternative. Like most revolutionaries or radicals of the day, in print Hayden has always
denied participation in political violence, other than as
an observer of events at the Democratic Convention at
Chicago in 1968, at the University of California at
Berkeley, at Columbia University, and at Newark. Yet,
in public speeches and interviews, he has refused to condemn violence, even though he does so in the Port Huron
Statement.[47]

Cleaver:[48] black nationalist and revolutionary[49]

      Cleaver's chief indictment of the American regime
or white "mother country" is its essentially colonialist
exploitation of people of color, both at home and abroad.[50]
He states that the regime denies blacks equality-- intellectually, politically, economically, emotionally, sexually,
and spiritually.[51] Cleaver has demonstrated his rage at

---

[46]Tom Hayden, "The Politics of 'The Movement,'"
The Politics of the Powerless, ed. Robert H. Binstock and
Kathleen Ely (Cambridge: Winthrop Publishers, Co., 1971),
pp. 304-311.

[47]In the spring of 1969, the author attended a public
speech and smaller private gathering afterwards with Tom
Hayden. His support for violence and revolution no longer
remained a question in this private setting.

[48]Eldridge Cleaver, Soul on Ice (New York: Dell
Publishing Co., Inc., 1970). See also George Jackson,
Soledad Brothers: The Prison Letters of George Jackson
(New York: Bantam Books, Inc., 1970).

[49]Note that the Black Panthers, at least in Oakland
in 1971-1972 under the leadership of Huey Newton and Bobby
Seale, now claim a willingness to work somewhat within the
system. In 1973, Seale was a democrat running for mayor of
Oakland.
      [50]Cleaver, Soul..., p. 111.

      [51]Cleaver, "Introduction" to Rubin's Do It, p. 8.

such white injustices to blacks in many ways. His demonstrations of rage include his workshop of violent
revolutionaries, his rape of a white woman (which he called
an act of insurrection),[52] and his belief that the Watts
riot had a cleansing effect.[53]

Cleaver criticizes the white regime's policies of
racial injustice on quite diverse grounds. For example,
he bases his criticism on the principles of equality in
the Declaration of Independence; and on the thoughts
of beatnick Jack Kerouac, ex-slave Frederick Douglass,
the Muslim's Malcolm X and Elijah Mohammed, and theologian
Thomas Merton. According to Cleaver, the ideals of the
Declaration of Independence are in conflict with the immoral
Constitution.[54] Nevertheless, he demands his constitutional
right to dissent.[55] For Cleaver, the only truly legitimate
regime must be egalitarian,[56] cooperative,[57] free, just,[58]
and humanistic.[59] Quoting Marx and Lenin, Cleaver says
such a just regime cannot be capitalistic. His goals are
possible only in a socialistic society. Unfortunately,
he doesn't explain exactly what he means by socialism. In
any case, the ultimate solution cannot involve continued
compromise over questions of right and wrong.[60] Thus,
he hopes to destroy the present structure.[61]

His method is to create a revolutionary coalition
among guilt-ridden white students,[62] the New Left, and
peace movements.[63] Cleaver finds guidance for his movement in writings and actions of the Russian revolutionaries of the nineteenth century, such as Backunin and
Nechayev, and the communist leaders and guerrillas of the
twentieth century, among them Lenin, Castro, Mao, and
Guevara.[64] In a sense, his separatist movement, like that
of the Muslims, seeks "national independence" or secession.

The Radical

The radical seeks to rule the regime in order to
transform it. He does not renounce it, as does the revo-

---

[52]Cleaver, Soul..., p. 26. [53]Ibid., p. 38.

[54]Ibid., p. 79. [55]Ibid., p. 114.

[56]Ibid., p. 97. [57]Ibid., p. 85.

[58]Ibid., p. 65. [59]Ibid., p. 111.

[60]Ibid., p. 18. [61]Ibid., pp. 84, 66.

[62]Ibid., p. 84. [63]Ibid., p. 112.

[64]Ibid., p. 30.

lutionary, nor does he seek merely to change its policies, as does the reformer. The radical sees a need for a fundamental transformation of the existing system. For radicals, the regime's illegitimacy in operation and in contemporary ideals is deeply rooted and wide ranging in the whole economic, social, and political structure of authority. Yet the total structure itself is not illegitimate, even though it may approach such complete illegitimacy.

Despite their ultimate belief in the legitimacy of the regime, radicals are closely related to revolutionaries and reformists in terms of their purposes and tactics. For that reason, few groups or individuals are easily categorized as radical. Nevertheless, the lucid political thought of A. S. Kaufman is illustrative of the radical.[65] According to Kaufman, the deficiency of the American system is deep-rooted: it goes beyond the realm of formal political institutions and processes. Kaufman says the malignancy of authority and middle class depravity permeate nearly all aspects of the American system.[66] For example, the workplace is dehumanized;[67] education is inequitably accessible;[68] and the distribution of economic products is unequal.[69] The social structure also contributes to the injustices of the overall system or regime. For example, the middle class is racist[70] and culturally and intellectually mediocre.[71] The middle class also tends to debase the aesthetic and intellectual tastes of others.[72] On the whole, philostinism and ugliness prevail in American culture.[73]

Despite these many faults, Kaufman and other radical liberals consider the regime to be at least tenuously legitimate. Radical liberals remain uneasily committed to the fundamentally valuable American system of political democracy.[74] "This conviction [in the value of regime protections] marks the most important differences between liberalism and Marxist Humanism."[75] In other words, the belief or disbelief in the essential legitimacy of the regime is the critical factor in the choice between radical reform or transformation and revolution.

---

[65]Kaufman, Radical.... Perhaps Justice Douglas would qualify. See Douglas, Points....

[66]Kaufman, Radical..., p. 27.   [67]Ibid., p. 21.

[68]Ibid., p. 20. [69]Ibid., p. 62.   [70]Ibid., p. 17.

[71]Ibid., pp. 25 and 118.   [72]Ibid., p. 20.

[73]Ibid., p. 50. [74]Ibid., p. 116.

[75]Ibid., p. 7.

At times, Kaufman's condemnation of the American regime would seem to leave no moral choice but violent destruction. Yet, with respect to those political tactics required to bring about a more perfect democracy, Kaufman has made extensive arguments for a politics of radical pressure, avoiding both the "politics of pseudo-realisms" and politics of self-indulgence." By pseudo-realism, Kaufman means the tendency of most reformist liberals to compromise with the forces of reaction and the moneyed power elite by believing pessimistically, not realistically, that very little is possible in American politics. Such pessimism is a self-defeating tactic and ends up being a self-fulfilling prophecy.[76] Thus, Kaufman believes that to avoid conflict is to make an immoral marriage with the present immoral politics of coalitions, consensus, and countervailing power. To gain power, one must press vigorously for the radical alternatives. By the politics of self-indulgence, Kaufman means a preoccupation with the moral correctness of one's own position, often accompanied by a neglect of the cause and people who are being championed. Kaufman believes the policies of self-indulgence are as ineffective as "the politics of pseudo-realism." For example, Kaufman believes the self-indulgence of the New Left makes it incapable of sustaining political action.[77] The people of the New Left move from one mass demonstration to another without making rational calculations of political efficacy and often refusing to compromise on insignificant matters.

Having eliminated the tactics of the pseudo-realist and the self-indulgent as ineffective, Kaufman advocates the politics of radical pressure. Radical pressure requires the use of "any device short of open rebellion or revolution to bring pressure to bear in support of liberal aims."[78] In other words, the radical uses whatever tactics are effective. Thus, Kaufman finds it practical to capitalize on the violence and disorders of others, such as black militants and the New Left, to dramatize unfulfilled human needs. For example, the rhetoric and violent action of Black Power advocates is a "momentary strategic option."[79] For Kaufman, transformation of the present system is possible through the positive political use of any effective tactic, whether self-imposed or by taking advantage of the tactics of others. Kaufman apparently is convinced that what he calls "the dialectic of disorder," provided by the gaps between rhetoric and reality, ultimately will either destroy or radically transform the present system.[80]

---

[76]Ibid., p. 115.   [77]Ibid., p. 54.

[78]Ibid., pp. 72-73.   [79]Ibid., p. 94.

[80]Ibid., pp. 57 and 153.

Reformers

The fourth group is the reformers. Reformers usually give overt support for existing structures of political authority but may participate in nonviolent deviance from the regime's laws, customs, or norms. Reformist groups are usually deeply committed to the fundamental regime principles and accept them as legitimate standards for judging the actions and policies of government. Reformers may find the regime wanting according to its own ideals, but they believe that it is capable of progress and social change. The high purposes of reformers are fairly specific. They often involve a single set of well-defined policy grievances, such as civil rights, labor legislation, or peace. The reformer may become involved in norm-oriented movements. Although seeking social changes, reformers require only minor changes in the rules, rather than changes in the basic forms or mystical principles of government. Such minor changes are seldom significant threats to any regime, except the most rigid. The political system can tolerate, control, or ignore reformers with little difficulty. As indicated earlier, however, because of unanticipated consequences or unarticulated goals, changes in rules may involve changes in fundamental values and not the mere alteration of minor or petty routines. Some examples of reform and protest movements and organizations which may sometimes lead to political violence are: labor movements, the civil rights movement, anti-war movements, agrarian uprisings, labor protests, democratic socialist movements, populism, progressivism, abolitionism, S.N.C.C., Americans for Democratic Action, Common Cause, S.A.N.E., the American Civil Liberties Union, young college democrats, social banditry, and some liberal intellectuals.[81]
The most common tactics of reformist movements or organizations are peaceful and legal demonstrations and protests-- such as strikes, "teach ins," and legal picketing-- and selective acts of civil disobedience against particular laws perceived as unjust. These protest or dissent tactics of reformers tend to be disruptive but are seldom meant to be violent. Some of these tactics, however, may degenerate into violence because of (1) the threatening kinds of interaction between police and reformers and (2) the presence of radicals, revolutionaries, anarchists, criminals, and super-patriots, who may be seeking violence. A few reformers may sometimes use violent tactics consciously in order to elicit responses by authorities to their grievances. Again, the reformist intention is the change of policies, not the radical

---

[81]The problem with this category is the mixture of purposes, situations, and tactics.

transformation or the overthrow of the governmental whole.
Given these purposes, reformer tactics are likely to be
very selective and planned acts of violence designed to
disrupt the flow of traffic or the use of other public
facilities. In Gurr's terms, violence connected with
reform is better categorized as turmoil, rather than
revolution, internal war, or conspiracy.

In contemporary American life, the most publicly
significant reformers tend to be liberal intellectuals,
such as Arthur Schlesinger, John Kenneth Galbraith, and
John Gardner. Traditionalists and members of the establishment may also seek some minor political changes or
adjustments which they would call reform, such as welfare
reform or "creative" or "new" federalism. Most of these
changes, however, would be fairly consistent with existing
regime norms. Moreover, their own actions are likely to
be nonviolent, and their reforms would meet with little
resistance, unless perceived as a drastic "roll back"
from previous political gains for particular interests or
groups.

The Establishmentarian

The establishmentarian actively supports the
existing regime and looks askance at any political violence,
though he may understand the use of violence by others. He
is a liberal Republican or middle of the road Democrat. He
belongs to and participates in any number of organizations,
which may dabble in politics. He is likely to belong to a
labor union or chamber of commerce. He is probably "inner
directed"[82] or has "public regardingness."[83] In short,
he is a "good citizen" or allegiant of the existing regime.

Traditionalists

The behavior of the traditionalist is characterized
by (1) the avoidance of any deviation from customary or
legal regime norms and values; (2) overt support for the
existing structure or political authority;[84] and (3)
avoidance of use of political, if not personal, violence.
He abhors especially the violence of students and blacks.

---

[82]David Riesman, The Lonely Crowd: A Study of the
Changing American Character (New Haven: Yale University
Press, 1961).

[83]James Q. Wilson and Edward C. Banfield, "Public-
Regardingness as a Value Premise in Voting Behavior,"
Perspectives on Urban Politics, ed. Jay S. Goodman (Boston:
Allyn and Bacon, Inc., 1970), pp. 333-354.

[84]Muller, "A Test...," p. 14.

The traditionalist is a supporter of the establishment or the system. On campus, he is a conservative or a vocationalist.[85] In the black community, he is an "Uncle Tom" who still votes Republican. Among the white middle class, he is likely to be prototypically an ordinary citizen of Orange County who does not belong to the super-patriotic John Birch Society. He pays his taxes and votes. He may even avoid traffic tickets. Along with establishment supporters, he may be a member of the so-called "silent" or "forgotten" majority-- he is a middle American. He may be an "ethnic" or a "hyphenated American" with ancestral roots in Eurpo?, such as a Polish, Italian, or Greek-American.

The traditionalist does not care much about politics or politicians, until they tear up his street, or his lights go off. His political participation is limited to voting and to a very occasional letter to a congressman. If he belongs to any organizations, it is a fraternal or veterans group, or perhaps even a church. He is not very interesting to most social scientists, or perhaps even to most politicians. In 1972, he may be using his vote to protest school bonds and busing to achieve racial balance: paradoxically, he may vote for either George Wallace or George McGovern. When and if he finds out what George McGovern stands for, he will probably not "throw his vote away" in the general election in November. He will vote for safe, secure, and uninteresting candidates, like Richard Nixon and "Chet" Hollifield. Generally, he splits his ticket for both Democratic and Republican candidates. Except for his low level of political interest and participation, the traditionalist is practically indistinguishable from an establishment type.

Deviants

A seventh category includes those criminal or deviant groups or individuals who usually perceive the regime as legitimate, but who have few scruples about the means used to redistribute its benefits to a few lawbreakers. In 1971, Gay Talese reported the anger of Mafia leaders at black rebellion and student disruption.[86] They

---

[85]Clark and Trow, "Organizational... ."

[86]Gay Talese, Honor Thy Father: The Inside Book of the Mafia (New York: World Publishing Co., 1971). Criminality is probably not genetically transmitted only through Italian-American genes. For reports on Irish, W.A.S.P., and Jewish criminals, see George V. Higgins, Friends of Eddie Coyle (New York: Alfred A. Knopf, Inc., 1971).

wonder what is happening to the country.[87] Probably most people are familiar with the tactics of organized and individual crime. These tactics are related to the particular kind of fun, profit, or vengeance sought. Young street-corner gangs probably use violence for kicks and fun, as well as for profit and some community control. Like all violence, these tactics have the same results-- harm, death, destruction, and disorder. The important difference is in the purpose of criminal tactics. Criminals are distinguished from the revolutionaries in that they generally accept the regime's fundamental values and lack a radical ideology.[88]

Although they support the regime, criminals violate its social norms, customs, rules, and laws. The modern gang depends on a kind of law and order, as does the legitimate businessman. Indeed, some gangs may provide a form of order for their neighborhoods, albeit outside of existing law. On the other hand, the revolutionary openly violates both norms and values.[89]

The Super-Patriots

The eighth and last category is the patriots, or more accurately, the super-patriots. Super-patriots are deeply committed to their own perception of the meaning of the purposes of the regime. Their avowed purpose is to maintain the system or regime or to push it back to a golden era when regime principles were supposedly more pure. It should be made clear that the super-patriot is a peculiar breed of citizen. Most ordinary citizens to about their daily activities normally convinced that their government can be trusted to take care of most important things rightfully and competently, albeit with some corruption and graft, probably seen as a normal part of the "dirty" profession of politics. Quite to the contrary, the super-patriot seeks vigorously to protect the regime. In fact, in his efforts, he will go outside the law to provide protection or "security" for the nation.

---

[87]Talese, Honor... . For a report on Francis Ianni's anthropological findings that Mafia members tended to be hawks on the war in Vietnam, see "Mafia Youth Leaving Fold, Expert Says," Los Angeles Times, May 27, 1971, p. 1.

[88]Some black gangs may combine both criminality and political radicalism.

[89]See William F. Whyte, Street Corner Society (Berkeley, Calif.: University of California Press, 1943); Yablonsky, Violent...; and Howard W. Polsky, Cottage Six: The Social System of Delinquent Boys in Residential Treatment (New York: John Wiley and Sons, Inc., 1962).

When this group resorts to violence in its effort to assist government (usually ignorantly and intolerantly), most people have categorized them as vigilantes. Examples of such vigilantism include the violence of "hardhats," police, nativist movements, know-nothings, reactionaries, North Carolina Regulars, Minutemen, and the John Birch Society. (Some black groups claim to be vigilante, but the system they may be defending is their own black culture, not the existing American regime.) Historically, in America preservative vigilante violence has probably been the dominant form of violence. According to Hofstadter,

> one is impressed that most American violence-- and this also illuminates its relationship to state power-- has been initiated with a "conservative" bias. It has been unleashed against abolitionists, Catholics, radicals, workers and labor organizers, Negroes, Orientals, and other ethnic or racial or ideological minorities, and has been used ostensibly to protect the American, the Southerner, the white Protestant, or simply the established middle-class way of life and morals.[90]

In the past, the vigilante's mob-like style was lynching, midnight raids, and tar and feathering. Usually, the ritual of a fair trial accompanied such tactics. Some contemporary acts of super-patriots may indicate their strong willingness to use violence in the future. The most frightening of these acts are the clandestine desert maneuvers and the stockpiling of weapons arsenals by some groups, such as the Minutemen and some southern white citizens' councils. Apparently, some super-patriots may become vigilantes in the near future.

If mass media reports are accurate, such vigilante movements in 1972 probably do not constitute a well-

---

[90]Hofstadter, "Reflections...," p. 12. On vigilante movements, see Richard Maxwell Brown, "The American Vigilante Tradition," History of Violence in America, ed. Hugh Davis Graham and Ted Gurr, A report to the National Commission on the Causes and Prevention of Violence (New York: Bantam Books, 1969), pp. 154-217. On labor violence, see Robert Hunter, Violence and the Labor Movement (New York: MacMillan Co., 1914); Stanley Frost, Labor and Revolt (New York: E. P. Dulton and Co., 1920); and Herman Feldman, Racial Factors in American Industry (New York: Harper and Bros., Pubs., 1931). On the Klan, see David M. Chalmers, Hooded Americanism: The History of the Klu Klux Klan (New York: Doubleday, 1965).

organized or actively regular political phenomenon.[91]
Some possible exceptions may be among some southern or
urban police departments, individuals within some
National Guard units, and factions within many police
departments. In contemporary American, super-patriotic
groups generally perceive their violent activity as
generally reactive to leftist or black violence. Ultimately, this group probably represents the greatest threat
to the regime. If organized and widespread, super-patriots
could conceivably mobilize greater public support, through
distorted appeals to traditional "American" values, than
perhaps the left or selected dissident minorities or subcultures.

---

[91]On existing vigilante groups in the Late 1960's
see Kirkham, Levy, and Crotty, Assassination..., pp. 281-
289; for a good historical overview of vigilante, racial,
and labor violence, see pp. 212-225.

CHAPTER V

A PARTIAL TEST OF ELITE OPINIONS
ON DEMOCRATIC LEGITIMACY
AND POLITICAL VIOLENCE

This chapter outlines the evolution of the concept
of democracy among political elites, such as political
philosophers, statesmen, intellectuals, and radical political activists. The United States of America is commonly
understood to be a democracy-- either in its practice, its
theory, or its ideals. The myths legitimating authority
in America are democratic. Consequently, almost everyone
judges it by their interpretation of those democratic
standards of political justice. There are many theories
of democracy. One difficulty of defining democracy is
generally that there are competing and even (sometimes)
contradictory understandings of the meaning of such central
ideas of the democratic myth as equality and liberty. The
greatest difficulty is perhaps in attempting to operationalize or to apply such ideals in the practice of political life
and in the study of politics. In practice, differing interpretations of such ideas as democracy, equality, liberty, and
legitimacy may give rise to contradictory political interests
and ideological conflicts, some of it violent.

Political Philosophers

The classical political thinkers, Aristotle and
Plato, rejected democracy because of its tendency in
practice to breed anarchy and ignoble citizens. If a
people were to make the unfortunate choice of democracy
for their government, they would have to temper it by
(1) the rule of law, and (2) indoctrination of the citizenry as to their duties. On the other hand, if there is
rejection of citizenly virtues as a political goal (in
the comprehensive sense of the ancients), as there is in
most of modern thought, then democracy may be a legitimate
form of government. That is, if the goal of democracy is
merely to be orderly, then a democratic government may
become legitimate through the widespread belief among its
citizens in their political obligation to obey.

The initial modern solution to the democratic problem of a violent and lawless rule by the many, with the significant exception of Rousseau, was primarily fear-- fear of the possibility of disorder and of the power of the absolute sovereign state. Hobbes argued that without the rule of an absolute sovereign, the lives of men would be mean, nasty, brutish, and short. It is this fear of violent death in the state of nature that drives men to seek civil society. Hobbes' myth of disorderly state of nature legitimates, at least in theory, all forms of political authority which maintain order.

Locke

Locke mitigated the harshness of Hobbes' teaching by arguing that besides the fear of disorder, it is in the acquisitive and material interests of all citizens to voluntarily consent to obey the state. First, the regime must prove itself worthy of obedience by protecting life, liberty, and property. Under this condition and in fear of disorder, citizens would voluntarily consent to governmental authority. According to Locke, this consent could extend to any form of government, provided it protects the natural rights of its citizens.

Locke also had much to say directly about legitimacy and revolution. His teachings had considerable influence on early American political thought concerning democratic legitimating ideologies or principles of citizens' obligations in a democracy. According to Locke, the legitimate purpose of any civil society is to preserve those natural rights-- life, liberty, property, and peace-- which all men had in nature before they instituted the social contract. If the state breaks the social contract, the people have a right to defend themselves against any efforts to threaten their natural rights. Yet citizens must bear petty injustices in order to preserve a government of laws, which is preferable to the lawlessness of the original state of nature. Desiring orderliness and self-preservation, the people are usually unlikely to resort to revolution except to provide that order necessary for their own comfortable self-preservation.

Rousseau

According to Rousseau, no particular form of government is inherently legitimate. The civil state, whatever its form, is legitimate through only one source-- the collective or general will of the people at large. No man, group, faction, or party can make law in place of the general will. Many have interpreted Rousseau's brilliant theoretical vision as support for a participatory democracy under the thoroughgoing and positive form of consent-- the general will. Yet Rousseau's doctrine of general will

unlike the ideology of participatory democracy, gave no
unambiguous support for democracy. Rousseau called democracy a "wild anarchy of self-interest." According to
Rousseau, representative government is also not legitimate
(except as an unavoidable necessity for large nations),
because the general will cannot be expressed indirectly.
Thus, for Rousseau, there is no clear principle for a
legitimate regime other than the general will. The people
as a whole must determine the form of government and laws
they want. Thus, any form of government is legitimate only
in terms of consent of the general will. Once the people
have established a government, they have few grounds for
revolution.

Despite their differences, the thoughts of Locke
and Rousseau form the basis of much of the political thought
of American statesmen in the period of the American Revolution and the formation of the democratic republic.
Collectively, Hobbes, Locke, and Rousseau provided a series
of arguments attempting to legitimate the state through
both fear and consent. Their doctrines of natural equality
also provided a central part of the legitimating myths of
American democracy.

Political Thought of American Statesmen

One means of reviewing the evolution of American
political thought on the meaning of democracy, equality,
and liberty, and their relation to legitimacy and political
violence is through the eyes of the principle American
statesmen at critical turning points in the history of the
nation. For example, Jefferson's Declaration of Independence stated principles of government justifying the American
Revolution. In 1800, he claimed to present a democratic
alternative to the monarchial tendencies of the federalist
government of Hamilton and Adams. As the principle authors
of The Federalist Papers, Madison and Hamilton (as Publius)
claimed to institute a democratic and competent form of
government. Lincoln said the Civil War was necessary to
maintain a democracy which might be more perfectible in the
future. Finally, Franklin D. Roosevelt claimed to make
American democracy safe from the big business interests
which had sold out the general welfare of the people. Each
of these statesmen made important additions to American
thinking about democracy, equality, and liberty. The ideas
of these men signaled important and not always subtle
changes in the legitimating myths of the American regime.
What they thought and did affected more than just the
formal arrangement of political offices and policies.
Their ideas not only set the tone and agenda for American
politics, sometimes for a generation or more, but also
had considerable impact on the meaning of the legitimating
ideologies of American democracy.

Jefferson[1]

According to Jefferson in the Declaration of Independence, a just and legitimate government, as least in principle, is any government which secures individual life, liberty, and the pursuit of happiness. Desiring such protections, citizens are likely to consent to a government which does indeed secure their natural rights to life, liberty, and the pursuit of happiness. They will choose a government which also defends the people against the domestic and foreign enemies of equality. Thus, government derives legitimacy from the principle of equality. This equality is reflected collectively in the consent of the people to allow government to rule them.

Jeffersonian equality is thus purely political, involving the right to consent voluntarily to government and to select their own representatives. There is no class of men so superior, either naturally or artifically through wealth or birth, as to have a natural or divine right to rule all other men. Such political equality entitles every man to equal protection of the law. As men are not equal in color, intelligence, religious belief, or economic interest, one cannot expect equality in such things. Jefferson applies equality of educational opportunity only to those capable of being natural rather than artificial aristocrats.

For Jefferson, liberty is essentially the equal opportunity of individuals to be secure in their lives and to be able to pursue their own happiness without undue governmental interference. Such liberty, if encouraged includes an adequate supply of cheap land (to insure an independent and free spirit) and the absence of political restraints by government or any "monocrats" or moneyed class of bankers and manufacturers. Perhaps one of the greatest problems of democratic government is achieving a balance between liberty of minorities and the consent of the majority. Though Jefferson says in his First Inaugural Address that absolute acquiescence to the majority is "a sacred principle," he also fears an "elective despotism." The source of that despotism was most likely to be the subversion of the will of the people by elected federalist representatives. In his famous letter to Madison on January 30, 1787, Jefferson testified to both

---

[1]See Harvey C. Mansfield, Jr., "Thomas Jefferson," American Political Thought: The Philosophic Dimensions of American Statesmanship, ed. Morton J. Frisch and Richard G. Stevens (New York: Charles Scribner's Sons, 1971), pp. 23-50; and Thomas Jefferson, The Complete Jefferson Containing His Major Writings, Published and Unpublished Except His Letters, assembled and arranged by Saul K. Padover (New York: Duell, Sloan, and Pearce, Inc., 1943).

this fear of federalist monarchial tendencies, which
would deny the peoples' liberty, and his continuing faith
in the American people's capacity for self-government.
Thus, Jefferson's interest in liberty does seem to have a
majoritarian bias-- liberty for the greatest number. In
accordance with this belief, he sought expansion of the
suffrage and direct democracy in local townships and wards.
Thus, for Jefferson, the only legitimate form of government
for the American people (if not for the French or for
Indians) is democracy. Such a legitimate government is
worthy of preservation.

Jefferson's view of liberty was not devoid of
restraints-- certainly all men have an obligation to obey
that government which secures their rights. As the
Declaration indicates, however, when government violates
natural rights, the people have a right to rebel. Yet,
as the doctrine of natural rights leads to a social contract,
citizens, as well as governments, have obligations.
Governments are not to be overthrown by revolution for
"light and transient causes." Rather the people must
suffer a "long train of abuses" with "patient sufferance."
They must demonstrate that there is a "design" of "absolute
despotism." These steps are necessary because revolution
is a serious business which may result in a return to the
state of nature, where there is "war of all against all."
Revolution is justifiable only after injustices have been
borne, demonstrated, and protested, and after that protest
has failed. In the Declaration, Jefferson outlines some
possible causes of legitimate revolt. Interestingly
enough, one of the charges against King George was that
America had indeed returned to a state of nature:

> the Legislative Powers ... have returned to the
> People at large for their exercise; the State
> remaining in the mean time exposed to all the
> dangers of invasion from without, and convulsions
> within.[2]

Though at first hopeful for the benefits of the
French Revolution, Jefferson later riled against it.
Apparently, the injustices Jefferson saw in the illegitimate
regime of monarchist France were not sufficient to justify
the violent excesses of the French Revolution, for prudence
and the survival of a political community sometimes do not
permit the immediate realization of justice. Taking a

---

[2] Declaration of Independence.

similar position on the evils of slavery, Jefferson said
in 1820, "We have the wolf by the ears and we can neither
hold him, nor safely let him go. Justice is on one scale
and self-preservation is on the other."[3] Jefferson claimed
to tremble over the future of American democracy because of
black slavery. Yet, according to Jefferson, the Republic
in 1820 was worthy of preservation even though black
slavery was an injustice to a minority. The injustice
had to be borne in order to preserve the higher public
good based on the "sacred principle" of majority rule.

Despite Jefferson's reluctance to resort to revolution once the Republic had been formed, many of his
readers have found revolutionary guidance in his writings.
The high ideals and justifications for revolution in the
Declaration of Independence; Jefferson's famous letter
on the need for "a little rebellion now and then;[4] and
his failure to provide an absolute case for the legitimacy
and necessary preservation of any regime-- all these
examples have lead many of his readers to believe he
provides a rather easy justification for revolution. Yet,
in order to understand Jefferson, one must remember his
thoughts on the obligations of the social contract; his
condemnation of King George on disorder; his later condemnation of the excesses of the French Revolution; and
his belief in the orderly, as well as independent, habits
instilled by land ownership. There is plenty of evidence
on both sides of Jefferson's views on order and revolution,
but surely, with his "law and order" view of the purposes of
limited government and his restricted view of equality and
liberty, his doctrines on revolution are not thoroughgoing.

Federalists[5]

The Declaration is a uniquely American creed on
the standard of legitimacy of government in general, but

---

[3]Jefferson, cited by Jaffa, Equality..., p. 135.

[4]Letter to James Madison, January 30, 1787, in
Jefferson, Complete..., p. 270.

[5]My thoughts on the Federalists are heavily influ-
enced by Martin Diamond. See Martin Diamond, Winston
Mills Fisk, and Herbert Garfinkel, The Democratic Republic
(2d ed.; Chicago: Rand McNally and Co., 1970), chap. iv,
"The Fundamental Political Principles," pp. 83-120; Martin
Diamond, "Democracy..."; Martin Diamond, "The Federalist,"
American Political Thought: The Philosophic Dimensions
of American Statesmanship, ed. Morton J. Frisch and Richard
G. Stevens (New York: Charles Scribner's Sons, 1971),
pp. 51-70; and Martin Diamond, "The Federalist," History

the Constitution formed the governmental institutions
which ruled the American people from 1787 until the
present (1972). Thus, the Federalist-- Madison's and
Hamilton's (Jay's role being rather small)-- understanding
of American democracy is crucial, for they were the chief
supporters of that constitution. The Federalists claimed
support for the democratic legitimating principle of
equality in the Declaration throughout their writings.
For example, their support is evident in their claims that
they were friends of popular government;[6] that representative government is one form of rule by the people;[7] that
the people retain the right to alter or abolish their
government;[8] and that government ultimately rests on the
consent of the people.[9] These expressions of support for
the people's consent is their view of a standard for
legitimating the Constitution.

The Federalists believed that democracy normally
provides scant protection for minority liberty and may
lead to unwise decisions detrimental to the common good
as well. For example, in The Federalist No. 10, Madison
said,

> To secure the public good and private rights against
> the danger of ... a [majority] faction, and at the
> same time to preserve the spirit and the form of
> popular government, is then the great object to
> which our inquiries are directed.[10]

For the Federalists, the abuse of liberty by minority
factions is a rather small problem easily safeguarded
against by energetic and stable government. On the other
hand, it is necessary to give liberty added insurance and
protections through temporary restraints on majority
passions and interests. According to the Federalists, the
Constitution insures that American democracy will be safe
for liberty and conducive to the common good through the

---

of Political Philosophy, ed. Leo Strauss and Joseph Cropsey
(5th ed.; Chicago; Rand McNally and Co., 1963), pp. 573-
593.

[6]Hamilton, Madison, and Jay, Federalist..., No. 10.

[7]Ibid.

[8]Ibid., Nos. 1, 22, 23, 28, 29, 39, 40, and 78.

[9]Ibid., Nos. 1, 22, 23, 37, 39, 49, 78, 84, and 85.

[10]Ibid., No. 10, p. 79. (Insert of "majority" is
mine and replaces only the word "such" which refers to
majority faction in Madison's previous sentence.)

implementation of discoveries of "the new science of politics," such as separation of powers, bicameralism, and the representative principle. The primary remedy, however, for the democratic disease-- "violence of factions"-- is a large commercial republic designed to break and control the "violence of faction," especially the violence of majority faction, through the multiplication of economic and political interests. The Federalists hoped further to insure the solution to this substantive problem of majority factions by strengthening the executive and judiciary and by extending the territory governed by a strong national government. The Federalists also expected the commercial advantages of the large republic to give plenty of fertile ground for the individual exercise of liberty and equality of opportunity. Finally,the Federalists believed that equality before the law obligates the people to support the regime which secures and protects life, liberty, the pursuit of happiness, and property.[11]

In one sense, the whole of The Federalist Papers is an argument for the legitimacy of the government institutued in 1787. In another sense, one can see the advocacy of the creation of a strong and stable government with "energy and stability" as an effort to provide the means to enforce order and to foreclose the possibility of the political violence of "domestic insurrections" or foreign interventions. On the whole, The Federalist Papers are Madison's and Hamilton's arguments on the legitimacy of the regime chiefly established in 1787.

Lincoln[12]

For Jefferson, the principle of equality provides the moral grounds for justifying revolution under the insufferable conditions of 1776. Since revolution is conditional and must be succeeded by the institution of a government of laws, the principle of equality implies a standard for a citizen's obligations as well as grounds for his individual rights. The Federalists institutionalized the principle of equality in their efforts in the Constitution to establish a democracy capable of defending

---

[11]Ibid., No. 43.

[12]My interpretations of Lincoln's political thought is heavily influenced by the writings of Harry Jaffa. See Jaffa, Equality...; Crisis...; and "Abraham Lincoln," American Political Thought: The Philosophic Dimensions of American Statesmanship, ed. Morton J. Frisch and Richard G. Stevens (New York: Charles Scribner's Sons, 1971), pp. 125-144.

itself from enemies, both foreign and domestic. In the
Constitution, equality becomes more clearly a principle
of obligation to a government which upholds its contractual
obligations to defend life, liberty, and pursuit of happiness (as partially restated in the preamble of the Constitution). Lincoln accepted the natural rights grounds of
the principle of equality and the obligations to law that
it entails.[13] He did, however, reinterpret the meaning
of equality.

For Lincoln, equality is a standard maxim, an
ideal of perfection, to be pursued as much as contemporary
prejudice permits. That is, Lincoln understood the equality
of the Declaration in its universal terms not only as
truth derived from nature, but also as a guide for the
future acts of statesmen. According to Lincoln, the
Declaration

> gave liberty not alone to the people of this country,
> but hope to all the world, for all future time. It
> was that which gave promise that in due time the
> weights would be lifted from the shoulders of all
> men and that all should have an equal chance.[14]

Another illustration of Lincoln's understanding of equality
as the political rights of the Declaration yet to be
achieved is his speech on the Dred Scott decision:

> I think the authors of that notable instrument intended
> to include all men, but they did not intend to declare
> all men are equal in all respects. They did not mean
> to say all were equal in color, size, intellect, moral
> developments, or social capacity. They defined with
> tolerable distinctions, in what respects they did con-
> sider all men created equal--equal in "certain inal-
> ienable rights, among which are life, liberty, and the
> pursuit of happiness." This they said, and this they
> meant. They did not mean to assert the obvious untruth,
> that all were then actually enjoying that equality, nor
> yet that they were able to confer it immediately upon
> them. In fact, they had no power to confer such a boon.
> They meant simply to declare the right, so that the en-
> forcement of it might follow as fast as circumstances

---

[13]For a general argument for obedience to the laws
of the republic, see Abraham Lincoln, "The Perpetuation of
Our Political Institutions," An address before the Young
Men's Lyceum of Springfield, Ill., January 27, 1838, On
Civil Disobedience, ed. Robert A. Goldwin (Chicago: Rand
McNally and Co., 1968), pp. 1-9.

[14]Lincoln's Independence Hall speech of 1861,
quoted by Jaffa, "Lincoln...," p. 142. (Italics mine.)

should permit. They meant to set up a standard maxim for free society, which would be familiar to all, and revered by all; constantly looked to, constantly labored for, and even though never perfectly attained, constantly spreading and deepening its influence, and augmenting the happiness and value of life to all people of all colors everywhere.[15]

During his debates with Douglas, which were concerned with the extension of slavery into the territories, Lincoln clarified his concepts of equality. Douglas had said that popular sovereignty or rule of the people required that a majority of citizens in the territories decide the slavery issue by vote. Lincoln's arguments against Douglas were in terms of both morality and the narrow self-interests of whites. Lincoln argued that for even a majority of the people to consent to the slavery of a black minority is to deny the equality of all men. Such universal equality is the moral grounds for the white majority's right to its own liberty and self-government. Thus, if a white majority denies the equality of the black minority, that majority also denies its own right to liberty and self-government. Lincoln also argued in terms of the narrow self-interests of whites. In 1855, he wrote a private letter to his old friend Joshua Speed, in which he said,

> I am not a Know-nothing. That is certain. How could I be? How can any one who abhors the oppression of ne-groes, be in favor of degrading classes of white people? Our progress in degeneracy appears to me to be pretty rapid. As a nation, we began by declaring that "all men are created equal." We now practically read it "all men are created equal, except negroes." When the Know-nothings get control, it will read "all men are created equal, except negroes, and foreigners, and Catholics." When it comes to this I should prefer emigrating to some country where they make no pretence of loving liberty--to Russia, for instance, where despotism can be taken pure and without the base alloy of hypocrisy.[16]

With this understanding of the possible effect of abstract ideas on political behavior, Lincoln sought to place slavery in "the course of ultimate extinction."

Thus, Lincoln's equality was political and had moral implications. The liberty resulting from the equality of men gives hope to the individual. This liberty consequently results in enterprise, industry, and economic prosperity for the nation. The party of Lincoln strongly believed in this economic prosperity. Unfortunately, there were many

---

[15]Lincoln, quoted in Ibid., p. 136. (Italics mine.)

[16]Lincoln, quoted by Harry Jaffa, "Reflections on

abuses to this economic liberty. The next section discusses
Franklin D. Roosevelt and how he corrected these abuses.

Franklin D. Roosevelt[17]

Just as Lincoln's interpretation of equality had
added to it a standard of perfection, so Franklin D.
Roosevelt reshaped and reinterpreted certain American ideas
in the course of instituting the welfare state. Many of
his critics have claimed that the welfare state was a
fundamental break with the American political tradition in
the direction of socialism. Nevertheless, Roosevelt's in-
complete brand of socialism was democratic. In the face
of an economic depression during the 1930's and the then
apparent prosperity of undemocratic totalitarian systems,
particularly in Nazi Germany and the Soviet Union, Roosevelt
successfully showed that capitalism or the economic liberty
of some could be regulated by government without the destruction of democracy (political liberty) for the many.
In one key sense, Roosevelt was committed to an energetic and competent national government dedicated to the
"general welfare" referred to in the preamble of the United
States Constitution.
     It is true that Roosevelt sought to restrict the
liberty of those who had abused it-- the large economic
enterprises and the wealthy. Yet this restriction, through
policies of economic redistribution, probably enlarged and
protected the economic liberty of most citizens. Thus,
the essential characteristic of Roosevelt's view of democracy is the greatest good for the greatest number. This
policy requires that government do more than secure or
guarantee the minimal conditions for happiness or attempt,
as Lincoln did, to enlighten a racist majority. This
policy requires more precisely that government should do
what it can to provide for the actual achievement of general
well-being and happiness for as many citizens as possible.

Thoreau and Lincoln: Civil Disobedience and the American
Tradition," On Civil Disobedience, ed. Robert A. Goldwin
(Chicago: Rand McNally and Co., 1970), p. 54.

     [17]My interpretations of Roosevelt rest entirely on
the single article by Morton J. Frisch, "Franklin Delano
Roosevelt," American Political Thought: The Philosophic
Dimensions of American Statesmanship, ed. Morton J. Frisch
and Richard G. Stevens (New York: Charles Scribner's Sons,
1971), pp. 219-236. For a contrary view that Roosevelt
and indeed most American statesmen were little influenced
by political principles, see Richard Hofstadter, The
American Political Tradition (New York: Alfred A. Knopf,
Inc., 1948); and Lasswell, Psychopathology....

With Roosevelt, the burden of obligations seems to shift
from citizens to their government, as Lincoln's "standard
maxim" of equality may have anticipated. Political rights
expanded under Roosevelt to include economic rights.

The preservation of democracy seems to require
that governmnet attempt to guarantee equality of opportunity
by its actions rather than by securing the liberty of
individuals to seek their own opportunities. In this
sense, Roosevelt goes beyond Lincoln's understanding of
the place of equality and liberty. Yet, in a more fundamental sense, Roosevelt and the welfare state were perhaps
a vigorous pursuit of Lincoln's standard of perfection.
Recently, some have interpreted perfection, democratically
understood, to mean ultimately government provision of
both materialistic egalitarianism and hedonistic libertar-
ianism.

Political Thought of Contemporary Americans

Lasswell, Dahl, Schlesinger, Douglas, and Stolz
are important social scientists and thinkers about American
politics. Although one would not necessarily think of
them in terms of their theories of American democracy, a
democratic theory. Sometimes unconscious or inarticulated,
does underly much of their work and interests. In a much
more comprehensive effort than this, Dwight Waldo revealed
that political theory underlies much of the public administration literature up to 1940.[18] Thus, these writers
probably provide a fair cross section of the political
thought of this era, even though they would not necessarily
be on everyone's list of democratic theorists. A discussion
of their thought is meant only to be illustrative but not
exhaustive of certain contemporary issues in democratic
theory.

Political Thought of Contemporary American Social Scientists

Although not always consciously, individual social
scientists have their own theories of democracy, equality,
and liberty. Like the political thought of American statesmen, these views have tended to expand and enlarge the
application of these values to areas of American life which
would have been beyond earlier democratic theories. It may
be in this sense, as well as others, that twentieth century

---

[18]See Dwight Waldo, The Administrative State (New
York: Ronald Press, 1948).

Americans tend to consider themselves so much more democratic than their ancestors.

Lasswell

According to Lasswell, democracy is a "preference
for the wide sharing...of decision making" or power.
Lasswell does not limit his theory of democracy to power
sharing only in formally political or governmental institutions. Power may also include the "entire network of
community institutions,"[19] such as trade unions, cooperatives
and corporations.[20] This all inclusive view of democratically based power may help explain Lasswell's preference
for a high level of citizen participation, in which "decisions are properly in the hands of [the] people."[21] For
Lasswell, democracy exists where referenda and elections
are frequent;[22] where there is a rapid turnover of officials;[23] and where participation is general.[24] Thus,
Lasswell is concerned with the "sharing of power" or the
degree of democratic participation in a wide range of human
relations. For Lasswell, the standard of perfection for
the good society is the "maximum sharing of all values ...
power, wealth, and other values..."[25] Power is only one
of the seven human values Lasswell discusses.

Lasswell seems to have a truly egalitarian view of
democracy . In addition to equality, all seven of Lasswell's
values reflect this expanded view. For example, security
is the sharing of the values of well-being, wealth, and
skill. Thus, security is not merely the governmental protection of life, liberty, and pursuit of happiness; security
also includes "a guarantee of basic income"[26]-- economic
equality. Thus, Lasswell's expansive view of security
means freedom from economic insecurity and fear.

Dahl and Lindbloom

Dahl and Lindbloom consider democracy, freedom, and
equality as goals for the whole of society. For Dahl,
society is an all inclusive concept encompassing economic,
educational, and political institutions. These societal
institutions govern the means and degree of individual
goal attainment. Adapted from Lasswell's values, these

---

[19]Lasswell and Lerner, World Revolutionary...,
p. 46.

[20]Ibid., p. 52.   [21]Ibid., p. 47.

[22]Ibid.   [23]Ibid., p. 48.

[24]Ibid., p. 51.   [25]Ibid., p. 17.

[26]Ibid., p. 60.

individual goals are: survival, physiological gratification, affection, respect, power, skill, enlightenment,
prestige, aesthetic satisfaction, excitement, and novelty.[27]
For Dahl and Lindbloom, freedom is "the absence of
obstacles to the realization of desires."[28]Social indoctrination is a major factor in determining one's perception
of these obstacles and desires. Thus, freedom is ultimately
dependent on what others want and will allow. Accordingly,
freedom should be roughly the same for everyone. Dahl
and Lindbloom's definition of freedom goes beyond mere
political freedom and includes all other spheres of human
activity where the fulfillment of individual needs may be
blocked.
Democracy is the system for "adjudicating" conflicts
caused by the pursuance of desires by individuals. The goal
of democracy is political equality attained through the
process of majority rule."[29] In Modern Political Analysis,
Dahl distinguishes between the ideal of democracy and
political reality. For example, Dahl uses the term polyarchy to refer to conditions where "power over state
officials is widely, though by no means equally shared."[30]
Equality is a goal which is probably unattainable.
Dahl and Lindbloom define equality as the sharing of
"control over government decision ... so that the preferences of no one citizen are weighted more heavily than any
other citizen."[31] In his later work, Dahl seems to find
the decision making process in politics nearly everywhere.
Thus, he applies the idea of equality as a standard for
judging nearly all human organizations, whether formally
political or not. According to Dahl and Lindbloom, the
final goal is subjective equality, or the expansion of
opportunities for an ever increasing number of persons to
achieve their goals. This egalitarian distribution would
include not only wealth but also education, housing, medi-
cal care, control, respect, status, and dignity-- economic
and social equality.
Yet achievement of such subjective equality, as
well as political equality, might threaten the minimum
level of agreement required in a polyarchy. Thus, "at
some point, it may prove desirable to put the brakes on

---

[27]Dahl and Lindbloom, Politics, Economics..., pp.
540-541.

[28]Ibid., p. 541.

[29]Ibid., p. 554.

[30]Dahl, Modern..., p. 73.

[31]Dahl and Lindbloom, p. 554.

equality rather than annihilate social agreement."[32] For
Dahl and Lindbloom, equality should thus be widespread
but should not be allowed to go beyond general consensus.
For these views on the dangers of disorder and his observations on the empirically low political participation
rates of American citizens, Bachrach and Walker have
called Dahl a "democratic elitist."[33] Dahl's incisive
analysis of American politics as decidedly polyarchial
and not democratic has perhaps contributed to a delegiti-
mization, at least among his many, many students, of the
democratic myths which support the present regime.

Political Thought of Contemporary
American Liberal Intellectuals [34]

This discussion of political thought must also
include that of American liberal intellectuals, as
representatives of the dominant political persuasion of
American political thought since Roosevelt.

Arthur Schlesinger
Arthur Schlesinger is committed to libertarian
democracy, "in which the rule of the majority at any
given time rests on the guarantee of the right of
minorities to convert themselves into new majorities."[35]

---

[32]Ibid., p. 562. Similarly, Stolz notes that Dahl
pronounces "the [violent] action that fashioned the Republic
... its mortal enemy." (Stolz, "The Liberal...," p. 1.)

[33]Note both of them are less uncertain than Dahl
about the costs of democratizing nongovernmental institutions. See Bachrach, The Theory...; and Walker,
"A Critique... ."

[34]I accept Schlesinger's identification of an intellectual as "one whose home is tne world of ideas."
(Schlesinger, Crisis..., p. 57.) He distinguishes this
world from worlds of power, nature, and images. By liberal,
I mean those generally supportive of the welfare state of
Franklin D. Roosevelt, which would include such individuals
as Arthur Schlesinger, John Kenneth Galbraith, John Gardner,
and Hubert Humphrey. This definition is, of course, very
imprecise and soon may be a relic of American political
history. I do not mean liberalism, as also represented by
the classical liberalism of modern economic conservatives.
For other sympathetic, if critical, discussions of liberalism, see Kaufman, Radical... .

[35]Schlesinger, Violence..., pp. 66-67.

Though condemning violence as detrimental to freedom, reason, and civility, Schlesinger agrees with much of the New Left critique of American democracy. This New Left critique and Schlesinger's argument are based on an expanded view of the scope of application of the principle of equality to all realms of human relations-- not just the equality of all citizens in relations with their government. Thus, Schlesinger says, "One can still understand ... why the contradictions [between the equality demanded by our constitutional structure and the equality denied by our social structure] ... weigh so heavily on the young."[36]

Even though change is necessary in libertarian democracy, Schlesinger realizes that the slow process of majority consent is " the best guarantee that policies relate ... to the greatest good of the greatest number."[37] Thus, despite his preception of an undemocratic social structure, Schlesinger remains optimistic about the inherent progressiveness and decency of American democracy. Yet his criticism of American society for failing to achieve the ideals of libertarian democracy may contribute to much of the current disaffection with these imperfections and contradictions between high ideals and low practices.

Justice Douglas

An Associate Justice of the Supreme Court, Douglas also indicates the possibility of widespread disillusionment with American progress and achievement among America's liberal intelligentsia. According to Douglas, American democracy is a sham, since momentuous decisions are being made by a "small club"-- the establishment and the military-industrial complex. Within this "small club," Douglas includes the C.I.A., the F.B.I., private enterprise, the agro-business lobby, and highway lobby. The unfortunate characteristics of such rule are conformity,[38] repressive force,[39] big brother, and Hitlerian rhetoric.[40]

This elitist dominance of decision making restrains and reduces individual liberty, as well as equality. Among those inequalities caused by elite rule which Douglas points out are political inequality and the great disparity between economic subsidies to industry compared to those subsidies given to the poor.[41] For Douglas, the equal dignity of all is not possible where equality of opportunity is not provided.[42] Thus, Douglas' chief concern is

---

[36]Ibid., p. 66.   [37]Ibid., p. 84.

[38]Douglas, Points..., p. 12.

[39]Ibid., p. 32.   [40]Ibid., p. 58.

[41]Ibid., pp. 70-72.   [42]Ibid., p. 45.

liberty-- freedom from fear of the politically powerful
and from economic want. Such genuine freedom will reduce
present feelings of futility, which lead to the violence
of the young and of the black. Douglas' vision is thus of
a peaceful, cooperative, and humane association of men
everywhere.

Douglas' ultimate complaint seems to be that
happiness is impossible in a corporate and technocratic
state which belittles, debases,[43] and deminishes men.[44]
His goal seems to be private happiness. The achievement
of private happiness is possible only by "increasing shows
of government largesse"[45] for the "poor, the unemployed
and the disemployed."[46] Law must "be responsive to the
human needs" of the hungry and the discriminated.[47] The
fulfillment of these needs will bring "freedom of choice."[48]
Thus, Douglas' understanding of liberty is not the freedom
to pursue happiness; it is the governmental provision of
the basic human needs for happiness without undue interference in private lives. According to Douglas, compliance
with his view of liberty might be revolutionary, but it
need not necessarily lead to violence. Yet, under existing
repressive conditions, Douglas says, "A speaker who resists
arrest is acting as a free man."[49] Justice Douglas seems
to find little need to talk about a citizen's obligations
to the law under the presently repressive system.

Matthew Stolz

Perhaps Stolz has made the most direct intellectual
analysis of the possible connection of ideas of democratic
legitimacy and violence. According to Stolz, the means to
the public good in America is democracy. For Stolz, violent
"conflict may be desirable and indeed legitimate, if it
enlarges or has the intention of enlarging democratic
freedoms and equalities."[50] Thus, democracy depends on
positive "efforts to prevent ... the unequal distribution
of power and resources in America."[51] In American history,
such unequal distribution is the result of "negative"
private violence against "the poor, the deviant and the
political radical."[52] "Through the selective use of
violence," the political structure has also impeded the
"redistribution of political power" and the extension of
"equality from promise to reality."[53] Government has

---

[43]Ibid., p. 33. [44]Ibid., p. 32. [45]Ibid., p. 78.

[46]Ibid., p. 92. [47]Ibid. [48]Ibid., p. 96.

[49]Ibid., p. 6.

[50]Stolz, "The Liberal...," p. 11. (Italics mine.)

[51]Ibid., p. 22. [52]Ibid. [53]Ibid., p. 24.

wedded itself to private property ... and corporate capitalism."[54]

For Stolz, equality is not limited to the political participation of equal citizens. It includes a more equal distribution of economic resources and social status. Equality is a principle of obligation for government, not for the people, as Jefferson might have said. Moreover, equality is no longer merely Lincoln's and Tocqueville's maxim of perfection. Equality should become a reality, not merely a promise or dream. The American dream of freedom from poverty, want, and necessity must now become a reality.

Having this egalitarian perspective, Stolz, as well as others, claims there is a radical contradiction between the equality of the Declaration and the restraints upon equality in the Constitution.[55] The constitution probably does contradict Stolz's egalitarian vision of equality, which is now widely accepted by many American intellectuals, politicians, blacks, and students. Stolz argues that the abolitionists sought to destroy the Constitution on grounds of the principles of the Declaration.[56] Stolz also points out accurately that "the extraordinary politics of the young and the black ... coalesce around the principle of equality."[57] The next section is a discussion of the ideals of some of these political activists.

Political Thought of Political Activists

Kaufman: radical liberal reformer

A. S. Kaufman eloquently condemns American society for not being fully democratic. He says American political processes are unduly submissive to and manipulated by corporate power (private and public) and by a moneyed elite.[58] This elitism is particulary hateful to Kaufman,

---

[54]Ibid. See also T. B. Bottomore, Elites and Society (Baltimore: Penguin Books, 1964), p. 120.

[55]As discussed earlier, Jefferson himself found the Constitution in nearly perfect agreement with the principles of the Declaration (see Mansfield, "Jefferson...," p. 42).

[56]Stolz, "The Liberal...," p. 33, refers to Aileen Kraelitor, Means and Ends in American Abolitionism (New YOrk: Pantheon, 1969), p. 201.

[57]Ibid., p. 44.

[58]Kaufman, Radical..., pp. 6, 49, and 69. Other

because he believes the protection of property rights now
takes precedence over other rights.[59] Kaufman further
criticizes the American system by saying it fails even by
its own standards. The system has demonstrated a recurring
failure to "match radical deed to radical word,"[60] thus
creating a gap between rhetoric and practice.[61] A specific
example is the "gap between the rhetoric of affluence
and the reality of poverty."[62] Such gaps create a
"dialectic of disorder," as promises feed aspirations
which far outpace actual achievement.[63]

    Kaufman's indictment of the American regime is
based on his particular vision of equality and liberty.
In reference to equality, Kaufman believes everyone
should "possess the resources of materials, mind and
spirit as well as opportunity to carve out a career in
conformity with that person's own nature and reasoned
choice."[64] In other words, everyone should have access
to those cultural and industrial resources which make
possible individual dignity and self-esteem.[65] Kaufman

---

elite theorists are: C. Wright Mills, The Power Elite (New
York: Oxford University Press, 1956); Marcuse, One-
Dimensional...; Barrington Moore, Jr., Political Power
and Social Theory (New York: Harper and Bros., 1958); and
Robert S. Lynd and Helen M. Lynd, Middletown in Transition:
A Study of Cultural Conflicts (New York: Harcourt, Brace,
Jonanovich, Inc., 1971). For critiques of elite power
theories, see Dahl, Who Governs...; and Nelson W. Polsby,
Community Power and Political Theory (New Haven: Yale
University Press, 1963).

    [59]Kaufman, Radical..., pp. 62-63. See also
Bachrach, The Theory...; and Walker, "A Critique... ."
Burns presents a similar view of the system's basic
structure alternatives. See James MacGregor Burns, The
Deadlock of Democracy (Englewood Cliffs, N. J.: Prentice-
Hall, Inc., 1963).

    [60]Kaufman, Radical..., p. 13.

    [61]Ibid., pp. 14, 89.   [62]Ibid., p. 161.

    [63]Kaufman's mentioning of a "dialectic" of disorder
seems to be a relative deprivation theory of political
conflict.

    [64]Kaufman, Radical..., p. 6. (Italics mine.)

    [65]Ibid., p. 10. Kaufman gives special attention
to the present "psychological inequalities" of blacks
(see pp. 78,80,83-84).

indicates that this equality of psychological, economic,
and cultural conditions is necessary for psychological
happiness and thus should be available to the "maximum
number of persons possible."[66]

Kaufman uses the example of education. He says
that education is absolutely necessary in order to
establish a virtuous citizenry capable of protecting
itself against the manipulators of the democratic
process.[67] Thus, "liberal education is essential for
the good like, and in general, liberal education requires
higher education."[68] Since everyone (except for the
"irremediably brain damaged")[69] is capable of benefiting
from higher education, there is a "presumptive right
to higher education."[70]

Kaufman supports the concept of participatory
democracy and thus seeks to extend the present practice
of political equality. He believes everyone needs to
participate in the making of social policies which affect
their lives,[71] especially in decisions involving welfare,
poverty,[72] and educational policies. Thus, Kaufman would
extend the concept of political equality to include
provision of more personal decision making structures
in all aspects of American life.[73]

According to Kaufman, the present system prohibits
individual development and liberty-- biologically, intellectually, and spiritually.[74] Freedom is sacrificed to
corporate power. For example, the elite deceives the
public by urging concessions of personal liberty in the
name of "national interest" and patriotism. Thus,
Kaufman believes liberty should be expanded in order to
provide opportunities for people to live more authentic
lives.[75] Kaufman insists on "the fullest possible freedom

---

[66]Ibid., p. 10.

[67]Ibid., p. 63. On manipulation, see also Joe
McGinniss, The Selling of the President (New York: Trident
Press, 1969); and Vance Packard, Hidden Persuaders (New
York: David McKay, Co., Inc., 1957).

[68]Kaufman, p. 116. (Italics mine.)

[69]Ibid., p. 117.   [70]Ibid.   (Italics mine)

[71]Ibid., p. 58. See also Students for a Democratic
Society, Port Huron Statement.

[72]Kaufman, p. 74.   [73]Ibid., p. 62.

[74]Ibid., p. 26.   [75]Ibid., p. 3.

to contest prevailing power by spreading alternative aims
and programs before the public."[76] Each individual
should have complete freedom to develop his own potentials,
"qualified only by the moral and prudential constraints
of civility."[77]

Hayden's New Left critique
of the system

The standard of justice by which Hayden condemns
the present system is a radical vision of both equality
and liberty:

> We seek the establishment of a democracy of individual
> participation governed by two central aims: that the
> individual share in those social decisions deter-
> mining the quality and direction of his life; that
> society be organized to encourage independence in
> men and provide the media for their common partici-
> pation.[78]

Hayden claims that in such participatroy democracy there
is neither egotistical individualism nor submergence
of the individual within the group's decision making.
According to Hayden, democracy should extend to all
institutions affecting people's lives, including industrial
firms and schools.[79] This "democratic socialist regulation"
would decrease the liberty of some groups, especially the
economic elite, while increasing the liberty of others
in certain areas.

According to Hayden, the military-industrial
complex rules the American system. Time and time again
he evokes images of an almost undefeatable power elite.

---

[76]Ibid., p. 6. See Marcuse, One-Dimensional...,
on how such alternatives may be obscured by existing
ideologies, even among social scientists.

[77]Kaufman, p. 10. (Italics mine.) For a criticism
of the Port Huron Statement for its neglect of the moral
foundations of civility, see Harry M. Clor, "American
Democracy and the Challenge of Radical Democracy," How
Democratic is America?, ed. Robert A. Goldwin (Chicago:
Rand McNally Inc., 1971), pp. 77-108.

[78]Hayden, "Port...," in Silverman, p. 83. See
Newfield, Prophetic....

[79]Tom Hayden, "Manifesto Notes: Problems of
Democracy," The New Politics: Mood or Movement?, ed.
James H. Burkhart and Frank J. Kendrick (Englewood Cliffs,
N. J.: Prentice-Hall, Inc., 1971), pp. 39-45.

America is a Leviathan, a police state, or an outlaw nation
where the people do not rule.[80] This system results in
systematic repression of individual liberty.[81] Such
repression takes two forms: (1) psychologically, due to
capitalistic materialism, and (2) physically, as a result
of the elitist dominated hierarchies of modern public and
private bureaucracy. True freedom, love, reason, and
creativity are impossible under the present system. Thus,
the achievement of the desired fraternal and communal
brotherhood of man can never culminate. The accomplishment
of Hayden's goals for society is even more precarious,
since the American majority is just as tainted as the elite.
Along with Lynd, Hayden condemns the majority as irredeemable because of its past sins to Indians and blacks.[82]

Abbie Hoffman: revolutionary and counter cultural anarchist[83]

Abbie Hoffman seems to condemn all authority and
all regimes-- except for that of Fidel Castro, whom he
quotes extensively. According to Hoffman, the evil of the
American regime lies in its imperialism (both military
and economic), racism, and poverty.[84] Most politicians
and their bureaucratic machinery have denied every individual his birthright to freedom.[85] Thus, the basis for
Hoffman's condemnation of the American system is his
radical vision of liberty and equality. According to
Hoffman, the most important liberty denied by the American
system is each individual's right to sensual experiences,
expecially those involving drugs and sex.[86] Thus, he
advocates the elimination of laws which create crimes

---

[80]Hayden, "Port...."

[81]For Hayden, repression is neglect of human needs.
This view of repression is an extension of the ordinary
meaning of deprivation. The affluent young student is deprived of his true freedom-- achievement of his potential.
His deprivation is expecially acute in his incapacity to
make decisions. See Hayden, "Port...."

[82]See Tom Hayden and Slaughton Lynd, "We Are Not at
War," American Radical Thought: The Libertarian Tradition,
ed. Henry J. Silverman (Lexington, Mass.: D. C. Heath and
Co., 1970), pp. 226-236.

[83]See similar activist sentiments in Rubin, Do It;
and Kunen, Strawberry....

[84]Hoffman, Revolution..., pp. 173-174.

[85]Ibid.   [86]Ibid., pp. 13, 106, and 173.

145

without victims, especially those laws prohibiting the
use of marijuana, psychadelic drugs, and cohabitation.
"Play" and "instant gratification"[87] are the hallmarks
of a liberty which involves the joy of doing.[88] Such
freedom to do as one likes, without harming an unwilling
person, would free the creative potentials found in everyone.[89]

    Hoffman also seeks "humanistic cooperation and
equality"-- a kind of communal and fraternal experience
that grows out of tribal meetings. "The meeting is the
message." Community control is the means to humanistic
politics. Hoffman believes achievement of economic equality
is possible by abolishing money, work, and private property.[90] Similarly, housing, transportation, food, clothing,
medicine, and public toilets should all be free,[91] since
everyone would take only what he needs.[92] Hoffman presents
a vision, but he provides only a few examples of a specific
political program or regime structures. Hoffman's scheme
does not include leaders: everyone simply adds his own
ideology to the group process, which he likens to a tribal
meeting.[93] He makes several references to peoples' rule
conducted by both computer tabulated telephone polls and
television referenda.

    These elite theories of democratic legitimacy do
not prove the hypothesized connection of mass opinion and
man behavior. They only provide a possible framework of
political thought which may or may not coincide with the
thought and actions of their political sympathizers or
followers. The following chapter measures subcultural and
national views of democratic legitimacy. Chapter VII tests
these views of individual activists in political violence.

---

[87]Ibid., p. 224.   [88]Ibid., p. 173.

[89]Ibid., p. 113.   [90]Ibid., p. 223.

[91]Ibid., p. 173.   [92]Ibid., p. 181.

[93]Hallmark says this view delegitimates the regime
by "retribalizing the society." (See Stephan Hallmark,
"Subcultures as a Focus of Analysis," Protagonists of
Change: Subcultures in Development and Revolution, ed.
Abdul A. Said [Englewood Cliffs, N. J.: Prentice-Hall,
Inc., 1971], pp. 10-19.)

CHAPTER VI

SOME NATIONAL AND SUBCULTURAL OPINIONS
ON DEMOCRATIC LEGITIMACY

Public opinion is often as difficult to interpret as
the flights of birds or the entrails of a sheep.[1]

It would be a bold man who would contend that statis-
tics bear more resemblance to facts than they do to
lies.[2]

To review, the major hypothesis of this thesis is
that members of certain subcultures, which have been
designated as under-privileged and over-privileged, may
harbor a larger portion of political discontents or
apoliticos than the national political culture as a whole.[3]
Such a sense of disenchantment, alienation, distrust,
anomie, and cynicism about the regime or its authorities
will, of course, vary from individual to individual within
the subculture. Similarly, not every discontented individual believes the regime is sufficiently unjust to be
worthy of either destruction by revolution or major transformation by radical reform. The ideological or partisan
intensity of individual political disenchantment may affect
the level of political conflict in terms of general purposes
as well as magnitude and intensity of tactics. Generally,
these purposes fall into three broad categories roughly
corresponding to the intensity of one's beliefs about the
legitimacy of the regime. These analytically distinct
purposes and their potentially related tactics are: (1)
reform of the present regime, (2) revolution to institute

---

[1]Dahl, Who Governs..., p. 322.

[2]Clive Barnes, "Special Introduction," The Report of
the Commission on Obscenity and Pornography, Commission on
Obscenity and Pornography (New York: Bantam Books, 1970),
p. xii.

[3]On anomie, see especially de Grazia, Political
Community...; and Durkheim, Suicide....

a new regime, and (3) revolution to institute essentially no government at all-- anarchy.[4] Empirically, of course, such purposes and tactics overlap and intermingle. More-over, there is considerable variation between individuals within the subcultural groups as to disenchantment, politi-cal tactics, and programs.

The purpose of Chapter VI is to analyze the mass opinions within the designated subcultures in an effort to determine generally the manifest levels of subcultural opinions on the democratic legitimacy of the regime and thus to estimate at least the latent levels or potential for approval or disapproval of the use of violence against the political system. Each section compares American political attitudes of national samples with those of the black and student political subcultures. Chapter VII, which will analyze the opinions on political violence among both subcultures and individuals who are known to be activists-- the arrestees and militants-- may provide a more direct test of the possible relationship between the various dimensions of both legitimacy and violence. The data for chapters VI and VII were derived from a persual of over a thousand questions included in nearly a hundred public opinion surveys conducted between 1936 and 1972 by Harris,.Gallup, Roper, the Survey Research Center, and other survey organizations and individual scholars. Some of the sources come directly from national polling organizations, such as Harris, Gallup, and Roper; others come from such valuable secondary sources as Cohen, Scammon, Lipset, Brink, Robinson, and the national and presidential commissions on disorder and violence.[5] The organization of the survey items in chapters

---

[4]See Chapter VII, below.

[5]Cohen (ed.), Los Angeles Riots...; Scammon and Wattenberg, Real...; Lipset, Rebellion...; Seymour Martin Lipset and Philip G. Altbach (eds.), Students in Revolt (Boston: Beacon Press, 1970); Lipset and Wolin (eds.), Berkeley...; Brink and Harris, Black...; Robinson, Rusk, and Head, Measures Political...; John P. Robinson and Philip R. Shaver, Measures of Sociological and Psychological Attitudes (Ann Arbor: University of Michigan, Survey Re-search Center, Institute of Social Research, 1969); National Commission on the Causes and Prevention of Violence, To Establish Justice, To Insure Domestic Tranquility, Prepared by a commision directed by Milton S. Eisenhower (New York: Award Books, 1969), hereafter known as the Eisenhower Com-mission; Hugh Davis Graham and Ted Gurr (eds.) The History of Violence in America, A report to the National Commission on the Causes and Prevention of Violence (New York: Bantam Books, 1969), Kerner Commission; Kirkham, Levy, and Crotty, Assassination...; National Advisory Commission on

VI and VII will be according to the following topics:
(1) the legitimacy and the justice of regime objects,
(2) the legitimacy and/or effectiveness of the tactic of
political violence, (3) the willingness to use violence,
(4) participation in and/or support for political violence,
(5) regime legitimacy and violence, and finally (6)
purposes of political violence.

Mass Opinions on Legitimating Ideologies of Political Justice in America

Chapter VI deals with such political attitude scales
and survey items used by survey researchers which are most
closely related to the concept of legitimacy. The chapter
covers mass affective evaluations of the most general
regime objects, such as the various aspects of the legitimating ideology of equality; the social, economic, and
political system; government institutions; public officials; specific policies; and finally, levels of governmental effectiveness and responsiveness.[6] That is, what
is the degree of regime legitimacy for particular regime
objects according to members of the potentially political
black and student subcultures? Chapter VII is a more direct
attempt to find the relationship between individual attitudes on regime legitimacy and violent politics. The
aggregate opinion data for political subcultures in Chapter
VI, if proven to be politically significant, may provide
an experiential context for those individual opinions
discussed in Chapter VII.

One argument advanced in this paper is that differing perceptions of equality and liberty, the central
concepts of American democratic legitimating ideologies
and myths, provide standards for judging political life
in America. Yet what are the mass opinions on these
ideological concepts? How do citizens apply equality and
liberty? Given the limited quantity and quality of other
data, the approach to views of justice in this paper is
through an analysis of those specific grievances or
"causes" of violence which blacks and students perceive
and which may arouse them to participate in political

Civil Disorders, Supplementary Studies for the National
Advisory Commission on Civil Disorders (Washington, D. C.:
U. S. Government Printing Office, 1968); President's
Commission on Law Enforcement and Administration of
Justice, The Challenge of Crime in a Free Society, Prepared
by a commission directed by James Vorenberg (New York:
Avon Books, 1968); and Scranton Commission.

[6] For a discussion on these objects of legitimacy,
see Chapter III, above.

violence. In other words, what may some blacks and students really want or value perhaps enough to resort to violence?

Difficulties in the Analysis of Opinion Data on Justice and Equality

The question of the salience of ideology to the average citizen

The evidence is somewhat mixed on the salience of aspects of democratic ideology to the average citizen. Such evidence often depends on the content of particular questions used to tap ideological dimensions of a citizen's affective and cognitive processes.[7] Muller has said that, "as a coherent system of ethical principles and applications of these principles, the legitimating ideology of the regime is not meaningful to most citizens."[8] Yet only two of the six items in his Legitimating Ideology Scale refer to democracy or minority rights. His scale seems only remotely ideological in content. In contrast, Prothro and Griggs found in Ann Arbor and Tallahassee that nearly everyone agreed with the following five abstract democratic principles: "Democracy is the best form of government," "Public officials should be chosen by majority vote," "Every citizen should have an equal chance to influence government policy," "The minority should be free to criticize majority decisions," and "People in the minority should be free to try to win majority support for their opinions."[9] When asked what "things about this country are you most proud of," 85% of Americans in Almond's 1968 national survey mentioned such potentially ideological aspects of the political system as political freedom, democracy, and the constitution.[10] Thus, the legitimating ideology of democracies may be an indicator of a latent standard of political justice.

---

[7]On the potential precedence of other values besides equality and freedom, see Chapter III, above; Melville Dulton, Men Who Manage (New York: John Wiley and Sons, 1959); Maslow, "A Theory...;" Gurr, Why..., especially pp. 25-29, 66-71; and Hadley Cantril, The Pattern of Human Concerns (New Brunswick: Rutgers University Press, 1965).

[8]Muller, "A Test...," p. 22.

[9]Prothro and Griggs, "Fundamental...," pp. 282, 284.

[10]Almond and Verba, Civic Culture..., p. 102.

Support for political justice
in the abstract
        One major focus of attention in this paper is on
widely held opinions on political justice in the nation,
in black urban centers, and on campus. At least in the
abstract, most people desire a democratic standard of
political justice. In 1968, 63% of whites in a national
poll responded affirmatively to the general statement:
"Until there is justice for minorities there will not be
law and order."[11] Similarly, there are widespread interpretations that some specific kinds of government acts
would be unjust and would be very strongly disapproved
of as well. In fact, with respect to some hypothetical
government actions with the factual situation given,
there does appear to be nearly universal agreement on the
meaning of political injustice. From 95% to 97% of a
national poll disapproved of (1) different tax bills for
people with the same income, (2) governmental prohibition
of criticism of government, (3) mass arresting and impris-
oning of Negroes without cause, and (4) arresting and
shooting of innocent people.[12] These government actions
would seem to violate such democratic ideals as political
equality (equal treatment before the law of tax payers,
Negroes, and innocents) and political liberty (the right
to free speech). These data probably indicate that equality
and liberty are at least ideally the standards of political
justice for most Americans, whether expressed in such
philosophical terms or not.[13]

Support for equality:
abstract and
applied
        Some widely shared notion of equality may also be
implied in the common experience of many social scientists
with "subjective" measures of socio-economic class. Most
Americans either never think of class or seldom place
themselves in a "superior" upper class or in an "inferior"
lower class position. Some actively refuse to pick any
class, claiming there are no classes in a democracy.[14]

---

[11]Louis Harris, "Most Think Law and Order Has Broken
Down in Nation," Washington Post, September 9, 1968. Only
27% disagreed, and 10% were undecided.

    [12]Kirkham, Levy, and Crotty, Assassination...,
p. 268.

    [13]Dudley A. Ward, The American Economist: Attitudes
and Opinions (New York: Harper and Bros., 1955).

    [14]See Milbrath, Political..., pp. 115-116. The
wording of such "subjective" class items is very critical.

The inculcation of this "classless" view may occur subtly
at an early age. In response to the question,"Are you
a special sort of person?" all the children (age 5-7) in
one interview said in some form that they were each
different, but all said they were no "better."[15]
     When there is an attempt to apply the ideal of
equality to contemporary political conflicts and to someone else, whites to blacks for example, few completely
support or believe such rights to be applied fully to
particular groups and/or concrete situations.[16] Surpris-
ingly, Muller found that a full 40% of blacks, not whites,
disagreed with the statement: "Minorities should always
be allowed to criticize the majority."[17] More directly
related to violence, in 1961 only 30% of whites nationally
saw the cause of riots to be the "failure to give equality
to Negroes."[18] Such mass white opinions, however, may be
changing. In a 1968 survey, there was a 73% agreement with
the statement: "Rights of many people can be endangered
in the name of law and order."[19] Thus, even though there
is general agreement on the desirability of justice and
equality for blacks in the abstract, black and white
perceptions of inequality as a basic cause of actual
conflict or violence are quite different.

Asked to respond to questions implying upper, middle, and
lower class, most Americans have indicated middle. Yet,
when asked to respond to questions implying "propertied,"
middle, and working class, 53% said working in 1964; 37%
said middle; only 5% called themselves propertied (Free
and Cantril, Political..., p. 206). Most Americans reject
class comparisons, and most do work for a living.

[15]Of course, the sample was small and not random,
but the answers were strikingly suggestive of support for
the idea of equality, even among young children. "Are You
a Special Person," San Jose Mercury, October 14, 1971.

[16]Dahl, Who Governs..., p. 318.

[17]Muller, "A Test...," p. 21.

[18]Louis Harris, "Aid Programs to Curb Riots Are
Backed by Both Races," Philadelphia Inquirer, August 14, 1967.
In 1963, only 39% of the white national sample said that
Negroes were seeking "equal rights" in demonstrations (see
Erskine, "Demonstrations...," for a report on Louis Harris,
"The Negro in America," Newsweek, July 29, 1963, pp. 15-22,
25-34). A Harris poll in April, 1968 found the figure to be
38% (Louis Harris, "Whites, Negroes Split on Causes of
Rioting," Philadelphia Inquirer, April 16, 1968).

[19]Harris, "Most...," September 9, 1968.

On numerous occasions, blacks have indicated that
inequality is the cause of black rioting. A substantial
majority of blacks believed the causes of violence were
"failure to give equality to Negroes" (70%)[20] and "lack
of progress to equality" (72% in 1967, 65% in 1968).[21]
According to 85% of blacks, the solution to violence is
to "speed up civil rights progress."[22] Yet the specific
meanings of such abstractions as justice, rights, liberty
and equality may vary somewhat between the white and
black communities.

The separate dimensions or applications of equality

The abstract commitment to political equality is
clear in the above examples. The inconsistency between
ideals and their applications may be less significant, if
indeed equality means different things to different people.
The application of the principle of equality today may not
be limited to the political relations of citizens to other
citizens or citizens to their government. Equality may
also apply to social and economic aspects of life in America. It may be possible to separate these components of
equality. Indeed, failure to do so may lead to empirical
as well as analytical difficulties. Robinson's analysis
of an article by Hervert McClosky is illustrative of the
empirical problem:

> Responses to the "Belief in Equality" scale indicated
> respondents ambivalent in that they were inconsistent
> among the three subscales political, social and
> ethnic, and economic equality . It seems probable
> that this instrument tapped several conflicting
> attitudes.[23]

---

[20]Harris, "Aid...," August 14, 1967.

[21]Louis Harris, "After the Riots: A Survey,"
Newsweek, August 21, 1967, pp. 18-19; and Harris, "Whites,
Negroes...," April 16, 1968.

[22]Louis Harris, "White Fears, Negro Militancy
Continue to Show Steady Rise," The Washington Post, June 5,
1967.

[23]Robinson, Rusk, and Head, Measures Political...,
p. 171, commenting on McClosky, "Consensus and Ideology...,"
pp. 361-382. The McClosky article is conveniently reprinted
in Raymond E. Wolfinger (ed.), Readings in American Political Behavior (2d ed.; Englewood Cliffs, N. J.: Prentice-
Hall. Inc., 1970), pp. 383-410.

As suggested by Robinson, Ransford has shown that political
inequality (powerlessness) and social inequality (dissatisfaction with racial discrimination) were independent attitudinal factors in his analysis of black opinions about
the Watts riot.[24]
    Thus, this paper attempts to make some suggestive
distinctions between several possible applications of the
concept of equality. This may improve our understanding of
black grievances, as well as of white inconsistencies.
The various dimensions to be discussed here are: social
equality, economic equality, and political equality. Most
of the data will be items on government policies and
grievances. Of course, specific government programs
and citizen grievances may have either overlapping or
contradictory purposes and consequences.[25]
    In lieu of more complete and refined evidence dependent
upon the future funding of my own research design, this
discussion must rely on the responses to the indistinct
questions written by others with other research interests.
Those responses or questions which are clearly a mix of
the various analytical components of equality have been
thrown out. On others, it has been necessary to make
some intuitive judgments, which may be imperfect, but
such judgments seem the best possible approach until it
is possible to use factor analysis and other techniques
to make sure these now intuitive distinctions indeed
measure empirically separate dimensions of equality. For
example, job discrimination probably has social inequalities
as its chief cause, but the consequences of it are economic
inequalities. Such items on discrimination are categorized
here as expressions of a black desire for social equality.
Of course, it is recognized here that the responsibilities
of American government and thus the meaning of American
politics and perhaps political equality may have expanded
into a more comprehensive concern for social and economic
equality than in our earlier history. Yet such commitments

---

[24]H. Edward Ransford, "Isolation, Powerlessness and
Violence: A Study of Attitudes and Participation in the
Watts Riot," Racial Violence in the United States, ed.
Allen D. Grimshaw (Chicago: Aldine Publishing Company,
1969), pp. 434-436.

[25]On the consequences of the poverty program, see
Daniel P. Moynihan, Maximum Feasible Misunderstanding (New
York: MacMillan, 1968). See also Aaron Wildavsky, "The
Empty-Head Blues: Black Rebellion and White Reaction,"
Law and Order in a Democratic Society, ed. Marvin R.
Summers and Thomas E. Barth (Columbus, Ohio: Charles E.
Merrill Publishing Co., 1970), pp. 165-178; Banfield,
Unheavenly...; and James Q. Wilson, Negro Politics: The
Search for Leadership (New York: The Free Press, 1960).

154

to the achievement of social and economic equality may be
proceeding at different rates among different segments of
the American population.[26]
In an effort to test for the existence of such
potential groups and subcultural differences, the political,
social, and economic distinctions are particularly necessary.
Social equality here means the same treatment of one human
by another human irrespective of other human differences,
such as race, religion, national origin, sex, hair length,
or color of eyes. Economic equality means efforts to make
the quantity of material conditions, income, or economic
life style the same or at least to narrow the gap by redistributive policies. In this paper, political equality
means the same treatment of all citizens in similar circumstances (equality before the law), including the enfran-
chised chance to participate in American politics.
This paper will give minimal attention to the
potential conflict between equality and liberty, as illustrated in the following example: if one person attempts
to give equality to someone else, another person may
perceive this act as a restriction of his liberty. In
1940 for example, over half of the "prosperous" and only
17% of the "poor" felt federal interference was a restriction of individual freedom.[27] There is also empirical
verification that those valuing liberty high and equality
relatively low with respect to other values are often
least committed to civil rights for blacks. In a summary
of a study by Rokeach, Robinson says,

The relationship between the average relative positions
of the values equality and freedom differentiates among
those who are "sympathetic and have participate [in]"
(freedom ranked #1, equality #3), "sympathetic, but
have not participated" (freedom ranked #1, equality
#6), [and] "unsympathetic" (freedom ranked #2, equality
#11) in civil rights demonstrations.[28]

[26]See James Q. Wilson and Edward C. Banfield,
"Political Ethos Revisited," American Political Science
Review, Vol. LXV, No. 4 (December, 1971), pp. 1048-1062;
and Wilson and Banfield, "Public-Regardingness... ."

[27]Fortune poll cited by Hadley Cantril and Mildred
Strunk, Public Opinion: 1935-1946 (Princeton: Princeton
University Press, 1951), p. 107; also cited by Lane,
Political Ideology..., p. 194.

[28]Robinson, Rusk, and Head, Measures Political...,
p. 463, commenting on M. Rokeach, Beliefs, Attitudes and
Values (San Francisco: Jossey-Bars, Inc., 1968), pp. 156-
178.

Certainly it is possible to use or abuse liberty to restrict another's equality and liberty. Tocqueville is probably right, however, in saying that in a democracy the masses praise equality more highly than liberty. Thus, this paper will give major attention to equality. There are two basic sets of data which may be coded usefully into the three dimensions of equality suggested here. Surveys of mass opinion have sought to discover (1) the perceived causes, reasons, or purposes of peaceful demonstrations and rioting, and (2) citizen grievances on the conditions of life.

Data coding problems

There are a few critical problems of coding responses to survey questions.[29] The most severe of these problems is the great variation in both the wording of particular questions and the use of prepared lists of responses. Such item variations in wording and choices tend to elicit a particular content in responses, if not a predetermined magnitude of responses as well. For example, to such wording as "what are your biggest gripes or complaints about living here?" the prevalent responses in Watts tended to indicate unhappiness with the shabbiness of the immediate neighborhood or the local quality of life (33%). Responses were much lower for social conditions (14%) or economic conditions (13%).[30]

Furthermore, most lists of questions seem to be dominated by either economic items or other less discernible categories. For example, the Kerner Commission and Harris surveys include mixed lists dominated by economic choices.[31]

---

[29] General agreement on criteria for coding was reached with Mr. Gary Moon at Claremont Graduate School.

[30] Cohen categorized the responses as (1) living conditions in the neighborhood (33% giving examples relating to neighborhood upkeep, etc.), as distinguished from (2) economic conditions (13%), and (3) mistreatment by whites, coded here as social inequality (see Nathan E. Cohen, "Press Release, August 1, 1967," Press release for the Los Angeles Riot Study [Los Angeles: University of California, Institute of Government and Public Affairs, August 1, 1967], pp. 6, 8; and Murphy and Watson, "The Structure...," p. 156).

[31] The Kerner Commission reported that the three black grievances receiving the highest responses were: police brutality (45%), unemployment (42%), and housing (36%). (Kerner Commission, pp. 143-144, 146-150, 175, and 178.) A 1968 Harris survey reported this order: housing (73%), education (68%), and jobs (63%). An earlier Harris survey reported this order: housing (68%), jobs (67%), and education (61%). In the Harris surveys of 1967 and

Since most of these lists by the Kerner and Harris surveys
tend to provide mostly economic choices (except for the
education and police brutality items), the figures for
the black economic grievance items (coded here as economic
equality) were quite high: 63-72%. Thus, both the
wording and limited choice approaches make it difficult
to determine precisely what is being measured, at least
conceptually or analytically. Despite such variations in
responses, depending particularly on the wording of the
questions, black responses elicited by most open ended
questions on the causes, purposes, or reasons for demonstrations or riots seem to show greater concern for racial
discrimination than for economic conditions. For example,
in response to such open ended questions as "what do you
think" are the causes, reasons, or purposes of riots, mass
black opinion shows almost universally greater concern for
social equality over economic equality, while only a few
(possibly the most violent) have singled out problems of
political equality (political power or specific governmental programs).[32] In various surveys, figures for
responses to discrimination, categorized here as a desire
for social equality, are: 36%[33] 21%, 27%, and 31%.[34]
Lower economic responses to the same open ended questions
are: 28%[35] 8%, 8%, and 19%.[36]

1968, white figures for each item were: education (46%-
51%), housing (39%-44%), and jobs (34%-38%). (Harris,
"Whites, Negroes...," April 16, 1968; and Harris,
"Aid...," August 14, 1967). See also Erskine, "Demonstrations...," p. 666.

[32]See Chapter VII, below.

[33]Harris, "After...," August 21, 1967, pp. 18-19;
responses were coded as unfair treatment, prejudice, and
promises.

[34]T. M. Tomlinson and David O. Sears, "Negro Attitudes Toward the Riot," The Los Angeles Riots: A Socio-
Psychological Study, ed. Nathan E. Cohen (New York: Praeger,
1970), p. 300: the answers to a question on the causes of
the riot were 4% discrimination, 21% mistreatment by police,
and 3% mistreatment by whites. On page 304, the question
asked was whether it was just chance or if there was a reason for some being attacked in the Watts riot; the reasons
given were coded as discrimination, mistreatment (6%), and
police brutality (26%).

[35]Harris, "After...," August 21, 1967: poverty,
slums, ghetto conditions.

[36]Tomlinson and Sears, "Negro...," p. 300, poverty

Data acquired from such open ended questions indicate that both economic and social inequality are important, but social equality-- that blacks be treated as equals in their relations with others-- takes the edge with responses from 8% to 21% higher than for economic equality on the same item. Economic inequality is a vital concern, but blacks seem to feel social inequality most deeply. Of course, social inequality has very real economic consequences, but there are fewer specific references to material and economic conditions than for social inequalities of racial relations-- such as prejudice, discrimination, segregation, and police brutality. Given such an apparent hierarchy of concerns and the problem of often limited choice responses, what is the content of such a sense of deep grievance with respect to social, economic, and political equality?

Black Opinions on Several
Dimensions of Equality

Social equality

A very substantial majority of blacks (58%-91%) are particularly concerned with such aspects of social inequality as segregation, racism, and discrimination. With respect to integration, 90% of blacks in one survey would prefer working in a racially mixed group.[37] In a 1969 national survey 78% of blacks preferred integrated schools; 74% preferred integrated neighborhoods.[38] In response to the direct question of whether the riots "were brought on mainly by white racism," 58% of blacks agreed, only 17% disagreed, and 25% were not sure.[39]

---

and economic depression; p. 304, 15% over-charging and selling inferior goods, 4% unemployment and poverty.

[37]Cohen, "Press Release...," p. 3.

[38]Louis Harris, "Report from Black America: A Newsweek Poll," Newsweek, June 30, 1969, pp. 17-26, 31-35. In 1966, 68% preferred integrated neighborhoods (Louis Harris, "Black and White: A Major Study of U. S. Racial Attitudes Today," Newsweek, August 22, 1966, pp. 12-27).

[39]Harris, "Whites, Negroes...," April 16, 1968. Only 35% of whites would accept this explanation. Signs of black racism, however, are low. One of the lowest responses on the Harris surveys of 1967 and 1968 was on the item: "Negro hatred of whites" (i.e., black racism)-- 20% and 16%. White agreement on these items was substantially lower, but the ordering from highest to lowest responses was essentially the same.

The Los Angeles Riot Study shows that nearly all blacks of whatever level of civil rights militance claimed to have experienced discrimination. The highest levels of discrimination (social inequality) were in private relations between the races involving housing (87%-90%), jobs (83%-91%), and landlords (65%-75%).[40] Housing, schools, and landlords were intimately related to the position of social inferiority and inequality imposed on blacks by many whites. Given generally segregated neighborhoods and schools in 1965, job discrimination, which reflects the highest level of experiences of social inequality at 83%-91%, was probably the most frequent contact blacks in Watts had with whites.

Economic equality

Since many blacks are poor, and everyone likes economic redistribution to be in his favor, it is not surprising that most blacks give a high level of support to policy suggestions for reducing economic disparities between the races. In a 1967 Harris survey, 58% of blacks thought welfare payments ought to be higher, while only 28% of generally middle class, tax paying whites agreed.[41] These figures may indicate that blacks give higher support for policies of economic redistribution or economic equality than do whites. Similarly, 91% of blacks, in comparison to 66% of whites, supported a proposal for federal programs to provide jobs for all the unemployed.[42] In the same survey, a small minority (30%) of blacks said that looting ("ripping off whites?") was "not as bad as stealing." This response might reveal, perhaps, a different attitude toward property rights, at least for a significant black minority. Yet resentment of white merchants and a desire for vengeance, rather than any ideological commitment to economic equality, probably account for a large proportion of those responses. Though government has assumed an increasing responsibility for alleviating the economic inequality of poverty, it is difficult to say, with the data given here, what portion of blacks now believe economic equality is a right beyond mere aleviation of economic hardship. In any case, probably twice (58%-28%, and 91%-66%) as many blacks as whites desire more vigorous government efforts to relieve economic inequities through welfare

---

[40]David O. Sears and John B. MacConahay, "Riot Participation," The Los Angeles Riots: A Socio-Psychological Study, ed. Nathan E. Cohen (New York: Praeger, 1970), pp. 258-260.

[41]Harris, "Whites, Negroes...," April 16, 1968.

[42]Harris, "Aid...," August 14, 1967.

and employment policies.[43]

Political equality
Political inequality or black grievances indicating
governmental referents make up only a small percentage of
all responses in nearly all surveys. Only 2% in one survey
cited organized (political?) groups as causes of riots.[44]
In another study, only 10% cited political agitation.[45]
One possible exception to generally lower levels of political grievances is widespread grievances with the police,
which ranks high. Yet even this overtly political grievance probably taps the particular dimension of unequal
treatment by some individual policemen or particular police
departments, not the police function itself. The problem
seems to be the racial discrimination of some policemen
who treat blacks as social inferiors. Indeed, blacks have
often supported police quite generously in bond elections.
Some neighborhoods have even organized their own policing
organizations, only some of it against the police. In riot
cities, the complaint of police brutality, while a grievance
against a public symbol of authority, does not seem to
reflect a lack of confidence and/or trust in at least
the national government leadership, which is high (92%).[46]
In reference to particular national programs, 24%-49%
responded favorably, depending on the particular program,
while only 5%-10% responded unfavorably.[47]
The analytical distinctions between social, economic, and political equality are not easy to maintain
where governmental programs imply a political obligation
to impinge on economic and social relationships. Yet
even here complaints about discrimination by public
authorities in public programs are usually relatively
low in comparison with more clear instances of social
and economic inequalities. For example, in the Los Angeles
Riot Study, black reports of discrimination or unequal

---

[43]Statistical "controls" for income to determine the
racial factor for this set of attitudes on economic inequalities would make little sense, since blacks are, as a matter
of fact, disproportionately poor.

[44]Tomlinson and Sears, "Negro...," p. 300, comment
on the Muslims, civil rights groups, organized groups, and
the Klu Klux Klan.

[45]Harris, "After...," August 21, 1967.

[46]David O. Sears, "Political Attitudes of Los
Angeles Negroes," The Los Angeles Riots: A Socio-Psychological Study, ed. Nathan E. Cohen (New York: Praeger,
1970), p. 700.

[47]Ibid., p. 687.

treatment by public authorities were: 34%-48% in welfare, 41%-48% in fire departments, 23%-40% in parks departments, and 26%-36% in garbage services.[48] The highest complaint for public discrimination, 70%-75% for the schools, is probably a better measure of neighborhood housing patterns, racial relations, and private white discrimination, than it is a measure of unequal treatment by public authorities. There is some evidence for this interpretation. The Lemberg study showed that racial segregation, a form of social inequality, was associated very highly with the statement that "city government is doing too little."[49] Thus, where public policy impinges on social and economic relations, black disenchantment with unequal treatment by politicians is the highest.

Political disenchantment is probably more intense for blacks than for whites. Indeed, Finifter found race was the second best single predictor of expectations of unfair or unequal treatment by political officials.[50] Probably a slim majority of blacks believe they have achieved formal political equality, if judged in terms of less unfair or unequal treatment by public authorities than private individuals. Yet there is considerable discontent with public authorities, such as the police and schools. These seem to be most reflective of a desire for equal treatment socially by whites than for general discontent with political inequality.

White Opinions on Equality

Generally, whites see the same purposes, reasons, and causes (i.e., the same dimensions of equality) for peaceful demonstrations in the same order as do blacks, but, as one survey shows, whites perceive these purposes with considerably lower magnitudes: social 27%, economic 5%, and political 2%.[51] Yet when riots, rather than

---

[48]Tomlinson, "Ideological...," p. 342.

[49]Lemberg Center for the Study of Violence, Six-City Study: A Survey of Racial Attitudes in Six Northern Cities; Preliminary Report (Waltham, Mass.: Brandeis University, June, 1967), p. 16). (Mimeographed.)

[50]Ada W. Finifter, "Dimensions of Political Alienation," American Political Science Review, Vol. LXIV, No. 2 (June, 1970), p. 399. The scale was labeled political "normlessness." When controlled for education and income, the correlation dropped only from .22 to .175.

[51]Twenty-seven percent social-- a desire to be

peaceful protests, are involved, whites are more likely
to see the cause as politically motivated agitation:
45% and 28% according to a national survey and a California
poll.[52] There is more specific evidence on attitudes
toward social, economic, and political aspects of equality.

Social equality

When confronted with questions during a period of
rioting, a significant minority of whites give responses
indicating their belief that blacks are actually inferior
to whites: 24% of responses in one 1967 national survey
may be so coded.[53] Scammon and Wattenberg report that
not quite half of all whites (44%) felt that blacks have
"less native intelligence than whites." Somewhat more
than six in ten whites felt that blacks have "less ambition
than whites."[54] These figures indicate some slight improvement over McClosky's findings in 1963, in which 49% said
"all races are certainly not equal."[55]

Generally 56% of whites felt that racial integration was proceeding "too fast" in 1964; only 20% said
the progress toward integration was "about right."[56] In
1966, whites found social contact with blacks of the most
intimate kinds highly undesirable, particluarly for dating
(88%) and marriage (89%). Yet only a small minority of
whites (16%-20%) in 1966 found contact in public accommodations undesirable, depending on the particular form of
public accommodation. Previously in 1961, only 39%

---

treated as an equal, a human being, have a place in the
world; 5% economic-- live like all others; 2% political--
have a voice in the country (Erskine, "Demonstrations...,"
p. 663, citing Harris, "Negro in America...," July 29,
1963).

[52]Harris, "After...," August 21, 1967; and Erskine,
"Demonstrations...," p. 664.

[53]Harris, "After...," August 21, 1967. The report
also indicated 13% of whites believed Negroes are lazy,
and 11% were undecided. See also Scammon and Wattenberg,
Real..., p. 87.

[54]Scammon and Wattenberg, Real..., p. 87.

[55]McClosky, "Consensus and Ideology...," cited by
Robinson, Rusk, and Head, Measures Political..., p. 175.
The other items in McClosky's scale either lacked a racial
content or asked for empirical judgments on race relations.

[56]Free and Cantril, Political..., p. 196.

of southern whites approved of contact in restaurants.[57]
Somewhat less than a majority of whites (42%) find integrated housing (42%) or having a Negro neighbor (46%)
undesirable.[58]   One 1970 survey of union workers may
indicate some movement toward social integration in housing.
Only 21% of these union workers said they would not like to
have a Negro neighbor;   38% said they would not object;   and
41% had a wait and see attitude.[59]
          Contact in public schools is generally highly unde-
sired.[60]   In 1961, 70% of southern whites approved of black
attendance at public schools.[61]   Yet a Gallup survey of
1969 shows that the number of blacks involved in school
integration is crucial: only 8% had objections to a few
blacks in school with their children, but 32% had objections to over half of the students being black. A full 64%,
however, had no objections to school integration involving
over one half black students.[62]   Issues related to busing,
"quality" education, and racial confrontations in the
schools may possibly have moved this figure of "no objections" downward by 1972. George Wallace's success in
northern as well as southern Democratic Party primaries
in 1972 may reflect a downward trend in white attitudes
about social equality.

Economic equality
          With the possible exception of educational contact,
less than a majority of whites are unwilling to grant social
and economic equality to blacks. Figures for surveys
throughout the 1960's and 1970's, however, have been
increasing, so that soon there may be the possibility of
full white majority support for black economic equality.
In fact, such overall support for black economic equality
may be evident in white support for black economic equality.

---

[57]Samuel Lubell, White and Black: Test of a Nation
(New York: Harper and Row Publishers, Inc., 1966), p. 113.

[58]Harris, "Black and White...," pp. 12-27.

[59]Harry Bernstein, "44% of Union's Workers Want Viet
Victory," Los Angeles Times, November 24, 1970, Pt. 3,
p. 27.

[60]Unfortunately, questions on school integration
frequently tap attitudes on other dimensions and issues,
such as "forced" busing, higher school taxes, and "quality"
education.

[61]Lubell, White and Black..., p. 113.

[62]Gallup, July, 1969, cited by Scammon and Wattenberg, Real..., p. 264.

In fact, such overall support for black economic equality
may be evident in white support for some federal programs.
In a 1967 Harris survey, a substantial majority of whites
supported several Kerner Commission proposals to prevent
future racial outbreaks: 66% supported work projects,
63% agreed with tearing down the ghettos, 59% approved of
rat extermination, and 55% approved of summer camps. Of
course, the black figures for the same programs were much
higher with almost universal approval: 91%, 84%, 72%,
and 78%.[63] Increasing support for black improvement is
also evident in the fact that white support for slum
clearance increased from 63% in 1967 to 83% in 1969.[64]
Without references to race, in 1963 McCloskey found a
small majority in support of governmental responsibility
for "a good standard of living" (55.9%) and providing
work (47.3%); only 28.2% said government ought to provide
good housing.[65] From 1965 to 1969, those feeling "bad"
about hunger went from 50% to 63%.[66] Similarly, white
desire for vigorous governmental action to provide jobs
jumped from 47.3% in 1963 to 67% in 1970.[67] In recent
years, a substantial majority, probably 60% to 85%, seems
in support of programs to alleviate economic inequalities.
In 1964, Free and Cantril found such support among those
ideologically defined as conservative, as well as among
liberals.[68]
     Many whites may also accept economic equality as
a goal. The belief that poverty (economic inequality) is
unjust is not, of course, the same thing as full acceptance
of a major redistribution of economic resources, especially
where blacks are perceived as the major recipients. For
example, in June, 1969 a Harris poll showed that a full
90% of whites were opposed to a program of church reparations to blacks.[69] Similarly, a poll of the middle class

---

[63]Harris, "Aid..," August 14, 1967.

[64]Harris, "Report from Black...." Also Scammon
and Wattenberg, Real..., p. 75.

[65]McClosky, "Consensus and Ideology...," in
Wolfinger, Readings..., p. 394.

[66]Harris, "Report from Black...;" also Scammon
and Wattenberg, Real..., p. 76.

[67]McClosky, "Consensus and Ideology...." Opinion
Research Institute, p. 64-77.

[68]Free and Cantril, Political..., pp. 190-191:
reduce unemployment (75%), public housing (63%), and do
away with poverty (72%).

[69]Harris, "Report from Black... ."

($5,000 to $15,000), representing 61% of the white population, shows that a large minority, 35% to 44%, of middle
class whites actually feel that blacks today have a better
chance of improvements in employment, education, and
housing than the middle class does.[70] A full 65% (about
40% of the wite population) felt that blacks also have
a better chance of getting financial aid if unemployed.[71]
These figures indicate a large white minority (21% to 40%)
"backlash" or reaction to impending black social equality,
economic competition, or perceived preferential treatment
of blacks.

Another significant minority of whites, however,
may support policies of economic redistribution, as possibly
indicated by the 20% to 40% Democratic Party voter preference for Senator George McGovern in some 1972 Democratic
presidential primaries. His election in November, 1972
would probably demonstrate such a sentiment among a
majority, ignoring, of course, all other issues or factors
affecting the boting decision. Similarly, the Nixon Family
Assistance Plan, a form of income guarantee at a low level,
also seems to be moving in the direction of economic equality. In summary, a majority of whites are probably
opposed to gross economic inequities, but only a minority
would actively support policies of economic redistribution
or full economic equality, at least in the immediate future.
Political leadership of both parties, however, may be
anticipating a movement in that direction or acting on
the presumption of possible majority acquiescence to
income redistribution.

Political equality
        Fully 95% of even southern whites approved of
blacks voting as early as 1961.[72] From 1958 to 1969,
those saying they would vote a qualified black for President, if their party nominated him, went from 38% to
67%.[73] Political equality for blacks, at least in principle, is hardly an issue among whites in 1972. It is
interesting to note that a majority of Americans, at least
in 1963, seemed to take a representative rather than a
participative view of political equality. McClosky found
that 47.8% to 62.3% of Americans expressed doubts about

---

[70]Only 21% to 28% of the total white population feel
blacks have a better chance of improvement than the middle
class. "The Troubled American: A Special Report on the
White Majority," Newsweek, October 6, 1969, pp. 28-52.

[71]Ibid.

[72]Lubell, White and Black..., p. 113.

[73]Scammon and Wattenberg, Real..., p. 99.

the knowledge, understanding, and ability of the people
at large to deal with complex issues or even their own
interests.[74]

Student Opinions on Equality

The survey data which this writer was able to com-
pile and categorize on this topic of student views on
equality was limited. The more complete data on other
hypothese may serve to rectify this deficiency somewhat.[75]
Many student attitudes toward political equality seem to
call for its logical extension. In one survey of a number
of generally prestigeous universities, 68% felt that
condidates ought to be chosen from the population at large
instead of being "men with government experience or
education."[76]

Summary of Opinions on Legitimating
Ideologies

In summary of his own studies, Lubell has said that
even in the South, "there was a general readiness to con-
cede the Negro political and economic rights, but opposition
mounted quickly on anything that touched social life."[77]
Similarly, Scammon detected general progressiveness on
economic issues but toughness on social issues. Social
equality as a goal for American society is in contention.
Larger precentages of blacks are more concerned about social
inequities by margins of 8% to 21%. Anywhere from 69% to
91% of blacks desire social equality, as reflected in desires
for integrated housing, schools, and employment. Yet any-

---

[74]McClosky, "Consensus and Ideology...," in
Wolfinger, Readings..., p. 392. McClosky interpreted the
data to mean that there was an absence of a consensus
on political equality. Strong support for McClosky's
items, however, would have indicated a desire for a more
direct participatory version of democracy, rather than
general support for democratic institutions.

[75]In an attempt to test run some items among this
writer's own students, the hypotheses on both egalitarian
and libertarian ideas hold. Yet the writer's data is from
an extremely unrepresentative population of exceedingly
"over-privileged" students. Moreover, the sample of this
population was neither random, representative, nor large.

[76]Ardery, "Special...," p. 637.

[77]Lubell, White and Black..., p. 113.

where from 25% to 40% of whites believe blacks are inferior,
and from 16% to 89% find racial integration undesirable,
depending on the degree of intimacy or numbers involved
in such social contacts.

While probably twice the percentage of blacks as
whites are concerned about economic inequities, a majority
of white opinion probably supports government programs to
relieve gross economic inequities. A white majority is
also probably moving in the direction of economic equality,
as reflected by increasing mass and elite support for some
forms of economic redistribution.

For most Americans, political equality is widely
held as an ideal. Most support its application as well.
Except for instances of police malpractice or where public
policies fail to promote social equality in particular,
blacks are probably generally satisfied with their level
of political equality. Though black power seems to be the
cry of only a very significant minority of the black subculture, the black majority's concern for social equality
and economic improvement may provide an acquiescent subcultural climate unlikely to vigorously oppose black power
revolutionists. As both James Wilson and St. Claire Drake
discovered in several studies of Chicago's black community,
the black community may legitimate almost any group which
works for "the race" or "the cause"-- Negro social equality.
In any case, few Americans of any race or status seem ready
today to accept the narrow notion of equality generally
attributed to Anatole France: "The majestic equality of
the law punishes rich and poor alike for sleeping under
bridges or stealing loaves of bread." The discussion now
turns to a set of survey opinions about more specific
objects of regime legitimacy than those so far indicated
by American legitimating ideologies on democracy.

Mass Attitudes Toward General Regime
Characteristics: Social,
Economic, and Political
Systems

Regime means the general or comprehensive organization of society politically, economically, and socially.
In America, the regime is the "American way of life" or
the American political culture. Some organic concepts
used by political discontents closely parallel this concept
of a regime. Some of these concepts are: "the system,"
the "establishment," the "corporate state," technocracy,"
capitalism, and the "middle class." Finally, inasmuch as
whites dominate blacks in the American system, many blacks
may designate the regime as "whites," the "white social
structure," or the "white power structure."

Black Attitudes Toward General
Regime Characteristics

This white domination of the American system is
precisely what many blacks find abhorrent. Black complaints which question the legitimacy of the general
system are directed precisely to their general desire
for social equality with whites. For example, the answers
to an open ended question reveal that "the main targets
attacked" in the Watts Riot were whites at 43% followed
by the police at 17%.[78] Thus, in the Watts Riot, the
"objects of hostility" were not other Negroes but white
people, especially merchants and policemen, who represented
for many blacks "symbols of constitutional authority."[79]
Further evidence of black discontent with the white regime
is the fact that 28% of blacks questioned in a national
survey favored "banding together against whites."[80]

Evidence as to black disaffection from a white
regime, however, is not totally clear cut. According to
Tomlinson, black citizens in Los Angeles "felt especially
disaffected with the local political system but much less
so about the federal government."[81] According to Campbell,
legitimacy depends on "some degree of community control
in minority communities."[82] Thus, black concerns seem
to center more on particular forms of unhappiness with
the government's operation than on general alienation
from the political system the government is supposed to
represent.[83]

Thus, except for a sizeable minority (28% to 43%),
black discontent with the American regime seems to lie in
their perception of specific operational policies, applications, and procedures reflecting social inequality with
whites and lack of community control within the existing
regime. Black discontent does not seem to reflect total
disapproval of the regime or its principles. For example,
although blacks desire greater economic benefits, as a
group blacks approve of capitalism. In fact, Muller found

---

[78]White merchants--14%; unspecified whites-- 28%
(Tomlinson and Sears, "Negro...," p. 303).

[79]Ibid., p. 305.

[80]Harris, "Report from Black...."

[81]T. M. Tomlinson, "Determinants of Black Politics:
Riots and the Growth of Militancy," Psychiatry, Vol. XXXIII,
No. 2 (May, 1970), p. 250.

[82]Campbell, Sahid, and Stang, Law..., p. 134.

[83]Tomlinson, "Determinants...," p. 250.

that blacks were actually <u>less</u> likely to support the break
up of large business corporations than whites (53% to 66%).[84]
In contrast, 79% in a 1972 national poll said that there
was "too much power concentrated in the hands of a few
large corporations."[85] Thus, blacks may be slightly more
supportive of the economic system than whites. The 30% to
40% of blacks who see the regime as illegitimate seem to do
so in terms of specific social aspects of the regime. They
do not condemn the whole of the economic and political
system-- the regime.

Student Attitudes Toward the Regime

<u>Society in general</u>
       As with the blacks, student disillustionment
generally is related to a perception of a broad range
of rather specific "inadequacies of society," rather
than disapproval of regime principles and government
institutions. According to 79% of students and 63% of
the general public, one of these inadequacies is that
"the American political system does not respond quickly
enough to meet the needs of the people."[86] Yet the
disillusionment of a significant minority of students
with the American system is perhaps more general than
that of blacks. Beginning with the evidence of the more
diffuse support or nonsupport, only 22% of the students
responding to a Gallup poll said their biggest gripe
was the "current inadequacies of society."[87] A majority
of students (72%) disagreed with the statement: "To do
anything rewarding one must work outside the regular
institutions of our society."[88]
       The most disillusioned segment of the student popu-
lation is that of the New Left.[89] Members of the New Left

---

[84]Muller, "A Test...," p. 21.

[85]"How Goes the Economy," <u>Life</u>, Vol. LXXII, No. 25
(June 30, 1972), p. 33.

[86]Gallup, "Special Report...," pp. 5-6.   [87]<u>Ibid</u>.

[88]Malcolm G. Scully, "Students Found Tolerant on
Sex, Marijuana, Even 'the System,'" <u>The Chronicle of Higher
Education</u>, Vol. V (Frebruary 15, 1971), p. 6, cited by
Lipset, <u>Rebellion...</u>, p. 57.

[89]A 1970 Gallup poll reveals that the "radical
left" is somewhat smaller than is sometimes believed. Only
4% of this student poll considered themselves to be members
of the "radical left" (George Gallup, "The Student Revo-
lution-- A Special Report," <u>Gallup Opinion Index</u>, No. 66

believe that the American system in practice is rotten to
the core. These people perceive the political system or
machine to be rule of, for, and by the "establishment," the
"power elite," "technocrats," and the "military-industrial
complex." According to some New Left spokesmen, this
ruling elite "dehumanizes" and "alienates" those for whom
"participatory democracy" is important. These elites support
the "immoral," "colonial," and "imperialistic" war in Vietnam; they promote white racism; and they destroy the
humanizing potential of the natural environment.

There is some data on the extent of support for
some parts of this New Left critique of America. A student
poll from a cross section of ten elite or large public
universities indicates some rather broad inadequacies of
American society which may reflect a tenuous condition of
quasi-legitimacy rather than illegitimacy.[90] In this
study, 41% of the students said American society is "sick";
41% called it "repressive"; 46% said it is "racist."[91]
According to Ardery, this "antirepression sentiment ...
when we come down to cases, is somewhat selective"
ideologically.[92] It is leftist. For example, while only
26% overall felt that "members of Marxist parties should
not be permitted to teach citizenship courses in the public
high schools," 40% would deny the same privilege to members
of "fascists parties." Similarly, only 12% thought members
of the Communist Party should not be allowed to teach in
college.

In a national student survey, while only 7% said
"repression" was the most important issue, these students
actually volunteered government repression as the single
most important issue in an open ended question.[93] Among

[June, 1970]; see also Lipset, Rebellion..., p. 60, where
he cites Louis Harris et al., "Youth Attitudes for Life
Magazine: Year End Issue" [New York: November, 1970]).

[90]These universities were: Yale, Williams, Sarah
Lawrence, Brandeis, Stanford, Reed, Marquette, Indiana,
South Carolina, Howard, and Davidsen.

[91]Ardery, "Special...," p. 645. Note that the
Carnegie study of a greater number of nearly all kinds of
American universities revealed much lower levels of discontent (see Lipset, Rebellion..., pp. 53-54, citing "Profile
of a Generation," multilithed report on a survey prepared
for C.B.S. News [New York: Daniel Yankelovich Associates,
April, 1969]).

[92]Ardery, "Special...," p. 638.

[93]"Playboy's Student Survey," Playboy, Vol. XVII,
No. 9 (September, 1970), p. 182.

these Playboy respondents, 43% felt that the Nixon administration policies of repressing dissent caused the killing
of the Kent State students by the National Guard.[94]
Similarly, 49% of students, in comparison with 27% of the
general public, said that "personal freedom and the right
of dissent are curbed in the United States."[95] Among a
significant minority of 10% to 40%, this fairly widespread
belief in the restriction of the right to dissent may
reflect a quite deep-seated opinion that a vital regime
principle, free speech, is being violated.

The use of such strongly descriptive terms as sick,
repressive, and racist by 40% to 50% of the students (at
least at the most prestigeous schools) suggests that a
larger minority of students than the general public tend
to believe the American system is illegitimate. Nevertheless, only 8% agreed with the statement: "The whole social
system ought to be replaced by an entirely new one; the
existing structures are too rotten to repair."[96] Similarly,
when asked whether change could be brought about by working
within the system, 73% agreed; only 27% were uncertain or
disagreed.

The political system

Despite student activism in protests over various
issues, the evidence provided by various national opinion
surveys indicates that the "alienated" actually include a
relatively small proportion of the student population (10%).[97]
For example, 78% in a 1971 Gallup poll said they could
"take pride in being an American."[98] This magnitude of
student pride in being an American corresponds with Almond's
findings in a 1958 national poll, in which 67% to 92%
expressed such pride.[99] Lipset reports further evidence of

---

[94]Ibid., p. 184.

[95]Gallup, "Special Report...," p. 6. Indeed, 40% of
the students in this poll believed that breaking the law
during the demonstrations should not be punished.

[96]Gilbert Marketing Group, "Omnibus Youth Survey"
(Gilbert Marketing Group, February, 1970), Tables 24, 25, and
31, cited by Lipset, Rebellion..., p. 57.

[97]Lipset, Rebellion..., pp. 48, 49, 53-54, and 72.

[98]George Gallup, "Four in Ten College Students
Think Change in U.S. Will Come through Revolution," Press
release of the American Institute of Public Opinion
(Princeton: January 21, 1971).

[99]Divided into three groups of high, medium, and
low subjective competence (sense of political efficacy),
92%, 87%, and 67% of Almond's respondents expressed pride

student support for the government and its institutions.
Only 14% of his student respondents "advocated fundamental
reform." Only 14% agreed with the statement: "There is no
point in trying to change existing political structures, if
one is interested in change he must work outside these
structures."[100] Lipset also reports that 37% of students
favored only "moderate change" in the Constitution, while
47% favored "no substantial change."[101]

The economic system

Finally, students also support the economic system
in America. Only 20% favored changes "to the point of
socialism."[102] Similarly, Samuel Lubell's study in 1966
found that 60% of the students he interviewed praised the
role of business: only 15% were critical.[103] In a more
recent study, 67% of the student respondents agreed with
this statement: "Those who knock free enterprise misun-
derstand what made this a great nation."[104] Greater
evidence of this sentiment is the fact that 72% of the
students in a C.B.S. News survey believed that "competition encourages excellence."[105] The C.B.S. News survey
also revealed that 75% of these students agreed with the
statement: "The right to private property is sacred."[106]

---

in their "governmental and political system." See Almond
and Verba, Civic Culture..., p. 19; Table 8, part 4.

[100]" A Study of the Inward Generation," Special
report published by Psychology Today (October, 1969),
cited by Lipset, Rebellion..., p. 55.

[101]Lipset, Rebellion..., pp. 56 and 60. Also
see pp. 48-49, where Lipset reviews the Gilbert Marketing
Group Study, "Omnibus...," Table 22.

[102]George Gallup, "The U.S. Campus Mood, '71: A
Newsweek Poll-- Students Avoid Party Labels; Also
Reject Radical Politics," Newsweek, February 22, 1971, p. 61.

[103]Samuel Lubell, "The People Speak," News releases
reporting on a study of American college students, No. 6
cited by Lipset, Rebellion..., p. 53.

[104]"Study of Inward Generation...," cited by
Lipset, Rebellion..., p. 55.

[105]"Profile of a Generation...," cited by Lipset,
Rebellion..., p. 54.

[106]Ibid.

The growth in radicalism

This student confidence may not be so complete if one considers Donald Stokes' finding that "basic evaluative orientations toward the national government," especially "political distrust was associated with a failure to identify the self on the political spectrum."[107] Thus, the fact that 45% of the students in Ardery's study denied affiliation with the two major political parties may reveal that student confidense may be considerably less than indicated above.[108] Indeed, only 14% of Ardery's sample expressed affiliation with the Republican Party, and 33% stated affiliation with the Democratic Party.[109] The Gergens' 1969-1970 survey of five thousand students in thirty-nine schools reported that 37% of the total sample were "liberals," "radical," or "disillusioned" with party politics and "otherwise alienated from party politics."[110] Indeed, only 15% (Sarah Lawrence) to 55% (South Carolina) of Ardery's sample agreed with the statement: "The present two-party system is satisfactory on the whole and should be essentially retained."[111] Similarly, 14% (South Carolina) to 57% (Sarah Lawrence) agreed with the statement: "I would support the founding of a third party that would represent the left more than either the Republicans or the Democrats do at present."[112] Another study reveals that in an average group of anti-war demonstrators, 62% would probably be Independents, while only 13% would be Republicans and 20% would be Democrats.[113] If failure to identify with the major political parties and participation in demonstrations against regime policies is adequate evidence of discontent with or distrust of the system, then these figures indicate that at least a large minority of students feel disenchanted with the system, perhaps to the point of approaching a denial of the regime's legitimacy.

---

[107]Stokes, "Popular...," p. 64.

[108]Ardery, "Special...," p. 637.

[109]Ibid.

[110]Kenneth Gergen and Mary K. Gergen, "Vietnam and the Students: A Brief Summary of Research Results," Department of Psychology, Swathmore College, June, 1970 (mimeographed), cited by Lipset, Rebellion..., p. 47.

[111]Ardery, "Special...," p. 642.

[112]Ibid.

[113]Gergen and Gergen, "Vietnam..," p. 2. cited by Lipset, Rebellion..., p. 47.

Several studies reveal that this student disenchantment, though still for only a small minority, has grown over
the last decade. This growth is particulary evident in the
increase of student self-identification as radical and
expression of radical ideals. The Harris organization
reports that the proportion describing their politics as
"radical or far left" increased from 4% to 11%.[114] Ardery
reports that 17% of his sample in twelve colleges identified
themselves as being radical; 25% took a specifically
socialist (as distinguished from liberal) position.[115]
Ardery also provides specific examples of increases in
radicalism: between the school years 1961 to 1962 and
1969 to 1970, "radicalism has grown six-fold at Yale
(3% to 18%), more than tripled at Stanford (5% to 17%) and
Harvard (8% to 29%), tripled at Boston (6% to 18%), and
almost tripled at Williams (5% to 14%)."[116] Ardery further
states that tolerance of Marxist or Communist teachers was
higher at "eastern elite schools" than in the Midwest and
South.[117] A Gallup survey provides further evidence for
this regional difference: 34% of those students from
eastern colleges had frequently demonstrated, while 71% and
78% from midwestern and southern colleges had never demonstrated.[118]

Although only a small percentage of students actually identify themselves as "radicals," a large proportion
have come to hold radical opinions. For example, the
special Harris survey conducted for the American Council
on Education found that 76% believed that "basic changes in
the system" are necessary to improve the quality of life in
America; 44% felt that social progress in America is more
likely to come about through "radical pressure from outside
the system" than through the actions of established institutions.[119] According to the Scranton Commission, this
growth in political radicalism has been accompanied by an
increase in student protests and "a greater willingness on
the part of some students to engage in-- or at least

---

[114]Harris survey of 1968 and Louis Harris, "Report
of the May 1970 Harris Survey of Students," May 20-28, 1970,
cited by Scranton Commission, p. 48. See also Harris
et al., Youth Attitudes..., cited by Lipset, Rebellion...,
pp. 47 and 49; and Louis Harris, "College Students
'Radicalized' by Vietnam War," Philadelphia Inquirer,
June 3, 1969.

[115]Ardery, "Special...," pp. 637 and 642.

[116]Ibid.   [117]Ibid., p. 638.

[118]Gallup, "Special Report...."

[119]Scranton Commission, pp. 48-49.

condone-- disruptive and violent protests."[120] Thus, 80%
of colleges represented by student respondents in one Harris
survey had experienced protests or demonstrations by May,
1970: 75% of the students of these schools expressed
approval of the goals of the protests; and 58% actually
participated in the protests.[121] Most studies, however,
indicate that the largest portion of demonstrators identify
themselves as either radical, far left, or liberal.[122]
"Though almost all self-described far leftists (91%), and
most liberals (74%) took part" in the 1970 Cambodian
incursion protests, only 37% of the middle-of-the-road
students did so.[123] Even though a large portion of students
express support of radical goals, most students are not
tactical extremists. For example, 68% do not accept
violence as an effective means of change.[124] Lipset
reports that 89% believed the radical left is as much a
threat as the radical right.[125] Indeed, Lipset suggests
that most surveys (i.e., Gallup, Harris, Roper, and others)
have overestimated the move to the left which occurred
during the sixties:

> There is some reason to believe that these organiza-
> tions have oversampled the more selective or higher
> quality schools, or that their respondents on given
> campuses were selected using quota sample rather than
> probability (randomly from list of students regis-
> tered) procedures. These "biases" may have resulted
> in an overestimation of the more radical or alienated
> segment.[126]

---

[120]Ibid., p. 49.   [121]Ibid.

[122]Harris, "Report May, 1970...," p. 140, cited by
Lipset, Rebellion..., pp. 47 and 93. See also Louis Harris,
"52% Decry Protests on Cambodia," Washington Post, June 1,
1970.

[123]Harris, "Report May, 1970...," p. 140, cited
by Lipset, Rebellion..., pp. 47 and 93.

[124]Scranton Commission, p. 49; and Harris, "Report
May, 1970...."

[125]Lipset, Rebellion..., p. 54.

[126]Ibid., p. 50. Ardery's study is probably the
best example of this.

Liberalizing effect of the
college milieu
        Despite the probability of overestimation of radi-
calism, several studies suggest either a liberalizing effect
on youth in universities or some student selection of radical milieus.[127] Whatever the source of student radicalism,
a 1970 Gallup poll reveals that "the noncollege youth have
been much more conservative on domestic, foreign policy and
cultural issues than students."[128] This study indicates
that the gap in opinions and behavior between the average
reaction of college students and others is not a generational one, but rather it is a difference between those on
and off campus, regardless of age. Although campus students
have become increasingly liberal, the noncollege population
has gradually moved in a more conservative direction over
the past half decade: "Increasing numbers [of the
noncollege population] identify theselves as conservatives
rather than liberals, so that by 1970 many more citizens
described themselves as conservatives (52%) than as liberals
(34%)."[129] A special C.B.S. survey in 1969 reveals the
extent of this discrepancy between college and noncollege
youth attitudes: 50% of the noncollege youth versus 37%
of college students were located in the "Moderate" category,
and 21% of the noncollege youth compared to 11% of college
students were identified as "Conservatives." Only 29% of
noncollege youth were on the left, versus 52% of college
students categorized as "Revolutionaries," "Radical Dissidents," or "Moderate Reformers."[130]
        Several studies suggest that college students merely
resemble the faculty in their political views. For example,
one Gallup poll in 1970 reveals that self-identified conservatives among the students are between 15% and 20%, among
the faculty about a quarter. Similarly, 5% to 10% of both
faculty and students identify themselves as left-wing
radicals.[131] A comparison of these figures with the find-

---

[127]For a discussion of both these factors in
explaining higher student than noncollege radicalism, see
Lipset, Rebellion....

[128]Gallup, "Student Revolution...," Index, No. 66,
p. 15; and Lipset, Rebellion..., p. 40.

[129]Lipset, Rebellion..., p. 41; and Gallup,
"Student Revolution...," Index, No. 66, p. 15.

[130]"Profile...," p. 35, cited by Lipset, Rebellion..., p. 48.

[131]Lipset, Rebellion..., p. 40; and Gallup,
"Student Revolution...," p. 15. See also Philip W. Semas,
"Students 'Satisfied' with Education: Most of Them and

ings of a 1969 Gallup survey suggests that the gap in
opinions of noncollege and college youth, as well as of
faculty and the general public, is indeed a difference
between college associated and noncollege associated individuals. According to this survey, 33% of the general
population, versus 42% to 46% of the college population,
identify themselves as "Liberal" or Moderately Liberal."[132]
Several studies also indicate that liberalism among college
professionals varies according to discipline and school
quality: "the liberal arts fields, particularly the social
sciences, and the most prestigeous schools ... are more
liberal."[133]

Summary of student attitudes
toward the regime
        The surveys just reviewed suggest several peculiar-
ities of student political opinion. For example, a clear
majority of students express general confidence and trust
in government and its institutions. Even an "overwhelming
majority of ... demonstrators place a high value on traditional American ideals."[134] Despite this expressed trust
in government, a substantial minority of American students
have become alienated from the conventional political
process, as indicated in the percentage who are not affiliated
with the two major political parties and identify themselves
as radicals or leftists of various types. Several studies
suggest this change in student opinions is in response to
specific issues, especially the war in Vietnam and greater
student recognition of black inequality. Other studies
indicate this student liberalism is due mostly to the influence of the college milieu, where youths are exposed to
faculties who are more liberal than the general adult population. Others stress that leftists select those schools

---

Teachers Agree," The Chronicle of Higher Education, Vol. V
(January 18, 1971), p. 2, cited by Lipset, Rebellion...,
p. 5.

        [132]George Gallup, Gallup Opinion Index, No. 50
(August, 1969), p. 6.

        [133]Lipset, Rebellion..., p. 188. See also Lawrence
C. Howard, "The Academic and the Ballot," School and Soci-
ety, Vol. LXXXVI (November 22, 1958), p. 416; Seymour
Martin Lipset, "The Politics of Academia," Perspectives on
Campus Tensions, ed. David C. Nichols (Washington, D. C.:
American Council on Education, 1970), pp. 85-118; and Paul
F. Lazarsfeld and Wagner Thielens, Jr., The Academic Mind
(Glencoe, Ill.: The Free Press, 1958), p. 402.

        [134]Gergen and Gergen, "Vietnam...," p. 2, cited by
Lipset, Rebellion....

most likely to reinforce their beliefs. In any case,
student discontent has definitely increased over the last
decade.

A 1971 _Playboy_ survey suggests that the student
demonstrations and protests of the sixties may not recur in
the seventies. This study indicates that the new amendment
allowing eighteen year olds to vote may provide students
with a more conventional means to reveal their dissatisfaction with the government and its officials and policies.
Only 3% of the students questioned in the _Playboy_ study
felt the eighteen year old vote could not have any significance: only 4% intended to stay away from the polls in
1972.[135] Even among the 43% who think the vote probably
won't make much difference, the great majority intend to
vote.[136] These figures indicate that student faith in
the democratic process, though tenuously held, is far from
dead.

Summary of Black and Student Attitudes
Toward General Regime
Characteristics

The evidence just reviewed of student support for
American institutions and their pride in being Americans
indicates that most students still consider the general
system to be legitimate.[137] The evidence also suggests
the majority of students are satisfied with governmental
institutions and do not advocate radical or revolutionary
changes, even though a passioned minority of probably 5%
to 20% do. A large majority of students (70% to 80%) are
concerned with unspecified social inadequacies but have
not rejected the system. Probably only 10% to 20% have
rejected the whole political system; 30% may have rejected
the economic system. For examples of more specific student
disillusionment, a large minority (40%) believe the system
is repressive of free speech (twice the rate of such
national opinions). A comparable minority also believes
the social system is racist. Thus, although most students
do not reject the system, probably a majority, perhaps as
large as 70%, seek major reform of the system. Therefore,
the legitimacy of the system may be in a tenuous state.
Indeed, 30% to 50% fail to identify themselves with the
major political parties. Similarly, a large number of

---

[135] "Student Survey: 1971," _Playboy_, Vol. XVIII,
No. 9 (September, 1971), p. 208.

[136]_Ibid._

[137]Gallup, "Four in Ten...."

students identify themselves as being on the left end
of the political system and admit to having participated
actively in protest demonstrations. Apparently, attitudes
of most students toward the social system, political
institutions, and the economy tend to reflect diffuse
support for the regime quite similar to that of the
general public.[138]

A very substantial minority of blacks (25% to 40%)
find the white dominated system defective and are concerned
about community control in the political system. Nevertheless, blacks are supportive of the economic system by a
wide margin. The evidence also indicates that up to 30% or
50% of American students and blacks may be close to denying
the legitimacy of the regime. Yet these studies also
reveal that such black and student discontent with the
American system is presently (in 1972) directed toward
specific policies rather than basic regime principles or
institutions. That support for the regime, however, is
not guaranteed for the future.

Trust in Governmental Institutions, Officials, and Policies

Evidence in the last section suggests that some of
the specific complaints about the American system by both
blacks and students may be related to some doubts about
the trustworthiness of specific governmental institutions
rather than a complete rejection of the "system," the
"establishment," or the "white power structure." Distrust
of government institutions may partially reveal a more
general lack of confidence in the whole political process.
This lack of confidence in turn may reflect indirectly a
marked tendency to see the system as less than fully legitimate.

Some Problems of Analysis

There are several problems involved in interpreting
most data on political trust. First, most of the political
trust studies attempt to cover a wide range of sentiments
about the honesty, justness, and benevolence of government.
These three sentiments may be separate dimensions of a
citizen's affective orientations. Most studies of political
trust probably tap only a portion of diffuse affective or
evaluative orientations or sentiments of legitimacy.

Another problem is that some studies of political
trust also lump together a wide range of governmental levels
and officials-- national, state, and local-- and institu-

---

[138]See Lipset, Rebellion..., pp. 53 ff, where he
discusses Lubell, "People Speak...," pp. 1-3.

tional services--- police, sourts, welfare, schools, etc.
The generally low salience of state and local politics and
the specific institutions of the national government for
most citizens make it difficult to get information on
diffuse support for institutional or authority objects.
For example, when asked to say something concretely about
the American political system, most citizens usually refer
to the national government. This greater salience of the
national government is evident in the greater voter interest
and participation in national rather than state and local
politics and elections.[139] Tomlinson reports that more
positive responses for blacks are toward the national
government.[140] Thus attitudes about the national political institutions may be more likely to reflect attitudes
toward the legitimacy of the regime than attitudes about
local government. The following is a summary of the extensive information on the specific attitudes toward trust in
national institutions. Due to the problems of analysis just
indicated, it should be clear that such evidence is only
one part of the puzzle of diffuse support for regime
legitimacy.

General Public's Trust in
National Government

Trust in government
        In 1958, 1964, and 1966, 73%, 77%, and 65% of the
respondents in several Survey Research Center studies said
they could always or almost always "trust government to do
what is right."[141] Similarly, in 1963 McClosky found 89.6%
of those questioned expressed such trust in government, and
58.9% said that most politicians could be trusted to do
what is right.[142] Some citizens seem to distinguish between

---

[139]For a good summary of the empirical evidence,
see Milbrath, Political.... Muller says, "If respondents
are forced to rank the levels, much ranking could be somewhat arbitary, reflecting, in part, the low salience of
state and local government for most people." (Muller,
"A Test...," p. 26.) See also M. Kent Jennings and Richard
G. Niemi, "Patterns of Political Learning," Harvard Educational Review, Summer, 1968.

        [140]Tomlinson, "Ideological...," p. 352.

        [141]Robinson, Rusk, and Head, Measures Political...,
p. 634.

        [142]McClosky, "Consensus and Ideology...," cited in
Robinson, Rusk, and Head, Measures Political..., p. 171.
Attitudes toward critical incidents involving the use of

authority roles and positions, governmental institutions, and the politicians who occupy government offices. A substantial majority of 60% to 90% believe that governmental authority is just in terms of doing "what is right."

Trust in democratic processes

In the study by Almond and Verba, 85% of the respondents specifically mentioned pride in government or political institutions, such as "the Constitution, political freedom, and democracy."[143] Similarly, most people believe rule in America is not by an economic elite. For example, in McClosky's study, a sizeable majority of 67.9%, 66.6%, and 57.1% expressed disagreement with questions indicating rule by an economic elite.[144] Only 32.1% believed the parties are controlled by the wealthy. Similarly, only 33.3% believed the laws of the land are "rich man's laws."[145] Studies in 1964 and 1966 reveal that only 24% to 29% felt that government pays more attention to big shots, big interests, and crooks than to ordinary people.[146]

Trust in specific branches of government

Some studies reveal that trust in specific governmental institutions may indicate rather high regime legitimacy. In a 1966 national survey, only 1% expressed distrust of the Supreme Court and Congress; yet, 32% said they didn't know.[147] In 1964, Free and Cantril found that

---

severe governmental punishments of citizens provide indirect inferences of the legitimacy of the regime's authorities. A national survey revealed that 77% of respondents could imagine it being right for a policeman to shoot an adult male, while only 27% could imagine it being right for a citizen to choke another citizen (David L. Baker and Sandra J. Ball, Mass Media and Violence, A report to the National Commission on the Causes and Prevention of Violence [Vol. XI; Washington, D. C.: U.S. Government Printing Office, November, 1969], p. 347).

[143]Almond and Verba, Civic Culture..., p. 64.

[144]McClosky, "Consensus and Ideology...."

[145]Ibid.

[146]Robinson, Rusk, and Head, Measures Political..., p. 644.

[147]Ibid., p. 506. Muller found that "belief in the legitimacy of the Supreme Court is strongly correlated with belief in the legitimacy of Congress, but otherwise shows

out of 10.0 possible in ladder ratings of trust, the averages
were 7.43 for the President, 7.23 for Congress, and 6.89
for the Supreme Court.[148] Muller indicates a continuing
low salience in which citizens "don't know" about their
own trust for specific institutions: the "don't know"
responses were 19% for the Presidency, 25% for Congress,
and 32% for the Supreme Court.[149] One national poll
revealed that only 19% of the public could identify the
three branches of government, and 33% could identify the
Bill of Rights.[150] This brief summary is probably consistent with McClosky's statement in 1964 that "a strong
majority of respondents did not question the legitimacy of
the system."[151]

Changes in patterns of trust

Between the fifties and sixties, such diffuse trust
in the government may have undergone considerable change.
For example, between 1958 and 1966, those saying they could
always trust the government declined from 57% to 17%.[152]
In 1969, Newsweek reported that only a little over half of
the respondents in a national poll of the American middle
class felt they could give "some trust in government and
the media to tell the truth."[153] Finally, the Survey
Research Center studies reveal a rise in the fear of
increased governmental powers: in 1952, 51% of the respondents said governmental power is "about right"; by 1964
and 1966, 44% and 56% expressed fears of increased governmental powers.[154] The decreasing electoral success of
incumbents and the success of Wallace in 1972 primaries
may perhaps reflect these dimensions of public alienation.

---

rather slight association with other legitimacy measures."
(Muller, "A Test...," p. 26.)

[148]Free and Cantril, Political..., p. 193.

[149]Muller, "A Test...," p. 22.

[150]Greenstein, Children..., p. 56, n. 1, citing
Hazel G. Erskine, "The Polls: Textbook Knowledge," Public
Opinion Quarterly, Vol. XXVII (Spring, 1963), pp. 137-140.

[151]McClosky, "Consensus and Ideology...," cited by
Robinson, Rusk, and Head, Measures Political..., p. 171.

[152]Robinson, Rusk, and Head, Measures Political...,
p. 634.

[153]"Troubled American...."

[154]Robinson, Rusk, and Head, Measures Political...,
pp. 511-518.

Trust in officials
and policies

If, as Hofstetter says, "disaffection with specific objects is cumulative, the end product of which is diffuse dissatisfaction, [or] disengagement," then dissatisfaction with particular officials and public policies may also reflect latent discontent with the regime or political system.[155] In their 1958 cross-national surveys, Almond and Verba found that citizens of the United States and Great Britain had more confidence in the fairness of their officials than did Mexicans, Germans, and Italians.[156] A national survey in 1969 showed that when Americans were asked to respond to the question, "What do you think is wrong with America today?", only 3% responded with answers coded as corruption or incompetence in national government.[157] The highest coded responses were: 14% for crime, lawlessness, and law and order: 11% for protests, college demonstrations, and unrest among youth.[158] Regime officials and institutions simply did not elicit responses suggesting that the system is in need of change or overhaul.

Other data about officials, however, show that such support is clearly not total. For example, approximately 40% in one study believed that a conspiracy was involved in the assassinations of President Kennedy in 1963 and of his brother Robert in 1968, strongly implying a cover up by the United States government officials in both cases.[159] American citizens believed in such a conspiracy and its cover up despite extensive investigations of both cases. Similarly, depending on the question, a clear majority in McClosky's 1964 study-- 54%, 55.1%, 65.3%, and 54.6%-- held sceptical views of politics, politicians, and political parties as involving differing kinds and degrees of dishonesty.[160] In 1971, 40% of Americans doubted the truthfulness of presidents, governors, mayors, and newspaper editors.

---

[155]Hofstetter, "Political Disengagement...," p. 174, n. 4.

[156]See Almond and Verba, Civic Culture....

[157]American Institute of Public Opinion, "What in Your Opinion Do You Think is Most Wrong with America Today?", AIPO, No. 775 (February, 1969).

[158]Ibid.

[159]George Gallup, "Public Sees Gun Registration as Most Urgent Step Needed to Curb Violence in America," Gallup Opinion Index, July, 1968.

[160]McClosky, "Consensus and Ideology...."

In 1972, a so-called "alienated" electorate may be turning to radical protest or special "message" candidates of both the right and the left, such as Governor George Wallace and Senator Goerge McGovern. This phenomenon has been called both populism and demagoguery. In July, 1972, a twenty-four hour Democratic Party telethon on national television asking for small monetary donations to save the two party system had very disappointing results. At the time of this writing (July, 1972) the Democratic Party seems to be worth about a dime for the average registered democrat. In any case, these examples may reflect some growing distrust between the people and their representatives. Whether such scepticism reflects a lack of support for the system as a whole is doubtful, but it is certainly not encouraging fo. existing political incumbents. This trend is evident in Muller's Waterloo finding in 1970 that 40% of whites and 40.1% of blacks agreed that "the Constitution is in need of major change."[161]

Thus, trust in the government or in most politicians is not universal or without reservation. This cynicism may reveal a frightening lack of confidence in the political process, or it may be a healthy sign of citizens' vigilance and scepticism. In addition, the widespread belief shown in several studies that politicians are crooks,[162] serve special interests, and are big shots[163] is not always of fundamental political importance, for criminality involves only a minor redistribution of the system benefits without necessarily threatening to change the basic purposes of the regime. Similarly, others may accept such political immorality as a part of human nature applicable to all human politicians rather than a reflection of the essential nature or character of the regime.[164] Similarly, Muller notes that an item suggesting that the nation wastes tax money (83% agreed) did not correlate with the twenty-three other items attempting to measure political trust.[165] Apparently, citizens may accept such immorality in politics as a "fact of life."

Summary

Nationally, about 73% to 90% trust government in terms of its justice or "rightness." Only 25% to 35%

---

[161]Muller, "A Test...," p. 21.

[162]See especially Sherrill, "Mass Attitudes..."; and Lane, Political Ideology....

[163]McClosky, "Consensus and Ideology...."

[164]Lane, Political Ideology....

[165]Muller, "A Test...," n. 39.

believe the government is undemocratic, as measured by
belief in rule by a wealthy elite contravening ideals of
popular government. Distrust of particular branches of
the national government is practically nonexistent.
Interest in the intricate workings of these institutions
also appears to be nonexistent.

In 1972, probably a narrow majority no longer
trusts government with the intensity once felt. Similarly,
a majority may fear an increase of governmental power.
Certainly, a very substantial minority of perhaps 40%
question the credibility of government. This cynicism
is probably simply healthy citizenly vigilance. Perhaps
only 25% acquiescently grant quasi-legitimacy to political
institutions and officials. Certainly, support for
alienated candidates of the left and the right is not
reassuring to incumbents and may perhaps reflect a trend
toward decreasing support for the regime.

Black Trust in Government

Black trust in government
institutions
Within the national context of substantial, if
uneasy, trust in government by the general citizenry,
to what extent do blacks trust government? Several
studies have shown that black children are generally
less trustful of the political authority structures
than white children.[166] More specifically, Muller says,

Expression of affect toward these institutions is a
direct monotonic function of level of education only
among whites; blacks with a high school-education
are somewhat less likely to express affect than those
with a grade school education. ... For both races,
neither Legitimacy Congress not Legitimacy Presidency
show a consistent tendency to increase as level of
education increases, although there is a somewhat
sizeable contrast between college-educated blacks and
non-college-educated blacks in diffuse support for
the Presidency: non-college-educated blacks are low
on Legitimacy Presidency, as opposed to 15 percent of
high school and grade school blacks who rank low on
this variable, 75 percent of the college-educated
blacks are high on Legitimacy Presidency, as opposed

---

[166]Ibid., n. 69, citing Schley R. Lyons, "The
Political Socialization of Ghetto Children: Efficacy
and Cynicism," Journal of Politics, May, 1970; and
Greenberg, "Children and Government...."

to 45 percent of high school and grade school blacks
respectively.[167]

Black trust in government
officials

A study of the Watts riot shows that 45% of blacks
said, "Elected officials cannot generally be trusted."[168]
Only 17% of the Los Angeles whites agreed.[169] Agreement
with a more positive phrasing of the question indicates
that only 50% of blacks, versus 79% of whites, generally
trusted elected officials.[170] Sears reports that 62% of
the Watts residents questioned believed they could trust
"Negro elected officials."[171] Muller found that race
correlated very highly with general trust for political
authority at .572.[172] Racial and social equality issues
seem to be criteria of other differentials in black
responses to political trust items.

Differentials in black trust
of political authorities

Tomlinson states that blacks have less confidence
in local political systems than in the federal government.[173] Apparently, blacks attribute their social inequality more to local government than to federal institutions. Certainly, local officials are closer to both
individual cases of social injustices and the implementation of federal urban programs. Thus, local governments
and officials are easier to identify and attack.

Knowledge of the political situation at the time
of the Los Angeles survey is necessary in order to understand this discrepancy between trust in the federal government and distrust of local government. Black trust in the
federal government may be attributed to the fact that this
survey was conducted during a time when a Democratic govern-
ment-- President Johnson, the Congress, and the Supreme
Court-- was enacting the most extensive civil rights legis-

---

[167]Muller, "A Test...," p. 24.

[168]Sears, "Political Attitudes...," p. 697.

[169]Ibid.   [170]Tomlinson, "Ideological...," p. 347.

[171]Sears, "Political Attitudes...," p. 697.

[172]Muller, "A Test...," p. 34.

[173]Apparently, this lack of trust is most prevalent
among the younger, better educated Negro respondents
(Tomlinson, "Determinants...," p. 250).

lation since the Emancipation Proclamation.[174] According
to a 1969 <u>Newsweek</u> survey, 74% of the blacks questioned felt
the federal government under President Johnson to be helpful
to Negro rights. Only 25% felt so toward the Nixon administration.[175]

    This preference by blacks for Democrats is parti-
cularly apparent in Sears's study in Los Angeles. This
study reveals that black attitudes toward the Democratic
Party and toward its two most "visible" leaders, President
Johnson and Governor Brown, were highly favorable, while
attitudes toward the "maverick" Democrat Mayor Sam Yorty,
the Republican Party, and Republican Senator George Murphy
were unfavorable.[176] Sears states that this preference
for Democrats, even in the wake of the riot, is evidence
that Los Angeles Negroes as a whole had not rejected their
main allies-- "white liberals."

> Not only were the Democrats and their leaders favorably
> evaluated, but so were the two most powerful legisla-
> tive bodies, the State Legislature and the U.S. Con-
> gress. Both were dominated by racial liberals at the
> time. So, most Los Angeles Negroes seem to have been
> maintaining their traditional partisan commitments.[177]

The continued support of blacks for the Democratic Party
and the liberal "establishment" is evident in heavy black
support for Senator Hubert Humphrey out of a wide field of
Democrats, including a black candidate (Shirley Chisholm),
in most of the 1972 presidential preference primaries,
except in California. This support for Humphrey may also
reveal general black confidence in the existing system:
most blacks may be reluctant to follow the more "radical"
leadership. Yet identification of President Nixon with
George Wallace and a "southern strategy" for Republican
victories at the polls may drive many moderate blacks into
the arms of the militant black radicals, some of them violent
and separatist. Indeed, 30% of Tomlinson's sample expressed
sympathy with the Black Muslims (the only black organization
that was both radical and highly visible at the time of the

---

[174]At the same time, Los Angeles local government
consisted of Mayor Sam Yorty and Sheriff Peter Pitchess,
with whom blacks had had several confrontations.

[175]Harris, "Report from Black...," p. 19.

[176]Sears, "Political Attitudes...," p. 678.

[177]<u>Ibid</u>. Samuel Lubell shows that even after
Franklin Roosevelt landslides, many Negroes clung to their
traditional loyalties to the Republican Party, probably
until as late as 1958 (see Lubell, <u>White and Black...</u>).

survey).[178] Aberbach and Walker found that

expressions of political trust and approval of black
power are indeed inversely related. The higher a
person's score on the various trust indices, the less
likely he is to favorably interpret black power.[179]

There was a -.52 correlation for trust of federal government and support for black power.[180]
Black distrust of public officials is especially
evident in their attitudes toward the police. In Watts,
only 41% of blacks, versus 92% of whites, trusted police.[181]
Both blacks and whites express discontent over the fairness
of police behavior. In an earlier 1966 survey, however,
black belief in the unfairness of police was less than among
whites: 33% of blacks versus 58% of whites.[182] The most
common sign of official malfeasance expressed by blacks is
police brutality. In 1964, 65.2% of black Watts residents
believed that blacks were beat up while in custody. The
respondents expressed decreasing percentages of this happening to friends (34.4%), actually seeing it happen
(20.8%), and it actually happened to the person questioned
(3.9%).[183] In one study, those having such actual experiences with police were also likely (correlation of .43)
to have low trust in national and local government as well.[184]

---

[178]Tomlinson, "Determinants...," pp. 250-251.

[179]Aberbach and Walker, "Meaning of Black Power...,"
p. 377.

[180]Ibid., p. 378. On the other hand, there was a
lower -.22 correlation for Detroit (local) government and
support for black power.

[181]Tomlinson, "Ideological...," p. 350. On Detroit,
see Joel D. Aberbach and Jack L. Walker, "Political Trust
and Racial Ideology," American Political Science Review,
Vol. LXIV, No. 4 (December, 1970), pp. 1199-1219.

[182]Harris, "Black and White...."

[183]Walter J. Raine, "The Perception of Police Brutality in Sourth Central Los Angeles," The Los Angeles Riots:
A Socio-Psychological Study, ed. Nathan E. Cohen (New York:
Praeger, 1970), p. 386. Note, however, that included within
the "brutality" index were: insulting language, rousting
and frisking, stop and search, and search of homes.

[184]Aberbach and Walker, "Political Trust...," p.
1204.

In an open ended question, however, only 14% cited
police brutality as the single action they most disliked
about the Watts riot.[185]

Summary of black trust
        Probably a bare majority of 50% of noncollege blacks
trust particular government institutions. Black trust for
selected local government institutions is quite a bit lower
than for national government institutions. Somewhat less
than a majority (40% to 50%) definitely do not trust government officials in general. Nevertheless, blacks generally
express approval of liberals and of the highly visible state
and national executives of the Democratic Party. This
differentiation in the trust of national and local institutions and liberal and conservative officials would seem to
indicate distrust founded on perceived party differences on
civil rights policies not any general disaffection from the
political system. General regime disaffection is probably
limited at most to the 30% sympathetic to black dissident
groups.
        Nevertheless, black trust in the national govern-
ment may be in a great deal of flux. Increased association
of local police malfeasance with national government could
conceivably spill over into less diffuse support for the
national government. Black confidence in the national
government also seems only somewhat less than that of
whites, as well as being less stable and more open to
change in response to policies and official acts with
respect to social equality. The legitimacy of the regime,
at least as reflected by blacks' attitudes toward the
national government, may have been tenuous at best in
recent years. Yet general disaffection is not yet evident
in 1972

                    Student Trust in Government

        Several surveys reveal that the students of the
nation express greater confidence in the government than
do blacks. For example, in an open ended question asking
for their biggest gripe, only 16% responded in answers that
were coded "government and adult authority."[186] Similarly,
a 1970 Harris poll revealed that only 24% had "hardly any
confidence" in the ability of the "government to solve the
problems of the '70's."[187] A 1965 Harris survey revealed
the degree of confidence students have in specific areas of

---

        [185]Tomlinson and Sears, "Negro...," p. 297.

        [186]Gallup, "Special Report...."

        [187]Lipset, Rebellion..., p. 59, citing Harris,
"Report of May, 1970...."

authority. The "hardly any" and "not sure" responses to
the question "How much confidence do you have in these
institutions?" were: 5% for banks and finance institutions,
7% for the U.S. Supreme Court, 8% for big corporations,
9% for the executive branch of the federal government, 9%
for Congress, 19% for the military, 15% for the Democratic
Party, 23% for the press, 32% for organized labor, and 35%
for the Republican Party.[188] This student confidence in the
government is apparent in the special 1970 Harris survey
commissioned by the American Council on Education, which
was conducted after the Cambodian incursion and the student
deaths at Kent State and Jackson State. The several studies
just discussed indicate a remarkably high level of general
student confidence in governmental institutions. These
studies also reveal that a substantial minority of 10% to
30% of students is quite disaffected.

Summary of Attitudes in Trust
in Government

To review the findings on trust in government, a
clear majority of citizens expresses confidence in the American government. Although most blacks believe that the
regime principles and government institutions are legitimate, blacks are somewhat less trustful, especially in terms
of local government. Students apparently are becoming more
and more discontented with the government, although the
majority of students is likely to express belief in the
legitimacy of the regime and trust in government. Except
for significant minorities, both black and student discontent seem to be limited to specific issues and governmental
policies toward these issues.

Responsiveness and Effectiveness
of Democratic Government

The concept of responsiveness of government is
closely related to trust in government and the belief in the
legitimacy of a democratic regime. According to Campbell,

> our citizens expect a dynamic balance between the twin
> goals of governmental competence and political account-
> ability and such a balance is thus essential to the
> strengthening of that legitimacy of government.[189]

---

[188]"Campus '65," Newsweek, March 22, 1965, p. 53.
Also Lipset, Rebellion..., p. 52.

[189]Campbell, Sahid, and Stang, Law..., p. 134. Note
Madison's comments on the need for a balance of energy and
stability with "inviolable" attention to liberty and republican form (Hamilton, Madison, and Jay, Federalist..., No. 37).

Presumably, democratic governments are responsive and attentive to citizens. How do citizens perceive governmental responsiveness?

Opinions on Governmental Responsiveness and Effectiveness in General

National samples

National disagreement with the statement, "I don't think public officials care much about people like me," ranges from 61% to 71% in Survey Research Center studies in 1952, 1960, 1964, and 1966. Agreement has ranged from 25% to 37%.[190] Similarly, 80% believed that "most Congressmen pay attention to the people who elect them when they decide what to do in Congress."[191] Finally, depending on the question, 70% to 90% of the national sample in 1964 felt that government was responsive to the people either "a good deal" or "some."[192]

Blacks

Blacks and the New Left do not share this confidence in governmental responsiveness. In a Los Angeles study, 60% of blacks compared to 27% of whites agreed that public officials "don't care."[193] Among a sample of blacks in Watts, nearly 50% felt that the Congress represented blacks only "a little" or "doesn't represent blacks at all."[194] Nearly 50% of blacks in Los Angeles gave neutral, ambiguous, or negative responses to the question: "How do you feel about the way you are represented?"[195] Not unexpectedly, only 9% of the blacks in Watts felt that their political interests were "really represented" by "white people."[196] In contrast, 62% of these Watts residents believed they could trust Negro elected officials.[197] Sixty percent of blacks versus 29% of whites agreed with the statement: "Public

---

[190] Robinson, Rusk, and Head, Measures Political..., pp. 636-638.

[191] Ibid., pp. 641-642. [192] Ibid.

[193] Tomlinson, "Ideological...," p. 347.

[194] Ibid., p. 353. Higher percentages feeling they were poorly represented were found among militants (56%) than among the uncommitted (50%) and the conservatives (38%).

[195] Sears, "Political Attitudes...," p. 695.

[196] Ibid., p. 696.

[197] Ibid.

officials don't care much what people like me think."[198]   In response to the open ended question, "Who really represents the Negro?", 24% said either "no one" or "don't know."[199]

Students

According to 79% of students, compared with 63% of the general public, the American political system "does not respond quickly enough to meet the needs of the people."[200] In another poll, 88% of the students believed "the American can respond effectively to the public need for change."[201] Finally, only 25% expressed "hardly any confidence" in the ability of the government to solve the problems of the 1970's.[202]

Summary of governmental responsiveness and effectiveness in general

In terms of the responsiveness of government, blacks are twice as likely as whites to believe that government fails to respond to their intersts. Students are probably only somewhat less confident than blacks in the speed of government responsiveness to their policy concerns. Even so, most students probably believe the government is responsive to needs for change and can solve the problems of the country.

Opinions on Policies Reflecting Nonresponsiveness

Such belief in the lack of responsiveness by government is related to particular problem areas and policies.

Blacks

A 1969 Newsweek survey reveals that black dissatisfaction with regime policies or programs is particularly severe toward the Vietnam War and the Draft, as well as the more significant policies on civil rights.[2 3] Moreover,

---

[198]Tomlinson, "Ideological...," p. 347; and Tomlinson, "Ideological," JSI, p. 105.

[199]Sears, "Political Attitudes...," p. 696.

[200]Gallup, "Special Report...," pp. 5-6. (Italics mine.)

[201]Lipset, Rebellion..., p. 54.

[202]Gallup, "The U.S. Campus...," p. 61.

[203]Harris, "Report from Black...," pp. 12-20.

black discontent on these issues was greater in 1969 than in 1966. For example, 33% in 1966 and 46% in 1969 believed the war in Vietnam was unfair to blacks.[204] Similarly, 25% in 1966 and 47% in 1969 believed the draft laws to be unfair to Negroes.[205] The black concern for the more fundamental inequities posed by civil rights issues has been covered much more extensively above.

Students

Most studies reveal general student support and approval of government institutions. Nevertheless, student disillusionment and activism on specific issues is high. According to Lipset, the "greatest hostility was directed against foreign policy and racial discrimination."[206] For example, when asked to rank six issues according to priority, the student respondents in a _Playboy_ survey chose the following order: the war in Vietnam, the race problem, the environment, repression, overpopulation, and the economy.[207]

The Gergens' 1969-1970 study attributes a radical shift in student political sentiment to opposition to the war in Vietnam.[208] Yet not until the spring of 1968 did the proportion of students who thought that "the United States had made a mistake in getting involved in Vietnam reach 50 percent."[209] Indeed, a Gallup poll of only a year earlier, spring 1967, revealed that 49% of college students classified themselves as "hawks" on the war in Vietnam.[210] By December, 1969, however, only 20% of the students would then classify themselves as "hawks," and 69% classified them-

---

[204]Ibid.   [205]Ibid.

[206]Lipset, Rebellion..., p. 56.

[207]"_Playboy's_ Student...," p. 182. The selection of these issues over economic concerns suggests, but does not prove, the strong influence of counter cultural values or the concerns of the privileged. The low rating of the economy in this priorities listing is surprising, since at the time of the poll in 1970, the national economy was beset by inflation and recession severe enough to contribute to substantial Republican losses at the polls (according to almost all political commentators).

[208]Gergens and Gergens, "Vietnam...," p. 1, cited by Lipset, Rebellion..., p. 47.

[209]Gallup, "Special Survey of College Students," Gallup Poll Release, June 29, 1968, cited by Lipset, Rebellion..., p. 41.

[210]Scranton Commission, P. 47.

selves as "doves."[211]Similarly, the 1971 Playboy survey
reveals that 9% of the students questioned in 1970, compared
to only 4% in 1971, wanted more aggressive action in Indo-
china.[212] In 1969, only 50% of students, versus 64% of the
adult public, "approved of the way President Nixon was
handling the situation in Vietnam."[213] Finally, in 1965,
only 6% of the students favored immediate withdrawal from
Vietnam; by May, 1970, 54% favored ending the fighting in
Vietman and bringing American troops home as soon as possible.[214] Such anti-war sentiment does not yet carry over
into a strictly anti-military or anti-defense posture.
According to one poll, only 25% felt that ROTC should
be completely removed from campus, while 37% felt that
it should be permitted on campus and should receive
academic credit.[215] Similarly, 72% believed that companies
doing defense business should be allowed to recruit on campus.

Another principal cause of the student shift to
radicalism is the "black issue." For example, the 1969
Urban Research Corporation study of incidents of student
protest on 232 campusis reported that "black recognition"
was a primary cause of campus protests. This survey
revealed that black issues were involved in 59% of the
campuses and 49% of the incidents.[216] Specific issues
included: "provide more courses on Black Studies" (32%);
"increase numbers of black students" (24%); "hire more
black faculty and staff" (23%); "end discrimination and
honor blacks" (15%); "provide more facilities for black
students" (9%); "increase black representation on general
committees" (8%); and "support off-campus black power"
and "hire black employees" (4%).[217] This study further
reveals that most of the incidents were mostly at white
institutions in the North, but such attitudes and issues
are also present and increasing among black students in
black colleges and universities in the South.

Strong feelings about the war and race carry over
into distinctive tactical responses for only a few. Thus,
although 62% in Ardery's student sample regarded the "black
power movement" as "an appropriate response to the condition

---

[211]Ibid., pp. 47-48.

[212]"Student Survey...," p. 208.

[213]Ibid.; and Scranton Commission, p. 48.

[214]Scranton Commission.

[215]Ibid.

[216]Ibid., p. 109.   [217]Ibid.

of the black person in America today,"[218] only 21% in
another study of student respondents reported they would
actually welcome "more vigorous protests by blacks"; 59%
said they would "disapprove of such protests."[219] This
lack of correlation between tactical responses and feelings
over war and race issues is also evident in student reactions to responses by authorities to student protests. For
example, 70% agreed that "school authorities are right" to
call in police when students occupy a building or threaten
violence. Even after the events of Kent State, 42% of the
students felt that "the National Guard has acted responsibly
in most cases" when it was called onto college campuses.[220]

The evidence in this section on political trust and
governmental responsiveness indicates that at least a minority of blacks and students (the New Left element) has a
strong feeling of illegitimacy or injustice concerning the
politics of the nation, if not toward the total political
system.

---

[218]Ardery, "Special...," p. 638.

[219]Lipset, Rebellion..., pp. 53-54.

[220]Scranton Commission, p. 48.

CHAPTER VII

INDIVIDUAL PARTICIPATION AND SUPPORT
FOR POLITICAL VIOLENCE

National Political Participation
in Normatively Sanctioned
Political Activities

One must approach participation in political violence in the context of other forms of political participation. Although most empirical data are concerned with voting, campaigns, and elections, that information may shed
some light on participation in political violence as well as
on normally sactioned political behavior. In order to
understand the role of political violence as a form of political participation, it is necessary to realize that levels
and forms of political participation are affected by several
factors. These influencing factors include the magnitude of
one's political interest, partisanship, information, personal
efficacy, political trust, and perceived responsiveness of
government. Thus, this first section of Chapter VII is a
discussion of participation in normally sanctioned political
activities in the light of these influencing factors.

Levels of Political Participation

Some forms of political activity are higher or
lower than others. Milbrath has estimated that perhaps 60%
of Americans are spectators, 33% are passive or apathetic,
and only 5% to 7% are gladiators.[1] Chart 2 indicates various levels of national participation for normal or regularly
sanctioned forms of political participation.[2] The types of

---

[1] Milbrath, Political..., p. 21.

[2] Adapted from ibid., p. 18; Lindblom, Policy
Making..., p. 45; and Julian L. Woodward and Elmo Roper,
"Political Activity of American Citizens," American Politi-
cal Science Review, Vol. XLIV (1950), p. 874. Milbrath's
figures are from Campbell et al., American Voter...; Robert
E. Lane, Political Life: Why People Get Involved in Poli-
tics (New York: The Free Press of Glencoe, 1959); and
Woodward and Roper, "Political...."

political activity differ somewhat from Milbrath's scheme.
The data surveyed in the chart reveal that although 40% to
70% of eligible voters do vote and participate in political
discussion, more active participation is low. Indeed, only
4% to 5% attend political caucuses or strategy sessions or
become active party members.[3] For the general public,
willingness to participate in normatively sanctioned politics, let alone peaceful protests and political violence,
is quite low.

Milbrath has suggested that the arrangement of political activities from least to most participation coincides
with the energy required for each. Accordingly, the data in
the chart can also be in the form of a hierarchy of the
opportunity costs of foregoing the investment of time to
other activities, such as work or leisure. In the light
of the fact that political violence requires such high
expenditures of time and energy-- not to mention incarcera-
tion, injury, or death-- it is not surprising that political
violence has not been a statistically significant form of
political participation and has also been of little interest
to political researchers. Thus, until recently, few have
given much attention to violence as a form of political
participation. Certainly, political violence is an extreme
form of political behavior, especially in the context of
low participation in even sanctioned varieties of political
activities.

Who then does participate in normally sanctioned
political activities? Demographically, the higher the educational level, socio-economic status, and age, the higher
the voter turn-out.[4] According to a study by Woodward and
Roper, the most active politically are: the upper-middle
(24%) to upper (36%) income groups (the upper 50% of the
population by income); those in the "higher" status occupations (executives [34%], professionals [32%], and stock
holders [28%]); and the college educated (24%).[5]

---

[3]Milbrath, Political..., p. 19.

[4]Campbell et al., Voter Decides...; and Bernard R.
Berelson, Paul F. Lazarsfeld, and William N. McPhee, Voting:
A Study in Opinion Formation in a Presidential Campaign
(Chicago: University of Chicago Press, 1966).

[5]Woodward and Roper, "Political...," p. 877.
"Finally, the economic security of most middle class occupations, the level of income they provide, the status they
confer, allow one to focus his attention on the subjective
and the ideational." (Melvin L. Kohn, "Social Class and
Parent-Child Relationships: An Interpretation," American
Journal of Sociology, Vol. LXVIII [1963], p. 447.) Even
children of higher socio-economic status families are more
often likely to give political referents on how to change
the world (Greenstein, Children..., p. 96).

CHART 2

APPROXIMATE PERCENTAGE OF AMERICAN CITIZENS PARTICIPATING IN VARIOUS FORMS OF NORMATIVELY SANCTIONED POLITICAL ACTIVITIES

Activities		Percentage	
		Per Activity	Total
Guardian Activities	Holding political office	less than 1	1-11
	Being a candidate	less than 1	
	Soliciting funds	less than 1	
	Attending a caucus or strategy meeting	4 - 5	
	Being an active party member	4 - 5	
Soldier Activities	Attending a political meeting	11[a]	7-21
	Contributing time in a political campaign	11[a]	
	Giving money	7-10[b]	
	Contacting an official	13-21[c]	
"Good" Citizen Activities	Displaying a button or auto sticker	15	15-40
	Belonging to a special interest group	33[d]	
	Attempting to talk another into voting a certain way	25-30	
	Initiating a discussion	25-30	
Passive Citizen Activities	Voting of eligibles[e]	40-80	40-80
	Exposing oneself to political stimuli	40-80	
	Identifying with a party	75	
Apathetic			20-30

[a]Woodward and Roper, "Political...," p. 874.

[b]Ibid.; and Milbrath, Political..., p. 19.

[c]Milbrath, Political..., pp. 19-20.   [d]Ibid., p. 108.

[e]Voting limited by residence requirements, illness, travel, barriers to blacks (Ibid., pp. 91-95; and Lane, Political Life...).

Conversely, only 15% of the next income group and 3% of the lowest income group are very active politically.[6] Similarly, the voter turn-out is usually low for the young, the less educated, the poor, and unskilled workers.[7] Of particular interest to this study, only 8% of the young adults (twenty-one to thirty-four years old) are very active, while 46% are very inactive. Similarly, 5% of blacks are very active, and 60% are very inactive.[8] A study done for the Violence Commission in 1968 came up with similar results but with one exception-- the young. Of those eighteen to thirty years old, 28% were very active in politics.[9] Unfortunately, the student sub-sample of this age group was too small for analysis. Apparently, the young today are more active than some earlier studies would indicate.[10]

---

[6]Woodward and Roper, "Political...," p. 877.

[7]Campbell et al., Voter Decides...; and Berelson, Lazarsfeld, and McPhee, Voting....

[8]Woodward and Roper, "Political...," p. 877.

[9]The highly active politically were those who felt they had a good financial future (57%), felt their economic status was getting better (56%), were salaried (45%), were suburbanites (36%), had some college education (29%), and the young (eighteen to thirty years old 28%). Note that of those above $15,000, 21% were active, while of those above $10,000 (the upper-middle class), 53% were highly active. According to this study, the highly active politically were those who said they had engaged in five out of the following political activities: political discussion, letter writing, contributions, petitioning, discussion with a government official, belonging to a political organization, demonstrating, illegal demonstrations, and rioting. See Sheldon G. Levy, "Attitudes toward Political Violence," Assassination and Political Violence, A staff report to the National Commission on the Causes and Prevention of Violence, Prepared by James F. Kirkham, Sheldon G. Levy, and William J. Crotty (New York: Bantam Books, 1970), pp. 510-513.

[10]The content of that activity is not necessarily, as many presume, mostly to the left. The age group twenty-one to twenty-nine gave higher support to George Wallace than any other age group in the 1968 presidential election. According to the Yankelovich poll of October, 1968, for Fortune, political support for Wallace by employed youth was 25% and by young manual workers, 31%. A pre-election Purdue Opinion poll showed 22% of high school students supported Wallace. These and similar results by Gallup, Harris, and the Michigan Survey Research Center are reported in Seymour Martin Lipset and Earl Raab, "The Wallace White-

Political Interest

According to Lazarsfeld and Berelson, political participation is partially a function of political interest.[11] Several studies reveal that most Americans are not very interested in politics. About a third are interested in elections, and another fifth may care a great deal who wins.[12] Such concern over who wins, however, may depend on the election. For example, in 1946, 50% said the election would make a great deal of difference.[13] Nevertheless, when asked to express their personal hopes and fears, Americans express little concern over political objects.[14] Such an attitude begins early. For example, when asked to name "a famous person you would want or not want to be like," most children choose the heroes of the popular culture rather than political figures.[15]

Perhaps, as Milbrath suggests in his analysis of participation in various political activities, interest in politics may relate to the time and energy required for personal necessities. Indeed, 66% polled in one survey said they just "don't have the time for politics."[16] Thus the low political participation among the young, the less educated, the poor, and blacks is probably due to the fact that these groups must spend greater time and energy on other necessary or more desired personal activities.

Lash," Ghetto Riots, ed. Peter H. Rossi (New York: Aldine Publishing Co., 1970), p. 154. See also Lipset and Raab, Politics of Unreason....

[11]Paul F. Lazarsfeld, Bernard Berelson, and Hazel Gaudet, The People's Choice: How the Voter Makes up His Mind in a Presidential Election (3rd ed.; New York: Columbia University Press, 1968); and Berelson, Lazarsfeld, and McPhee, Voting....

[12]Campbell et al., Voter Decides...; and Lazarsfeld, Berelson, and Gaudet, People's Choice....

[13]Cantril and Struck, Public..., p. 582. Fred I. Greenstein, "Benevolent Leader: Children's Images of Political Authority," Readings in Modern Political Analysis, ed. Robert A. Dahl and Deane E. Neubauer (Englewood Cliffs, N. J.: Prentice-Hall, Inc., 1968), p. 347, n. 3.

[14]Free and Cantril, Political..., p. 100.

[15]Greenstein, Children..., p. 99.

[16]Jack Jensen, "Political Participation: A Survey in Evanston, Illinois" (unpublished Master's thesis, Northwestern University, 1960), cited by Milbrath, Political..., p. 75.

Apparently, the affluent , students, and intellectuals are better able to budget their time and energy. Maslow's hierarchy of values may be suggestive here. Perhaps food, sex, sleep, safety,[17] and affection may have higher priorities for most individuals. On the other hand, as government seeks to regulate or redistribute activities and good related to food (welfare, food stamps, jobs), sex (abortion and birth control), and safety (automobiles and additives in food), these groups with previously low political participation-- the young, less educated, poor, and blacks-- may become more active politically. Certainly, such government activities affect a broad range of everyday personal interests and thus may stimulate interest among a wider range of poeple.

Several studies indicate that low levels of political interest are reflected in low levels of political information. For example, Greenstein reports that

> only 19 per cent of the adult electorate can name the three branches of government, a third can identify the Bill of Rights, and about half know who is Secretary of State.[18]

Similarly, according to a study by Walter F. Murphy and Joseph Tananhaus, 34.7% of a 1966 national sample of Americans had no idea what the main job of the Court is.[19] Finally, in the midst of an era of political violence, 37% of whites and 51% of blacks had never heard of the Students for a Democratic Society (S.D.S.).[20]

---

[17]Of over 28 million people receiving manufacturers' recall notices involving the safety of their automobiles, 28% did not respond to the call (Jack Anderson, "Washington Merry-go-round," San Francisco Chronicle, April 5, 1972.

[18]Greenstein, Children..., p. 56. See also Erskine, "Textbook...," pp. 137-140. For a general discussion of voter information, see Fred I. Greenstein, The American Party Systems and the American People (Englewood Cliffs, N. J.: Prentice-Hall, Inc., 1963), pp. 12-16, and the other references cited there.

[19]Muller, "A Test...," p. 63, n. 51. See Walter F. Murphy and Joseph Tanenhaus, "Public Opinion and the United States Supreme Court: A Preliminary Mapping of Some Prerequisites for Court Legislation of Regime Changes," Frontiers of Judicial Research, ed. Joel B. Grossman and Joseph Tanenhaus (New York: Wiley, 1969).

[20]Muller, "A Test...," p. 29.

The level of political information may be a function of the energy required to become informed. Sources of political information in the 1956 election were: 74% television, 69% newspapers, 45% radio, and 31% magazines.[21] Among these sources of political information, those requiring the greatest expenditures of energy are newspapers and magazines. Thus, the failure of newspapers and magazines during the 1960's and 1970's may indicate even lessening energies devoted to obtaining political information and probably less political information as well. Such low levels of political information certainly indicate low levels of political interest.

Almond and Verba's review and comments on the literature on citizen interest and participation pose not only a methodological problem but also the prospects for the success of a highly participatory democracy:

> Recent students of political behavior call the rationality-activist model into question for it is becoming clear that citizens in democracies rarely live up to this model. They are not well informed, not deeply involved, not particularly active; and the process by which they come to their voting decision is anything but a process of rational calculation. Nor does this model accurately represent the civic culture we have found in Britain and the United States. It is true-- and this point is both substantively important as well as indicative of the usefulness of comparative data-- that the informed, involved, rational, and active citizen is more frequently found in the successful than in the unsuccessful democracies.[22]

Almond and Verba's claim that participatory democracy is more successful is probably not empirically verified and raises several doubts. As the ideological demands for greater participation and the rewards and stakes of politics increase, political conflict may also increase. Such increases in political conflict may be due to the arousal of previously latent political interests or the increasing role of intensely partisan majorities or minorities. Whether such political conflict will be more violent or not may be evident in the events of recent American politics. In any case, a crucial variable in explaining political interest and hence political participation is political partisanship.

---

[21]V. O. Key, Jr., Public Opinion and American Democracy (New York: Alfred Knopf, 1961), p. 346, cited by Lindbloom, Policy-making..., p. 52.

[22]Almond and Verba, Civic Culture..., p. 338. For a discussion of rationality in voting, see Berelson, Lazarsfeld, and McPhee, Voting....

Political Partisanship

Partisanship has many degrees of intensity and dimensions of content. It can range from heated discussion to violence or from the abstract to the particular. Ultimately, a situation becomes partisan when it involves personal interests. Thus, if an issue is abstract and involves someone else's interest and not one's own, political interest and activity is usually low. For example, the intensity of American responses to a hypothetically "unjust or harmful national law" was low. Though 77% said they would do something, less than 1% would use violence; most (59%) would contact political leaders.[23]

Perhaps unspecified laws or most principles are too abstract to arouse the average citizen. One study showed that only 15.5% of Americans had "well structured" ideological perceptions.[24] Indeed, another study reveals that only 50% know the meaning of "liberal" or "conservative."[25] According to McClosky, party activists are more likely than the public at large (1) to be strongly liberal or conservative, or (2) to want to "change things for the better" (86% to 66%).[26] Only well educated professionals and intellectuals do much philosophizing. Accordingly, these groups are also most directly motivated by clearly defined abstract doctrines and principles.[27] On the other hand, most citizens are probably motivated by political decisions and issues which affect them concretely and directly.[28] Indeed, only 17.5% in one national study voted apparently without any reference to any political issues.[29] Similarly, 45% probably vote according to group benefits.[30] Nevertheless, Americans as a whole are not politically organized.

---

[23]Levy, "Attitudes...," pp. 499-501.

[24]Campbell et al., American Voter..., p. 249.

[25]Philip E. Converse, "The Nature of Belief Systems in Mass Publics," Ideology and Discontent, ed. David Apter (Glencoe, Ill.: Free Press, 1964), p. 222.

[26]McClosky, Hoffman, and O'Hara, "Issue Conflict...."

[27]Lane, Political Life..., pp. 97 ff; and Campbell et al., American Voter..., pp. 188-215; and Blondel, An Introduction..., p. 480, n. 3.

[28]Dahl, Who Governs..., p. 267.

[29]Campbell et al., American Voter..., p. 249.

[30]Ibid.

For example, although probably more organized than any other
national population, only 38% of Americans belong to special
interest groups with peripherial and temporary political
interests.[31]
Despite low levels of political organization among
citizens, the pre-existing political parties and their
candidates provide citizens with vehicles to express their
preferences in terms of personal interests. Indeed, Campbell and Lazarsfeld suggest the political parties and
candidates may actually arouse personal interests (partisanship), expecially where the party system is highly
competitive.[32] For example, the "out" party or group is
usually more partisan than the "in" party or group.[33] Thus,
42% of conservatives, versus only 18% of liberals, gave
political referents to their personal hopes and fears in
1964 when liberalism was clearly ascendant.[34] Similarly,
when citizens perceive or believe a particular election
involves a crisis[35] or presents clear alternatives,[36] voter
turn-outs are much higher.
Apparently, the intensity of partisanship is related
to whether or not one believes one's interests are represented properly (one's party preference is in power) or, stated
another way, the degree of tolerance one has for the other
point of view. Thus, a high degree of partisanship may reflect a low degree of tolerance for one's opponent.[37] Cer-

---

[31]Milbrath, Political..., p. 24.

[32]Ibid., p. 45; Campbell et al., American Voter...;
and Lazarsfeld, Berelson, and Gaudet, People's Choice....

[33]R. S. Milne and H. C. Mackenzie, A Study of Voting
Behavior in the Constituency of Bristol North-East at the
General Election, 1951 (London: Hansard Society, 1954),
cited by Berelson, Lazarsfeld, and McPhee, Voting..., p.
332. For a review of voting behavior findings during 1940-
1952, see Berelson, Lazarsfeld, and McPhee, Voting...,
pp. 331-347.

[34]Free and Cantril, Political..., p. 100.

[35]Lane, Political Life...; Milbrath, Political...;
and V. O. Key, "A Theory of Critical Elections," Journal of
Politics, Vol. XVII (1955), pp. 3-18.

[36]Angus Campbell, "Surge and Decline: A Study of
Electoral Change," Public Opinion Quarterly, Vol. XXIV
(Fall, 1960), pp. 397-418; Angus Campbell, "The Passive
Citizen," Acta Sociologica, Vol. VI, fasc. 1-2 (1962), pp
9-12; and Milbrath, Political..., p. 105.

[37]Campbell et al., Voter Decides....

tainly, those who turn out on the street or on campus to do battle indicate a low degree of tolerance for the politics of those in power. Thus, such intense partisanship, reflecting a desire for both political power and moral politics, is probably that kind of partisanship most likely to lead to violence. Fortunately, in his study of national attitudes, Almond categorized only 10% as intensely partisan, while 82% were mildly partisan, and 8% were apathetic.[38]

Which issues are most likely to result in intense partisanship? According to Kirkham's study of the politically vengeant (those desiring the death of some politicians or political opponents), the most intense partisanship revolves around racial issues.[39] Thus, partisan racial attitudes are the most probable source of political violence. Nationally, only 12% were politically vengeant. Those with lower incomes and education were the most politically vengeant, while those with incomes over $10,000 (5% to 6%) and with some college education (6% to 7%) were the least vengeant. Among the politically vengeant, 45% of the high vengeant whites preferred George Wallace for President. This fact clearly indicates the possibility of racial attitudes among whites leading to political violence. This may be particularly true in the South, where 16% of whites were politically vengeant.

Kirkham's summary of political vengeance among blacks may also help reveal where black political violence may appear. According to Kirkham, 28% of eastern blacks, 21% of southern blacks, and 20% of all blacks were politically vengeant.[40] Black allegiance to the Black Panthers and the Black Muslims may also reflect this partisanship. One study found this potentially anti-regime allegiance to be relatively low: 13% of blacks expressed allegiance to the Panthers, and 29% expressed allegiance to the Muslims.[41] Nevertheless, those blacks expressing allegiance to the Panthers and Muslims were also the most likely to express approval of political violence. Apparently, the greater the intensity of partisanship, whether among blacks or whites, the greater the potential for violence.

---

[38] Almond and Verba, Civic Culture..., p. 114. Partisanship measured by attitudes toward cross-party marriage.

[39] Kirkham, Levy, and Crotty, Assassination..., pp. 245-264.

[40] All the above figures are gleaned from Ibid.

[41] Muller, "A Test...," p. 30. See also Tomlinson, "Development...."

Political Efficacy

Even with the existence of political interest largely enhanced by the existence of partisan doctrines, issues, and interests, active political participation beyond voting and letter writing is limited. Only a few have an adequate sense of their own efficacy,[42] competence,[43] or capabilities to actively participate in and influence political outcomes. Those having high beliefs in their own political efficacy and capabilities tend to come from higher educated and income groups. Greenstein reports that

> in 1960, the following three partially overlapping categories of citizens stood at the top of a ranking of groups by their turnout in the presidential election: College educated (90 percent voted); professional and managerial occupations (88 percent); other white-collar workers (84 per cent). At the other end of the ranking were three different, and also overlapping, groupings; unskilled workers (68 per cent voted); grade school educated (67 per cent); Negroes (54 per cent).[44]

Depending on the survey item, 20% to 36% of the variation on political efficacy correlates with education and income, but education generally "explains" more of the variance in political efficacy scales than income in the Survey Research Center studies of 1952, 1956, 1960, and 1968. Those least likely to feel powerless are the educated (-.44), professionals (-.32), and those in higher income groups (-.31).[45]

---

[42]See Robinson, Rusk, and Head, _Measures Political..._, p. 628; Berelson, Lazarsfeld, and McPhee, _Voting..._; and Campbell _et al._, _Voter Decides..._. Survey Research Center index of political efficacy includes items on (1) "how much say" the average citizen has in politics, (2) whether voting is the "only way to influence politics," (3) whether "politics is too complicated," and (4) whether officials "care" about the average citizen. Some of these items are also used in other scales and perhaps could be replaced by other questions which might tap the dimension of political efficacy more precisely. See Robinson, Rusk, and Head, _Measures Political...._

[43]Almond and Verba, _Civic Culture...._

[44]Greenstein, _Children..._, p. 184. See also Campbell _et al._, _Voter Decides..._, pp. 187-189.

[45]Finifter, "Dimensions...," pp. 398-399.

The educated are, of course, more likely to have the requi-
site skills for understanding political issues, and those in
the higher income groups may have more leisure time and
energy to devote to political interests.[46] It seems reasonable and almost totally unremarkable that the educated would
be able to recognize their own cognitive, verbal, and social
skills. On the other hand, the less educated are less likely
to have developed such skills. Similarly, non-professional
and low income people often have less flexibility in the use
of their time and energies.

Yet, as an alternative explanation, the wording of
the items used in the political efficacy scales may tend to
sort out such demographic groups. The affluent and well-
educated are particularly unlikely to respond to items which
require them to compare theselves invidiously with others.
Such persons are hardly "average" or likely to respond to
such folksy phrases as "people like me." The well-educated
are also unlikely to respond to items which require them to
advertise their ignorance-- "the world is too complicated"--
or to say that "voting is the only form of political participation." Such items do not merely determine a psychological sense of political efficacy or competence, they also
elicit distinctly class related responses. The problem is
how to measure attitudes of self-assurance among the poor
and the less educated.

Political Efficacy, Political Trust,
and Political Violence

Many studies reveal that generally a sense of one's
own civic competience,[47] self-esteem,[48] capabilities, or
political efficacy[49] is directly related to participation
in conventional forms of political activity. Conversely, a
low sense of political efficacy presumably encourages non-
conventional political activity-- perhaps even violence.[50]
Several studies have found that those with a low sense of
personal efficacy, self-esteem, or subjective competence and
power[51]-- the extremists, authoritarians, cynics, cabalists,

---

[46]See Greenstein, Children..., pp. 90 and 94, where
he reports on the work of Dahl, Who Governs..., and others.

[47]Almond and Verba, Civic Culture..., pp. 190-196.

[48]Lane, Political Ideology....

[49]Almond and Verba, Civic Culture....

[50]Campbell, Sahid, and Stang, Law..., pp. 129-134.

[51]Neal and Seeman, "Organizations...," pp. 216-225.

and conspirators-- are most likely not to support democratic
ideologies, rules, institutions, or authorities. They are
also less likely to participate in democratic politics.
They feel a sense of inferiority, powerlessness, and normlessness. As some militants have suggested, they may even
sense an absence of their "manhood" or equality. Thus,
"demonstration-prone individuals are more likely to have
higher feelings of political efficacy than riot-prone
individuals."[52]
   According to Campbell, Sahid, and Stang,

   the perception of personal effectiveness in politics,
   or "political efficacy" is related to satisfaction
   with government and ... a strong sense of political
   efficacy seems to be necessary to motivate persons
   to express their demands in conventional, nonviolent
   modes.[53]

Political satisfaction and political trust[54] are usually
considered to be a function of the degree to which citizens
believe the government responds to or represents the people.
Thus, low levels of responsiveness apparently lead to low
levels of satisfaction, high distrust, a low sense of political efficacy, and ultimately to violence. There is evidence that some citizens perceive government to be nonresponsive and nonrepresentative. For example, studies
in 1964 and 1966 reveal that 24% to 29% felt that government
pays more attention to big shots, big interests, and
crooks than to ordinary people.[55] Similarly, 27% to 35%
of a national sample in several Survey Research Center
studies from 1952 to 1968 agreed with the statement:
"People like me don't have any say about what the government
does."[56] Thus, a significant minority (25% to 35%) of the

---

[52]Everett F. Cataldo, Richard M. Johnson, and Lyman
A. Kellstedt, "The Urban Poor and Community Action in
Buffalo," A paper presented at the annual meeting of the
Midwestern Political Science Association, Chicago, May 2-3,
1968, cited by Campbell, Sahid, and Stang, Law..., p. 128.

[53]Campbell, Sahid, and Stang, Law..., p. 127.

[54]See Robinson, Rusk, and Head, Measures Political..., p. 628. The Political Trust Scale includes diverse
items on waste in government, general trust in government,
crooks in government, government people being similar to
ordinary people, and government being representative of the
big people.

[55]Ibid., p. 644.

[56]This item is from the Political Efficacy Scale,

national population seems to have little faith or trust in
the political system.

Yet, how much of this distrust is due to political
efficacy or to nonresponsive government? The degree of
political trust in 1958 and 1964 Survey Research Center
studies did not seem to be influenced by demographic variables, which do affect a personal sense of political
efficacy.[57] Similarly, Almond and Verba found a span of
only 8% to 12% for level of education in citizen's expectations of "equal and considerate treatment" by the American national government.[58] Thus, personal competence is
probably a dimension quite separate from one's sense of
trust as reflected in one's perception of government
responsiveness. Nevertheless, a lack of political trust,
based on low levels of perceptions of government responsiveness, lead potentially to political cynicism and
ultimately to violent political participation. According
to Campbell, this feeling of cynicism or

> the sense that ... the policies of government neglect
> the individual ... becomes important because a recent
> study suggests that those who "participate" in uncon-
> ventional fashions-- demonstrations and rioting--
> share a strong cynicism.[59]

Several other studies have also recognized that a
personal sense of anomie, cynicism, or alienation results
in low levels of conventional political participation.[60]

---

but seems to tap the political trust dimension. Campbell
summarized data from the Survey Research Center and a
1968 Harris poll prepared for the Violence Commission.
The figures on four year increments from 1952 to 1968
were: 31%, 28%, 27%, 29%, 34%, and 35% (Campbell, Sahid,
and Stang, Law..., p. 130).

[57]Most correltions were low, falling below -.06
for sex, race, education, income, age, community size, and
party identification (Robinson, Rusk, and Head, Measures
Political..., p. 628.

[58]Almond and Verba, Civic Culture..., pp. 73-74.

[59]Campbell, Sahid, and Stang, Law..., p. 128,
reporting on Cataldo, Johnson, and Kellstedt, "Urban
Poor...."

[60]Milbrath, Political..., pp. 78-79, summarizes
data from Agger, Goldstein, and Pearl, "Political Cynicism..."; Campbell, "Passive..."; Litt, "Political Cynicism..."; and Morris Rosenberg, "Some Determinants of
Political Apathy," Public Opinion Quarterly, Vol. XVIII
(Winter, 1954-1955), pp. 349-366.

Yet, whether this form of alienation can be attributed to low levels of political responsiveness or political efficacy is not certain. Some researchers have interpreted agreement with the statement that "voting is the only way people like me can have a say about how government runs things" reflects a sense of political cynicism or political futility about government. Certainly, black agreement with this statement and the fact that blacks have low voter turn-out may reveal that they have little confidence in their capacity to participate effectively in any conventional form of political activity. The futility felt by blacks is even more apparent in the findings of the Los Angeles Riot Study, in which 78% of blacks, versus 41% of whites, agreed with the statement: "Voting is the only way people like me can have a say about how government runs things."[61]

Yet there is some evidence that among whites voting alone may be at least a fair measure of political trust and support for the political system. The results of Survey Research Center national surveys during 1952, 1956, and 1960 reveal that 81% to 92% of the national sample believed voting is a duty.[62] In these studies, a full 44% to 55% believed that voting is a duty even if one doesn't "care how an election comes out."[63] Similarly, 75% of the Woodward and Roper national respondents reported voting "once or more in the last four years."[64] In view of these national results, low black voter turn-outs in the context of wide national support for voting may reveal the extent of black disillusionment over the effectiveness of their vote. Such low voter turn-outs among blacks, however, are not necessarily an indication of low levels of political trust.

Some Difficulties of Interpretation

Even after a survey of the data, the hypothetical connections between political efficacy, political trust, and violence are not without considerable problems of interpretation. As already indicated, the influence of demographic characteristics of education, occupation, and wealth on political efficacy indicate that political efficacy may be

---

[61]Tomlinson, "Ideological...," p. 346. For a report on Survey Research Center and 1968 Harris Poll prepared for the Violence Commission, see Campbell, Sahid, and Stang, Law..., p. 130.

[62]Robinson, Rusk, and Head, Measures Political..., pp. 639-640.

[63]Ibid.

[64]Woodward and Roper, "Political...," p. 874.

a status biased measure, rather than a measure of those phychological states likely to lead to violence. Such demographic data may be "surrogate" variables actually standing for something else, such as one's objective capabilities, independent of both one's political trust and one's likelihood to engage in political violence.[65]

Many writers have claimed a low sense of political efficacy to be reasonably predictive of extreme political behavior by lower socio-economic groups-- poor whites and poor blacks.[66] Since the more educated and the middle and upper classes are politically more active or at least feel more capable of high political participation,[67] they usually score high in political efficacy and low on political extremism. Thus, few predicted the present political dissent and revolt among a sizeable minority of upper-middle class white college students, professors, and intellectuals-- the politically efficacious. Similarly, as of 1972, a large number of behavioralist-oriented political scientists have been incorrect in predicting the development of an American brand of fascism, authoritarianism, and a racial blood bath derived from the intolerance of the relatively under-educated lower-middle class whites. These behavioralists, of course, have been reasonably accurate with respect to a small group of southern white terrorists. Yet they have only parenthetically predicted the present Negro revolt, and most have misdirected their attention to lower status whites. In response to this problem, Olsen attempted to show that different classes were predisposed to different kinds of political alienation: the lower classes are more likely to have feelings of _incapacity_, and the upper-middle class is more likely to have feelings of _discontent_.[68]

Similarly, items in the scale of cynicism and futility may not measure what they claim to test. For example, McClosky's survey reveals several items which he says may contribute to the lack of influence in politics which 61.5% of his respondents felt. Among these factors are perhaps realistic recognition of the complexity of politics (67.5%) and the existence of considerable political wheeling and dealing (60.5%).[69] Perhaps these factors

---

[65]Muller, "A Test...," pp. 36 and 40.

[66]See Kirkham, Levy, and Crotty, Assassination...: Adorno et al., Authoritarian...; and Campbell, Sahid, and Stang, Law....

[67]Campbell et al., Voter Decides....

[68]Olsen, "Two Categories...," quoted in Robinson and Shaver, Measures Sociological..., pp. 164, 181-182.

[69]McClosky, "Consensus and Ideology..."; and Campbell, Sahid, and Stang, Law..., p. 30.

reflect extreme scepticism or even an objective sense of political realism rather than a deep-rooted cynicism about the power, authority, and influence of the solitary, unaffluent, and uneducated citizen.[70]

Moreover, for those citizens believing American democracy means representative government rather than a high level of citizen participation, voting is an adequate political right and perhaps the only political obligation as well.[71] Where possible, a protest vote on such issues as open housing,[72] taxes,[73] welfare,[74] and school busing[75] may be adequate to alleviate the irritations some citizens feel toward some specifically irksome policies of the otherwise legitimate system. Indeed, 71% of Almond's respondents found satisfaction in voting.[76] Survey Research Center studies in 1964 show that most citizens believed that elections did indeed make government pay attention to the people: 65% felt elections did so "a great deal," while 25% felt they did so only "some."[77]

A citizen's lack of such perceptions of his own political efficacy or capacity to actively participate becomes a problem only if he really desires much greater participation because of some deep-seated dissatisfaction. Finally, participation in political violence is probably not a function of low sense of political efficacy. Hardly any studies of black or student violence show that the "riff-raff" participate. It is probably true that participation in political violence, as in all forms of politics, is based on a high sense of personal esteem, competence, confidence, and efficacy. For example, Tomlinson points out that "racial partisanship and alienation" are most apparent

---

[70]See Lane, _Political Ideology...._

[71]Robinson, Rusk, and Head, _Measures Political...,_ pp. 639-640.

[72]Runsford Fair Housing Act, 1964.

[73]Taxpayers' revolt in local and state bond issues during the late 1960's and early 1970's.

[74]Elections of Ronald Reagan in California and Rockefeller in New York.

[75]Michigan and Florida presidential primaries, 1972.

[76]Almond and Verba, _Civic Culture...,_ p. 108.

[77]Robinson, Rusk, and Head, _Measures Political...,_ p. 641.

among the "younger, better educated Negro respondents."[78]
Even though low political efficacy and nonresponsiveness
may be reflected in low levels of political trust, such
feelings are not necessarily connected with political violence at all. Indeed, quite the opposite is true. Those
with a low sense of political efficacy are more likely to
withdraw, while the revolutionary is the one most likely to
have a high sense of his political competence.

Finally, the usual answer to perceptions of a nonresponsive government is to seek "maximum feasible" participation. Yet, according to Berelson, high participation
may lead to debilitating cleavages, while low participation
softens and blurs divisions.[79] There is some small empirical evidence to back up such an only apparent democratic
elitist hypothesis. Finifter found a sense of normlessness
(defined as a sense of a fairness and equality of treatment
by political authorities) was not affected by political
participation:

> Neither organization membership, nor being an officer,
> nor political participation can explain as much as 2%
> of the variation in the perceived normlessness scores.
> ... Participation has practically no effect on whether
> or not one perceives norm violating behavior by govern-
> ment officials.
> ....
> Cynicism about the behavior of public officials is
> evidently sufficiently persistent that participation,
> even in the political process itself, does not serve
> to reduce [normlessness] substantially.[80]

Actually, participation may tend to increase perceptions of
normlessness.[81] Though Finifter presents no direct
statistical evidence,

> the fact that men and native-born citizens ... have
> higher normlessness scores than do women and the
> foreign-born (who participate less) strengthens the
> implication that high scores on normlessness are
> partially a function of knowledge and experience with
> the political system.[82]

---

[78]Tomlinson, "Determinants...," p. 250.

[79]Berelson, Lazarsfeld, and McPhee, Voting...,
p. 316.

[80]Finifter, "Dimensions...," pp. 401, 404.

[81]Ibid., p. 406.

[82]Ibid.

In various studies, there is some evidence that mobile, college-educated people with higher participation have higher levels of alienation.

Thus, political alienation, distrust, and a sense of the illegitimacy of the system are probably independent of government responsiveness and participation in conventional forms of political activity. Yet, participation in political violence may be influenced by the same factors as participation in conventional politics. Active participation in conventional politics is generally low and depends on the existence of contributing factors, such as political interests, the availability of time and energy, partisanship, and political trust. Participation in violent politics probably requires an intensification of political interest, political partisanship, and self-confidence before political distrust can be converted into political violence. Indeed, Kirkham reports that "the politically active do account to a highly significant degree for revolutionary violence."[84]

Political Participation and Support for Political Violence

Participation in Political Violence

In other than a spectator capacity,[85] actual violent participation in urban and campus disorders is not high and includes only about 2% to 20% of those living in the vicinity.

Students
        In 1964, the student occupation of Sproul Hall and capture of the police car involved only about 2% of the student body of Berkeley.[86] At Columbia in 1968, approx-

---

[83]Ibid., p. 406, n. 49.

[84]Kirkham, Levy, and Crotty, Assassination...,
p. 273.

[85]According to the Kerner Commission, p. 128, in Detroit, 20% to 25% were admitted spectators, and another 14% tried to counter the rioting. My personal impression is that higher percentages watched the Watts riot in 1965.

[86]Calculated from figures in Glen Lyonns, "The Police Car Demonstrations," The Berkeley Student Revolt: Facts and Interpretations, ed. Seymour Martin Lipset and Sheldon S. Wolin (Garden City: Doubleday-Anchor Books, 1965), pp. 519-530. See also Peterson, "Student...," pp. 202-231.

imately 3% were involved in the occupation of several
buildings, ransacking of President Kirk's office, and
holding a dean prisoner. (Nearly 10% of the student body
was arrested in demonstrations in reaction to police
actions at Columbia.)[87] Many students admit to milder
forms of protest behavior. For example, in one Harris
survey, 18% of the students admitted to having
engaged in civil disobedience, and only 4% had gone to
jail.[88]

Blacks

The participation of urban blacks in riots is
higher than for students, but it still involves only a
small portion of the whole black population. Nationwide,
from 8% to 16% of blacks admit they would join or have
already participated in a riot.[89] The most common figure
in a great number of surveys is approximately 15%, which
corresponds closely to actual participation as estimated
by Cohen for the Watts riot of 1965 and by the Kerner
Commission for the urban riots in 1967.[90] For cities
having actual riot experience, the figures are somewhat
higher. For example, the figure for South Central Los
Angeles is 22%.[91] In all studies, whether for campus or
ghetto populations, young teenage males have participated

---

[87]See Daniel Bell, "Columbia and the New Left,"
Public Interest, No. 13 (Fall, 1963), pp. 61-101.

[88]Louis Harris, "Aversion to Vietnam War Reaches
High Among College Students, Harris Survey," Scranton
Tribune (Scranton, Penn.), June 30, 1969.

[89]Campbell and Schuman, "Radical...," p. 56; also
Tomlinson, "Determinatns...," p. 247, where he reports on
a Barss-Rietzel Corporation study.

[90]The Kerner Commission reports admitted participation for blacks was 11%. Other figures reported and their
sources are: 11% with an additional 13% leaning toward the
use of violence (Phillip Meyer, "Aftermath of Martyrdom:
Negro Militancy and Martin Luther King," Public Opinion
Quarterly [Summer, 1969], p. 161); 12% (Campbell and
Schuman, "Racial...," p. 52); 15% (Brink and Harris,
Black...,p. 265); 15% (Cohen, "Press Release...," p. 4);
11% (Harris, "Report from Black..."); 15% plus 24% not
sure (Harris, "Black and White..."); 16% (Barss-Rietzel
Corporation study, cited by Tomlinson, "Determinants...,"
p. 247). Muller found 7% of blacks with "intentions to
engage in political violence" in Waterloo, Iowa in 1970
(Muller, "A Test...," p. 16).

[91]Murphy and Watson, "The Structure...," p. 172.

214

at a rate approximately twice as high as teenage females.[92]
For example, in Sears and MacConahay's study in Los Angeles,
32% of all young people (fifteen to twenty-nine years old)
reported active participation in the Watts riot, while over
41% of the yong males from fifteen to twenty-nine reported
active participation.[93]

Nationally
        Campbell and Schuman report that approximately 6% of
whites think that if Negroes riot again, whites should do
some counter rioting. The male figure is 8%, the female
figure is 3%. For young white males sixteen to nineteen
years old, the figure is 12%, only somewhat less than the
figure of 15% for the black population as a whole.[94]

Summary of participation in
political violence
        Given the high risks, the uncertain benefits, and
low levels of participation in all forms of political activity, it should not be surprising that only a minority of
even an extremely disenchanted community would participate
in the most severe forms of violence. According to the
Kerner Commission, only one-half of 1% of arrests during
the 1967 black riots in nineteen cities were for arson.[95]
Most arrests were for looting and violations of police
curfew orders. Levels of moral support and approval are
a great deal higher than figures on actual participation.
Such moral approval is analytically more important for the
hypotheses of this paper involving the relationships
between verbal justifications and participation in political
violence.

Support for Political Violence:
Approval and Effectiveness

        Muller provides some statistical evidence for a
strong relationship between approval of and participation
in violence:

---

        [92]Among males, 20% said they were ready to join a
riot, versus 10% of females (Campbell and Schuman,
"Racial...," p. 52).

        [93]Sears and MacConahay, "The Politics...," p. 416.

        [94]Campbell and Schuman, "Racial...," pp. 56-59.

        [95]Kerner Commission, p. 334.

> Somer's d (symmetric) is .53: [that is] 53 percent of
> the total ordinal variation in APV [Approval of Politi-
> cal Violence] and IEPV [Intention to Engage in Political
> Violence] is shared in common. Assuming interval meas-
> urement, r^2 is .47r: [that is] 47 percent of the vari-
> ance in APV and IEPV is shared in common.[96]

Yet relatively lower participation than actual support for
political violence is understandable from several angles.
Muller says,

> Some of the elderly either say explicitly that they are
> too old, or else this can be inferred from their
> advanced age; also, quite a few of the respondents say
> they are afraid of reprisal from the state-- the state
> has too much coercive power.[97]

The individual costs of energy and life are high for actual
participation in political violence, while the direct benefits for the individual may be uncertain.

Normative approval of political violence

Though few in the past have admitted to being
willing to engage in violence, a third or more of the black
population and a similar figure on selected campuses give
positive endorsement to political activity more severe than
peaceful mass demonstrations. In contrast, the American
public disapproves overwhelmingly of such activity. For
example, 58% of the nation disapproved of riots so much
that they supported the shooting of looters.[98] These views
are in marked contrast to those in the urban centers and on
campus. In response to a more general question of whether
violence is sometimes justified to change American society,
only 14% of the national sample agreed, versus 44% of college students.[99] Muller discovered that 58% of whites,
versus 34% of blacks, were "unwilling to engage in any
deviant dissent behavior."[100]

Nationally

Nationally, the responses have been in overwhelming
opposition not only to campus and urban violence, but also
to peaceful demonstrations. In 1969, only 17% said that
protests by students, blacks, and anti-war demonstrators

---

[96]Muller, "A Test...," p. 17.   [97]Ibid.

[98]Gallup, "Public Sees...."

[99]Gallup, "Four in Ten...."

[100]Muller, "A Test...," p. 15.

should be continued.[101] On the other hand, in an incredible
act of empathy, 26% of whites indicated in 1967 that they
would be "mad, resentful and [would] fight back" if "discriminated against as a Negro."[102] Generally, affirmative
support of violence is higher for samples of blacks and
students than it is in the national population as a whole.

Blacks
        Among blacks, the figures vary from 13% in Oakland
believing violence is justified where self-defense is <u>not</u>
involved to 34% in Watts making comments coded as favorable
to violence.[103] In a 1969 <u>Newsweek</u> national survey, 31% of
blacks believed that past riots had been justified.[104]
Further indirect evidence of approval of violence is that
19% of the black community in 1966 supported the then
relatively unknown but violent-talking black militants
Floyd McKissick and Stokely Carmichael.[105] By 1969 in

---

[101]Louis Harris, "Protests Hit a Rut," <u>Boston Globe</u>,
September 8, 1969.

[102]Harris, "After...." See also Erskine, "Demonstrations...."

[103]William McCord and John Howard, "Negro Opinions
in Three Riot Cities," <u>American Behavioral Scientist</u>, Nos.
2, 4 (March/April, 1968), p. 26; and Cohen, "Press Release...," p. 4. Other figures and sources are: 27% made
favorable comments on what happened in the Watts riot, and
30% gave approval to riot participants (Sears and MacConahay,
"Riot Particiaption," p. 271); 20% in Houston and 29% in
Watts justified violence for a variety of reasons other than
self-defense (McCord and Howard, "Negro...," p. 26); 36.4%
of males and 23.5% of females made favorable comments about
the Watts riot (Murphy and Watson, "The Structure...," p.
174); 14% said violence is essentially good (Roger Beardwood, "A <u>Fortune</u> Study of the New Negro Mood," <u>Fortune</u>, Vol.
LXXVII, No. 1 1968, cited by Allen D. Grimshaw, "Brief
Note on the Sociology of Poll Interpretation," <u>Racial
Violence in the United States</u>, ed. Allen D. Grimshaw
[Chicago: Aldine Publishing Co., 1969], p. 318; and 20%
expressed moral support in Waterloo in June, 1970 (Muller,
"A Test...," p. 15).

[104]Harris, "Report from Black...," p. 21.

[105]Harris, "Black and White...." Muller reports
that political efficacy of violence items (violence "helps
or hurts") correlated .457 with dissident group allegiance
to Panthers, Muslims, and the S.D.S. (see Muller, "A
Test...," Table 2.13).

Los Angeles, 57% of blacks endorsed the idea of black
power.[106] In 1970 in Waterloo, 13% of blacks expressed
allegiance to the Panthers, and 29% expressed allegiance to
the Muslims.[107]

Where the long term political interests of the
black community may be at stake, it is not surprising
that violence ostensibly for the improvement of the race
would go essentially uncondemned. Approximately one-
third or more of the black community may actually favor
the use of violence. This support may be increasing.
For example, in 1966, 10% of blacks in a national survey
gave approval to black students arming themselves.[108]
Three years later, 25% of blacks felt the Negro community
should arm itself.[109] Certain indirect evidence suggests
that the actual reservoir of potential approval of violence
in the future may be very high. Certainly, blanket disapproval of violence is low in the black community. A Bedford
Stuyvesant survey indicates that only 27% would say that
violence is wrong.[110] Muller discovered that only 34% of
blacks, versus 58% of whites, were unwilling to engage in
any dissent behavior, with item choices heavily loaded
toward violent dissent.[111]

---

[106]Ten Houten and Ten Houten study, cited by Tomlinson, "Determinants...,"p. 247.

[107]Muller, "A Test...," p. 30.

[108]Harris, "Black and White...."

[109]Harris, "Report from Black...," p. 23. Of
course, some portion of this may be due to the perception of
the need for self-defense after the 1967 and 1968 riots.
Similarly, a small percentage of whites reacted by making
a run on the supply of guns, at least at the height of the
Watts riot. Such desire for protection may be evident in
the fact that in a Spring, 1971 bond issue election, blacks
gave overwhelming support to police bonds. Their support
for taxes in 1971 was less enthusiastic.

[110]Brink and Louis, Black..., p. 264.

[111]Muller, "A Test...," p. 15. Similarly, the
figures for always opposing violence are 20% in Oakland, 23%
in Watts, and 45% in Houston (see McCord and Howard,
"Negro...," p. 26). McCord and Howard also report that only
21% of college educated blacks "completely eschewed the use
of violence," versus 28% of elementary and 49% of high
school graduates (McCord and Howard, "Negro...," p. 27).
In Watts, only 1% objected to the Negro riots and Negro
assaults in general, though disapproval of specific actions
were higher, at 29% for burning, 21% for killing, and 13%

When blacks were asked to express their dislikes of
what happened in Watts, 40% failed to mention killing,
burning, and destruction of property.[112] In a national
survey, however, a full 47% of blacks thought that fire-
bombers deserve to be shot.[113] Though those supporting
violence may range from 30% to 40%, a considerable majority
is opposed to the more severe forms of violence and support
at least general police services, despite the existence of
deeply felt grievances. In any case, as Campbell says,

> The small proportion of Negroes who participate in a
> riot are able, at least for the present, to count on
> a much wider context of moral and perhaps more tangible
> support from the black community. The rioter does not
> stand alone.[114]

Muller has suggested that the true potential for violence
is a summation of approval of political violence, intention
to engage in political violence, and actual participation
admitted.[115] His test of his scales argues persuasively for
the accuracy of such an interpretation:

> The correlation (r) between Intention to Engage in
> Political Violence and Potential for Political Violence
> is .90; the correlation (r) between Approval of Poli-
> tical Violence and Potential for Political Violence is
> .93. Thus, Potential for Political Violence can be
> interpreted as measuring practically the same thing as
> IEPV and APV, but as further taking into account any
> APV-IEPV discrepancies.[116]

Students
        Normative support for violence on campus is also much
higher than the low participation rates of 2% to 10% would
suggest. According to Barton, 42% of Columbia University

---

for coercive police action (Fogelson and Hill, "Who
Riots...," p. 242.

[112]Tomlinson, "Ideological...," p. 359. In another
study, 76% did report dislike for harm to persons (29%) and
property (47%). (Tomlinson, "Determinants...," p. 247).

[113]Harris, "Report from Black...."

[114]Campbell and Schuman, "Racial...," p. 55.

[115]Muller, "A Test...," p. 13.

[116]Ibid., pp. 17-18.

students in 1968 felt that S.D.S. tactics were justified.[117]
Somers reports that in 1964 34% of Berkeley students
supported Free Speech Movement (F.S.M.) tactics.[118] These
early surveys may not tap the change of attitudes on
college campuses that may have occurred in the late 1960's
and early 1970's. A January, 1970 Gallup survey of the
nation's students found that 42% of the students felt that
America might have to be changed by revolution, and 44%
said violence is sometimes justified to bring about change
in American society. (Only 14% of the general public
responded affirmatively to this second question.)[119]
     The evidence, however, is mixed, as is evident in
the fact that a substantial majority of students disapproved of unrest and particularly of violence in one 1969
survey by the Foleys. The Foley poll reveals that 62% of
the student respondents are "getting tired of all the campus
unrest," and 80% felt "that students who break the law in
campus fights should be arrested and expelled."[120] To be
sure, the 20% who evidently did not believe in arrests for
fighting are a very substantial minority.

Effectiveness of violence

Blacks
     Perceived effectiveness of violence among blacks.--
Depending on the particular question, many blacks believe
violence not only to be justified or proper in some way but
also to be effective. A number of surveys have asked blacks
whether riots have helped or hurt Negroes. As many as 58%
in a Watts survey described favorable effects, versus only
18% who expressed unfavorable effects from rioting for Negro

---

[117]At Columbia, 31% of the faculty gave support for
S.D.S. tactics. Faculty support declines according to
degree of violent techniques used: approximately 7% of the
faculty there supported holding the Dean prisoner; 11% of
the student teachers supported this tactic. A full 17% of
the student teachers supported "examining the President's
files." About 22% of instructors supported the occupation
of buildings. See Allen H. Barton, "The Columbia Crisis:
Campus, Viet Nam and the Ghetto," Public Opinion Quarterly,
Fall, 1968, p. 341.

[118]Robert H. Somers, "The Mainsprings of the Rebellion: A Survey of Berkeley Students in November, 1964,"
The Berkeley Student Revolt: Facts and Interpretations,
ed. Seymour Martin Lipset and Sheldon S. Wolin (New York:
Doubleday Anchor, 1965), p. 538.

[119]Gallup, "Four in Ten...."

[120]James A. Foley and Robert K. Foley, The College
Scene (New York: Cowles, 1969), quoted by Lipset, Rebellion..., p. 36.

rights.[121] The lowest figure in this area was right after the Watts riot in 1965, when 8% of blacks nationally expressed the belief that rioting was helpful. The figures seem to be on the rise: in 1970 in Waterloo, Iowa, 42% of blacks believed rioting was helpful.[122] Another perspective is gained from the small percentages that saw nothing but bad effects, In a national survey of blacks, 60% said the rioting hurt civil rights, while 40% did <u>not</u> say so.[123] After the Watts riot, only 28% of blacks said the riot would hurt the Negro cause.[124]

Effectiveness for the black cause.-- An interesting question to ask is what do many blacks think riots are effectively promoting? An earlier section discussed specific grievances and hopes for social, economic, and political equality, but here it is necessary to see these specifics in more general terms. Only 12% of blacks in Watts saw rioting as the "most effective method."[125] On the other hand, 13.7% of blacks in Watts said the riot would hurt the Negro cause "a great deal."[126] Even so, 21% of blacks in one survey saw "some good" arising out of

---

[121]Tomlinson and Sears, "Negro...," p. 294.

[122]Muller, "A Test...," p. 32. Other figures and sources are: in Oakland, 51% said riots help Negro causes (McCord and Howard, "Negro...," p. 26); in Watts, 38% said the riot there helped Negro causes (Cohen, "Press Release...," pp. 4, 8); in a national survey, 34% said riots Helped Negro causes (Harris, "Black and White...," p. 27); in fifteen cities, 33% said riots helped Negro causes (Campbell and Schuman, "Racial...," cited by Grimshaw, <u>Racial...</u>, p. 317, n. 1); in another national survey, 32% said there was more to be gained than lost by rioting (Harris, "After..."); according to 30% of Houston blacks, riots helped Negro causes (McCord and Howard, "Negro...," p. 26); in Detroit, 25% said there is "more to gain than lose" in rioting (Phillip Meyer, <u>The People Beyond Twelfth Street: A Survey of Attitudes of Detroit Negroes After the Riot of 1967</u> [Detroit: University of Michigan Press, 1968], p. 318).

[123]Harris, "After...."

[124]Tomlinson and Sears, "Negro...," p. 294.

[125]<u>Ibid</u>., p. 312.

[126]Murphy and Watson, "The Structure...," p. 177.

violence.[127] In another national survey, 30% of blacks
expected government might "do something" in response to
black rioting.[128] Usually, blacks see that "good" or
"something" as a Negro cause. For example, from 38% to
48.5% claim violence will help the Negro cause.[129] Usually,
the Negro cause is Negro rights. Depending on the survey,
27% to 41% see violence as a necessary means, among others,
for advancing such rights.[130]
    A requisite for such rights is favorable reactions
by whites. Some blacks expect riots "to gain attention" to
Negro problems. For example, 26% in Houston, 27% in Oakland, and 13% in Watts expected riots to draw attention to
their problems.[131] Certainly, those whom blacks expect to
be more attentive to Negro rights are whites. Indeed, in
Watts 84% of blacks thought that whites would be more
"aware," and 62% did not expect relations with whites to
get worse.[132] Similarly, 51% expected whites to be more
sympathetic.[133] Tomlinson and Sears found that 43% expected

---

[127]Don R. Bowen et al., "Deprivation, Mobility and
Protest of the Urban Poor," American Behavioral Scientist,
Nos. 2, 4 (March/April, 1968), p. 20.

[128]Harris, "Black and White...."

[129]Cohen, "Press Release...," p. 4 (43% male and
35% female); and Craft study cited by Murphy and Watson,
"The Structure...," p. 177 (53% male and 44% female).

[130]Joseph R. Feagin and Paul B. Sheatsley, "Ghetto
Residents Appraisals of a Riot," Public Opinion Quarterly,
Fall, 1968, p. 359; and Brink and Harris, Black and
White..., p. 244. Figures for Watts study by the Barss-
Reitzel Corporation were 31% believing violence was
necessary to gain rights (cited by Tomlinson, "Determinants...," p. 247). According to Beardwood, 35% of blacks
believe violence is "necessary to achieve Negro objectives"
(Beardwood, "Fortune Study...,"). A Harris national survey
of black opinion said 21% denied that rights could be won
without violence (Harris, "Black and White...;" p. 23). In
a Ten Houten study, 41% said blacks could not win their
rights without violence (Tomlinson, Determinants...,"
p. 247).

[131]McCord and Howard, "Negro...," p. 24.

[132]Tomlinson and Sears, "Negro...," p. 308.

[133]Cohen, "Press Release...," p. 4. Also Raymond J.
Murphy and James M. Watson, The Structure of Discontent:
The Relationship between Social Structure, Grievance, and
Support for the Los Angeles Riot (Los Angeles: University

white help.[134]   Finally, 42% expected to change whites for
the better.[135]

Whites
        The white perspective on the effectiveness of Negro
riots has been almost universally negative. In a national
sruvey, only 6% of whites said the riots either helped (2%)
or made no change (4%) in Negro rights, while 87% said the
riots hurt the Negro cause.[136]   Ranging from 75% to 94%,
whites see Negro violence as ineffective, whatever the poll.
In one national survey, 94% of whites said Negroes have more
to lose than to gain by rioting.[137]   According to 76% of
Los Angeles whites, riots hurt Negro causes.[138]   Similarly,
in a 1966 Harris survey, 75% of whites said riots hurt
Negro causes.[139]   In a more recent poll, 80% of whites
in Waterloo said riots hurt Negro rights.[140]

Students
        In 1964, 25% of the students at Berkeley found
student politics ineffective for achieving their purposes
and supported "civil disobedience" instead.[141]   In a
college poll of November, 1970, 24% of students agreed
that "revolutionary tactics are necessary to affect significant social and political change in America."[142]

---

of California, Institute of Government and Public Affairs,
1967), cited by Grimshaw, "Brief...," p. 317, n. 1. See
also Raymond J. Murphy and James M. Watson, "Ghetto Social
Structure and Riot Support: The Role of White Contact,
Social Distance, and Discrimination," Racial Violence in the
United States, ed. Allen D. Grimshaw (Chicago: Aldine
Publishing Co., 1969), pp. 325-252.

        [134]Tomlinson and Sears, "Negro...," p. 305.

        [135]Tomlinson, "Ideological...," p. 346.

        [136]Louis Harris, "Riots Have Hurt Negro Cause, 87%
of America Believes," Washington Post, August 17, 1964.

        [137]Harris, "After...."

        [138]Tomlinson and Sears, "Negro...," p. 294.

        [139]Harris, "Black and White...," p. 27.

        [140]Muller, "A Test...," p. 32.

        [141]Somers, "Mainsprings...," pp. 554, 557.

        [142]College poll cited by Lipset, Rebellion...,
p. 61.

Summary of effectiveness
of violence

The evidence indicates that blacks and students are probably more willing than the general public to engage in violence and are more apt to believe violence is effective for the achievement of certain goals believed to involve question of right and wrong. As suggested above, these goals probably involve support for greater social, economic, and political equality. Muller has suggested that views of the effectiveness of violence are related to distrust of political authority or a belief in the illegitimacy of the regime. Muller says,

> Perhaps diffuse affect for the structure of political authority operates to some extent as a "filter" through which men view violent dissent against the regime: if men feel that the regime is illegitimate, they might tend to interpret violent dissent against it as having been helpful to the cause of the dissidents, whatever the objective circumstances; if men feel the regime is legitimate, they might tend to interpret violent dissent against it as having been detrimental to the cause.[143]

As evidence, Muller says, "Trust for Political Authority and Effectiveness of Political Violence show a moderate degree of correlation [of -.419] and the direction is negative, as one would expect."[144]

Many are dixcouraged from using violence, probably because of age, regime coercion, or lack of courage. Certainly, most of the young, most blacks, and most students avoid political violence. Even though Muller found that young blacks could account for 20% of the potential for political violence,[145] it is also necessary to find other explanations than age, race, or student status to account for the participation of a few in political violence. These additional explanations include the subcultural context of political objectives, substantial minority support for violence, and community majorities acquiescing in the existence of political violence.

Regime Legitimacy and Violence

A number of studies have shown some direct relationship between perceptions of legitimacy and the willingness to use violence. As indicated above, it is possible to

---

[143]Muller, "A Test...," p. 37.

[144]Ibid.

[145]Ibid., p. 33.

categorize regime legitimacy according to regime objects
of diffuse affective support. The categories are: legitimating ideologies, general trust in government, trust in
regime authorities, and trust in governmental policies.

Legitimating Ideology and Violence

Nationally
        According to Campbell and Schuman in a survey of
fifteen American cities, there is almost universal agreement among American citizens as to what constitutes a political injustice.[146] For example, in Violence Commission
surveys, almost everyone agreed that the following hypothetical government actions would be unjust: regressive
taxation (95%), prohibition of free speech (95%), arrests of
Negroes without cause (96%), and shooting of innocents
(97%). Moreover, high percentages indicated willingness to
take some form of political action in response to these
injustices. The degree of response seems to vary directly
with the severity of the injustice. Only 1% would use
violence against policies of regressive taxation. Yet 48%
said it would be "all right" for a citizen to use violence
against a government policy of shooting innocents: 41%
said they would do so themselves.[147]
        Given low levels of political participation in
general, perceptions of injustice seem to be tremendous
motivators for political action, some of it violent. In
fact, among those with very low political participation in
the past, 4% and 3% respectively would use violence to
rectify a breach of free speech or unfair taxation. Thus,
nationally perceptions of injustice would motivate from 1%
to 41% to actually participate in political violence for
regressive taxation and the shooting of innocents respectively.[148] Most of the Kirkham items would seem to measure

---

[146]"The advocacy of violence is associated with a
variety of grievances and ideological beliefs" (Campbell
and Schuman, "Racial...," p. 9).

[147]Kirkham, Levy, and Crotty, Assassination...,
p. 268.

[148]Ibid. In this study, the proposed situations
were: (1) "Your Senator has blocked legislation which you
believe is essential to protect the rights of every citizen.
The Senator has come to your town and is making a speech in
a public auditorium to gain support for this point of view."
(2) "Imagine that Congress has passed a law that makes you
pay just as many dollars in taxes as people who make a lot
more money than you do-- would you strongly approve, just
approve, disapprove, or strongly disapprove of this law?"

cases of violation of the principle of political equality,
particularly equal protection of the laws. Evidently, a
very large minority (40%) of the American public would rise
up in response to violations of this aspect of the democratic legitimating ideology. The level of violence depends,
of course, on actual perceptions of the most severe forms
of political inequality and injustice.

Blacks

Among blacks, the obvious source of perceived
injustice is that of the absence of social equality in their
relations with whites. In Newark, rioters were more likely
than non-rioters to engage in discussions of Negro riots
once a week or more often (66.1% versus 42.8%).[149] The
rioters were also more likely to have already participated
in a civil rights group (39.3% versus 25.7%).[150] The
rioter, who was one and one-half times more likely than non-
rioters to be politically conscious about civil rights
and to be active in civil rights groups, was also two times
less likely to think the country was worth fighting for in
both Detroit and Newark.[151] In Detroit, 39.4% of rioters,
compared to 15.5% of non-rioters, said that the country was
"not worth fighting for in a major world war": in Newark,
52.8% of rioters, compared to 27.8% of non-rioters, agreed
with that statement.[152] Anger over civil rights and an
unwillingness to fight for the country are strongly suggestive evidence that rioters, probably a majority of rioters,
do not believe the present regime is legitimate. This
belief probably relies on rioters' ideological perspectives.
A study of the Harlem riot of 1943 provides similar
evidence of a connection between a sense of racial injustice
(contravening the regime's legitimating ideology) and a
willingness to use violence among 60% of the rioters. Of

---

(3) "Imagine that Congress has just passed a law prohibiting
anyone from saying anything against the government-- would
you ...?" (4) "Imagine that the government has just arrested
and imprisoned many of the Negroes in your community even
though there had been no trouble-- would you ...?" (5) "Imagine that in order to keep control of the country, the government starts arresting and shooting large numbers of innocent
people, including members of your family-- would you ...?"
The possible violent response to the above casses of injustice was: "Of the following list of actions, which do you
feel are all right as responses to the above action? ...
If nothing else worked, participate in a physical assault or
armed action because of feelings about what is happening."
(See especially, pp. 267-268.)

[149] _Kerner Commission_, p. 178.

[150] _Ibid._   [151] _Ibid._   [152] _Ibid._, p. 78.

those accepting the riot, 45% associated the cause with
general injustice to blacks. Another 15% attributed it
specifically to bad treatment of black soldiers.[153]
Similarly, in Ransford's study of violence in Watts in 1965,
the 48% with high feelings of racial discrimination were the
most willing to use violence. In the same study, 84% of
those with a low perception of powerlessness and 83% of
those with a low sense of racial discrimination were
unwilling to use violence.[154] About 41% with high feelings
of powerlessness were also more willing to use violence than
those who did not have such feelings. Blacks feeling both
racial discrimination and powerlessness usually attribute
such feelings to a white power structure.

In a study of the mass meaning of the slogan "black
power," Aberbach and Walker found that 57% of those who
interpreted the term as meaning a "fair share for black
people or black unity" said they would join a riot.[155] The
call for black unity or community control or separatism is
a black response to their perception that whites will never
permit individual social equality. This relationship is
evident in the fact that 84.1% of those reporting no riot
activity in Watts scored low on experience with discrimination. On the other hand, a full 30.4% of those scoring high
on discriminatory experience were active in the riot.[156]

Some of Tomlinson's studies show an even higher
correspondence betweeen political attitudes and violence,
because he correlated individual and sub-group responses
rather than merely aggregate ones. Tomlinson divided his
Watts respondents into three approximately equal groups
according to their political attitudes. He designated these
groups as militants, uncommitted, and conservatives.[157]

---

[153]Kenneth B. Clark, "Group Violence: A Preliminary
Study of the Attitudinal Pattern of Its Acceptance and Re-
jection; A Study of the 1943 Harlem Riots," Journal of
Social Psychology, Vol. XIX (May, 1944), p. 319. This
article is also available in Racial Violence in the United
States, ed. Allen D. Grimshaw (Chicago: Aldine Publishing
Co., 1969), pp. 421-433.

[154]H. Edward Ransford, "Isolation, Powerlessness and
Violence: A Study of Attitudes and Participation in the
Watts Riot," American Journal of Sociology, Vol. LXXIII,
No. 5 (1969), p. 441. This article is also available in
Racial Violence in the United States, ed. Allen D. Grimshaw
(Chicago: Aldine Publishing Co., 1969), pp. 434-446.

[155]Aberbach and Walker, "Meaning of Black Power...,"
p. 388.

[156]Murphy and Watson, "The Structure...," p. 158.

[157]A more appropriate label for conservative might

The chief interest in this paper is with the militants, those who responded favorably to questions on how well the Black Muslims and their leaders were doing.[158] Militants were more likely to admit riot participation than others: "By a ratio of two to one they claim to have participated actively in the riot."[159] Tomlinson also states that 9% of militants, versus 4% of conservatives and only 2% of the uncommitted, claimed very active participation.[160] These figures are very small, but when Tomlinson combined the figures for the active and the very active, 34% of the militants versus 20% of conservatives and 16% of the uncommitted participated.[161]

Why did they participate? Tomlinson suggests that a riot ideology may be developing among black communities of America. For example, Tomlinson's militants lived in the subculture of Watts, where higher percentages of all groups saw the Watts riot as a protest, but the militants did so at a higher rate (70% versus 61% of conservatives and 55% of the uncommitted.[162] Though many blacks saw the riot as an expression of political purposes or as a tactic with political purposes, the militants, at 48%, were more likely to volunteer terms indicated more revolutionary political purposes than were the conservatives (36%).[163] Moreover, higher percentages of militants believed violence was

---

have been moderate or centrist, expecially since few Watts residents were subscribers to right wing ideals, politics, or magazines.

[158]In 1964-1965, the Black Muslims were the only nationally know black organization which was aggressively defiant of American society. Muller found considerable evidence of an association between Dissident Group Allegiance (Black Panthers and Muslims) and Trust for Political Authority, Potential for Political Violence, and Efficacy of Political Violence:

"Potential for Political Violence correlates with Dissident Group Allegiance at .486; Potential for Political Violence correlates with Efficacy of Past Violence at .458. Also, as expected, Dissident Group Allegiance and Efficacy of Past Violence are highly correlated themselves-- r is .457. ... Dissident Group Allegiance not only is strongly correlated with Efficacy of Past Violence, it also correlates strongly with Trust Political Authorities-- r is -.467." (Muller, "A Test...," p. 32.)

[159]Tomlinson, "Development...," p. 228. Also Tomlinson, "Ideological...," p. 373.

[160]Tomlinson, "Ideological...," p. 356

[161]Ibid.   [162]Ibid.   [163]Ibid.

both legitimate and effective for the achievement of Negro political goals, whatever they might be. "Three times as many militants (30%) as non-militants endorse the use of violence as a legitimate last resort."[164] When forced to choose between negotiation, non-violence, and violence, nearly three times as many militants (26%) as non-militants (9%) chose violence as the most approved choice of tactics.[165] Given a list of tactics, most militants did not put violence at the top of it, but they were nine times more likely to do so than were the conservatives and uncommitted groups-- 9% militants, 1% conservatives, and .5% uncommitted.[166] In response to the open ended question of what they "liked or disliked" about the riot, the militants used terms coded favorable over twice as often as did non-militants (37% versus 22%).[167] Militants were also less likely to use unfavorable terms for the rioting (27% versus 43% for conservatives and 40% for the uncommitted).[168] These responses would seem to indicate that militants perceived violence as legitimate. Militants were also more likely to believe violence to be effective: only 20% of the militants, versus 40% of the conservatives, said the riots hurt the Negro cause.[169]

Of Tomlinson's three political sub-groups, nearly all (67% to 91%) experienced high and nearly equal levels of discrimination involving some general private economic conditions and relations, such as housing, jobs, and landlords. Yet, with the exception of the one public service, the schools, the militants claimed to have experienced greater discrimination than the conservatives or the uncommitted. In such public services as welfare, fire departments, parks, and garbage, the militants indicated higher discrimination than did the uncommitted and conservatives. The breakdown for feelings of discrimination among the groups is: 48% of militants, 38% of uncommitted, and 34% of conservatives for welfare; 48%, 41%, and 46% for experience with fire departments; 40%, 23%, and 27% for experiences with park officials; and 36%, 29%, and 26% for exper-

---

[164]Tomlinson, "Development...," p. 28.

[165]Tomlinson, "Determinants...," p. 262.

[166]Tomlinson, "Foundations...," p. 114.

[167]Tomlinson, "Ideological...," p. 359.

[168]Tomlinson, "Foundations...," p. 109.

[169]Tomlinson, "Ideological...," p. 365.

iences with garbage collectors.[170] Militants showed greater
tendencies toward higher levels of discontent for injustices
of all kinds, private and public-- the "American way of
life" or perhaps the regime in general. The militants are
more likely to see the source of the problem as being
whites-- the majority supporting the regime. The Militants
were also considerably more active or supportive of violence.

Thus, the evidence may indicate that higher percentages of blacks as a community thatn the population as a whole
may be predisposed to violence to rectify perceived racial
injustices or social inequalities. Tomlinson's studies
indicate that when one's belief in the effectiveness of
violence and discontent over injustices are intense, that
person is very likely to use violence. Apparently, such a
person believes violence is a legitimate means to attack an
unjust (illegitimate) regime and society.

Students
Most student issues, such as the war in Vietnam and
civil rights, seem specific and instrumental rather than
ideological or revolutionary in overtones, but some evidence
suggests that more may be involved than mere free speech or
reform. Indeed, students may be seeking more radical
reforms in American society. For example, although anywhere
from 40% to 79% of students in twelve selected campuses
agreed that the "black power movement [is] an appropriate
response to the condition of the black person in America,"
such student support for black power may not mean support
for black power may not mean support for violence, but
rather, it may mean support for increased black participation in the existing system.[171] Indeed, about 82% of
student activists in campus disruptions in one study agreed
that "basically, the United States is a racist society."[172]
Similarly, only 11% of the activists said America was not
a racist society.[173]

For a large percentage, this rejection of the racial
social inequalities of American society goes deeper than
mere disapproval or racism. Indeed, several studies reveal

---

[170]Ibid., p. 342.

[171]Ardery, "Special...," p. 645.

[172]Sarah Cirese and Jeff Koon, College Seniors View
Campus Unrest and National Issues-- Spring 1970, A report
for the Center for Research and Development in Higher Education (Berkeley: University of California, September, 1970),
p. 10.

[173]Ibid.

that student activists are frequently leftists. For example, of those involved in holding a police car captive at Berkeley, 36% of the self-proclaimed socialists (democratic and revolutionary) were involved, while only 2% of the conservative Republicans participated.[174] Similarly, at Harvard the main source of support for the disruption there in 1968 was those with a leftist ideology. Of those on the two most leftist categories on a nine point scale, 65% thought that "the takeover of the building was justified," while only 2% of the three most conservative groups agreed.[175] In 1970, a national survey revealed that 91% of self-described far-leftists participated in the protests over the President's Cambodian incursion. Of course, most liberals (74%) and over one third (37%) of the middle-of-the-road students also participated.[176]

In his report on a study of three Michigan State University sub-groups-- political activists, non-activists, and student government leaders-- Peterson found that political activists scored much higher on the liberalism and the social consciousness scales than did the two other student groups. The political activists scored above the 97% line on a scale for liberalism (the highest liberalism score of any student group ever tested), compared to 69% and 59% for the other groups. Most such scales of liberalism involve items indicating government responsibility for improving social and economic opportunities-- an almost egalitarian and libertarian view of the application of the democratic legitimating ideologies of equality and liberty. Thus, it is not surprising that the political activists were one standard deviation higher than the other groups on a scale of social consciousness. Their scores were 84%, versus 50% for non-activists and 35% for student government leaders. The social consciousness scale attempts to measure "moral concern for human injustice."[177]

Among a substantial number of those with a leftist ideology, there is the belief that America is racist, repressive, and exploitive of blacks and the poor. Some leftist students are rejecting the economic, social, and political system as a whole as being illegitimate. Some are suggesting a socialist or other alternative standard of legitimacy. Many studies reveal that it is this leftist group which contributes a disproportionate percentage of supporters of violence and disruption.

---

[174]Lyonns, "Police Car...."

[175]Lipset, Rebellion..., p. 69.

[176]Harris, "Report May, 1970...," cited by Lipset, Rebellion..., p. 47.

[177]Peterson, "Student...," pp. 217-218.

Summary of legitimating
ideology and violence

Muller reports an inverse relationship (correlation
of .474) between student support for legitimating sentiments
and avoidance of protest.[178] Yet he argues that "the ethical principles on which the legitimating ideology is based
are presumably more meaningful to the students than to the
average citizen."[179] The relationship does not hold for
other groups in the population. Thus, for his broad sample
of citizens in Waterloo, Muller says that the "inclusion of
the Legitimating Ideology in the Potential for Political
Violence prediction adds nothing to the explained variance."[180] He decides then to use his Trust for Political
Authority scale alone. Yet the evidence presented above
that national recognition of violations of some norms of
political equality would mobilize nearly a majority (41%)
of Americans on some issues; that a high intensity of felt
racial discrimination activates a large minority of blacks;
and the connection of radical leftist ideology with campus
activism-- all these suggest that Muller's evidence is at
least open to question. In Muller's scale, only two items
out of six refer to democracy or a situation of free speech;
the others refer to such at least analytically distinct
objects of diffuse support as the economic system, the work
ethic, obedience to the law, and the Constitution. This
fact may explain why legitimating ideologies, as tested in
Muller's scale, did little to determine any relationship
between legitimating ideologies and political violence.
(Of course, it is possible that Muller and most other social
scientists are correct in assigning a low level of ideological understanding to the masses.)

As suggested above, it may be more useful to measure
diffuse regime support on several hypothesized levels of
probably decreasing importance for over-all system legitimacy. Kirkham's study provides some evidence of these
separate dimensions of legitimacy. Kirkham found

> Political Vengeance Against Government Authorities and
> Politicians had practically no correlation (.068) with
> Revolutionary Violence, which are the items on responses
> to injustice covered above. These seem to be the sepa-
> rate dimensions of legitimacy already suggested of legi-
> timating ideology and structural legitimacy.[181]

---

[178]Muller, "A Test...," p. 6.

[179]Ibid., p. 65, n. 62.   [180]Ibid., p. 22.

[181]Kirkham, Levy, and Crotty, Assassination...,
p. 244.

The next section is a discussion of these other separate
dimensions of regime legitimacy structures (economic,
governmental, and social), incumbent officials, and efficacy
of specific policies.

Diffuse Affective Support for Regime
Authority Structures and
Political Violence

Several studies suggest a very close relationship
between lack of support for regime authority structures and
political violence. For example, in his study of a mixed
sample of blacks and whites in Waterloo, Muller found his
scale of Trust for Political Authority correlated -.464 with
the Potential for Political Violence-- a higher correlation
than any other variable.[182] Similarly, Kim found that those
who believed that the "governmental directives should be
binding" (authoritative) were those least willing to attack
the government.[183] Kirkham's staff report for the Violence
Commission showed that those supporting clear elements of
the "established order" were less likely to resort to violence, while those opposed to the existing system were more
likly to support violence. The Kirkham Commission con-
structed a scale labeled Political Vengeance which included
the following three items: "The government in Washington
is the enemy, not the friend of people like me"; "Some
politicians who have their lives threatened probably deserve
it"; and "Sometimes I have felt the best thing might be the
death of political leaders." In terms of the relationship
between levels of support for "established order" and levels
of support for political violence, the "government as enemy"
item correlated .196 with "best thing might be the death of
political leaders," and .167 with "some politicians deserve
death."[184]
    The specific evidence is more persuasive. The poli-
tically vengeant constituted only 11% of those very interested in elections, 11% of non-switching party loyalists,
10% of Republicans, 10% of those supporing the 1968 Vietnam
policies, 9% of those favoring integration, 8% of those
favoring either Humphrey or Nixon for President, and only 6%
of those favoring pursuit of lower levels of racial integration. In contrast, those least likely to accept the
existing system, its current policies, or leaders were the
highest contributors to Kirkham's Political Vengeance Scale.

---

[182]Muller, "A Test...," p. 27.

[183]Kim, "Authority...," cited by Gurr, Why...,
p. 190.

[184]Kirkham, Levy, and Crotty, Assassination...,
p. 242.

Of those blacks not much interested in the 1968 elections, 30% scored high on Political Vengeance, as did 22% of those wanting the use of nuclear weapons in Vietnam, 19% of those unsure of party preference, 17% of Republicans switching to the Democratic Party, and those dissatisfied with the pace of integration as either too slow, 16%, or too fast, 14%.[185] Thus, vengeance itself is very closely tied to low levels of political trust and adherence to leftist or rightist positions upon the various political candidates and issues of 1968. Nationally, then, those with the greatest political dissatisfaction seem more likely to be supportive of violence than those highly supportive of the political system. Some of the issues, candidates, and groups particularly point to the problem of racial equality and it disaffective impact on diffuse support for the governmental structure.

Blacks

Similarly, among blacks those who are least supportive of the political system are those who are most likely to be supportive of violence. For example, in a study of black residents in Detroit, Joel Aberbach and Jack Walker

> found that 54 percent of those at the lowest ordinal position on a measure of trust in the political authorities reported that they could imagine a situation in which they would riot, whereas only 17 percent of those at the highest ordinal position on trust said they could imagine a situation in which they would riot.[186]

In Watts, "those who did not trust elected officials in general 37% and Negro elected officials 35% in particular were active in the riot."[187] Similarly, in Newark, only 7.7% of rioters versus 15.3% of non-rioters thought they could "trust the Newark govenment to do what is right" always or most of the time.[188] The Newark rioter was over twice as likely to say that "anger with politicians" had a great deal to do with causing the riot (43.2% versus 19.6%).[189] The Newark rioter was also more likely than non-rioters to attribute anger with police as a more particular cause (70.5% versus 48.8%).[190] Finally, in Rossi's

---

[185]Ibid., pp. 257-264

[186]Muller, "A Test...," p. 6, n. 24, commenting on Aberbach and Walker, "Political Trust...," pp. 1199-1219.

[187]Sears and MacConahay, "The Politics...," p. 429.

[188]Kerner Commission, p. 178.

[189]Ibid.   [190]Ibid.

study, respondents in riot cities were less likely than
those living in non-riot cities to believe that the local
political leaders were imaginative (66% versus 79%).[191]
Similarly, 67% of the respondents in riot cities versus 72%
of those in non-riot cities believed that the average citizen can find "someone to listen" in government.[192] These
differences are statistically significant but refer only to
the general political milieu as perceived by the whole
sample.

Even greater differences are evident in studies
concerned with those arrested during riots. For example,
arrestees in Watts, as compared to the rest of citizens in
the riot curfew area sample, generally felt more bitter and
distrustful about politics.[193] Indeed, only 14% of the
Watts arrestees trusted Negro politicians, and 12% trusted
politicians in general.[194] Similarly, 62% of the curfew
zone sample and only 47% of the arrestees gave trusting
responses; 29% of the curfew zone sample and 41% of the
arrestees gave distrustful responses.[195] The net response[196] of all the Watts arrestees to trust of national
and state elected executive officials was clearly negative
though not totally so: -18% versus 5% for the random
sample.[197] A majority (64%) of the black community assigned
some responsibility to the police for the riot, but 85% of
the arrestees did so.[198] Among self-proclaimed participants, 35% had specific grievances against local government
agencies, persons, or groups.[199] A substantial minority of

---

[191]Peter H. Rossi et al., "Between White and Black:
The Faces of American Institutions in the Ghetto," Supple-
mental Studies for the National Advisory Commission on Civil
Disorders (Washington, D.C.: U.S. Government Printing
Office, July, 1968), p. 86.

[192]Ibid.

[193]Sears, "Political Attitudes...," p. 699.

[194]Sears and MacConahay, "The Politics...," pp. 430-
431.

[195]Ibid., p. 438.

[196]Arithmetic differences between favorable percentages and unfavorable responses.

[197]Positive responses were to President Johnson and
Governor Brown. Sears, "Political Attitudes...," p. 700.

[198]Ibid., Table

[199]Sears and MacConahay, "The Politics...," p. 439.

participants (32%) also made negative evaluations of welfare
agencies. These grievances indicate perhaps more reformist
attitudes than calls for a major overhaul or revolution.
        On the other hand, the militants, already identified
as individuals approving of the more radical Muslim critique
of the American regime, were less likely to be reformists in
attitudes and were more likely to make negative evaluations
of parts of the political system. Among Muslim supporters,
only 45% expressed trust for elected officials. This
figure is significantly less than for conservatives (58%)
and the uncommitted (56%).[200] Nevertheless, 60% of the
militants expressed trust for Negro officials; this figure
is a great deal higher than their 45% trust for elected
officials in general.[201] More specifically, Tomlinson
reports that though

> a majority of Los Angeles Negroes did not trust the
> police-- more militants felt this was (63%) than
> conservatives (54%) or uncommitted (51%)-- and most
> of the respondents believed that the police were
> guilty of grave misconduct.[202]

Militants were nearly twice as likely to have claimed
experience with the unnecessary use of police force--
17% versus 9% for conservatives.[203]
        Underlying or amplifying these specific grievances
or general feelings of alienation, those supporting or
engaging in violence were more likely to have experienced
or felt outraged by discrimination or other injustices than
were other members of the black community as a whole. The
target of violence and the source of the perceived injustices were generally whites. Of the complaints by the
arrestees, 51% were coded as general mistreatment and
expressions of hostility toward white objects of attack.[204]
Tomlinson and Sears suggest that the arrestees seemed less
politically articulated or motivated, at least in their lack
of specific targets other than the police with whom they had
tangled.[205] Yet the immediacy of their encounter with the
police may have influenced the higher percentage (42%) of
their grievances in this direction.[206] If such attitudes
toward the police do reflect a general disaffection from
authority, then the arrestees were very politically moti-

---

[200]Tomlinson, "Ideological...," _JSI_, p. 105.

[201]_Ibid_.   [202]_Ibid_., p. 101.

[203]_Ibid_., p. 100.

[204]Tomlinson and Sears, "Negro...," p. 318.

[205]_Ibid_.   [206]_Ibid_., p. 317.

vated indeed-- perhaps against the whole white regime. On
the other hand, as Tomlinson and Sears also suggest, the
soldiers need not be articulate ideologically in order to
be politically motivated or mobilized for violence.[207] A
majority of arrestees (53%) seemed to categorize those who
supported the riot as the "good guys" or "everyone", while
only 16% mentioned undesirables as being involved.[208]
Apparently, those blacks who were most active in these
various riots were those who were particularly distrustful
of regime authorities.

Students
        Trust also appears to be a reliable predictor of
student violence. For example, Muller found that the single
greatest predictor of students avoiding protest (-.474) was
the Trust Political Authorities dimension of legitimacy
sentiment.[209] Most evidence of student attitudes, however,
has focused on specific policies and issues. Cirese and
Koon report that three times (27% to 9%) as many students
predisposed to campus disruption[210] had already participated in a wide range of actions protesting government
policies. Only 25% of the activists had not previous protest experience, indicating no previous disaffection.[211]
        Others have studies the character of that disaf-
fection. Certainly, student responses to some specific
issues indicate that most student protests are generally
reformist in nature. At Berkeley, 82% of the militant
students saw the issue as one of free speech, versus 69% of
the conservatives, who denied that free speech was the
issue. Of the student militants, 85% thought that the
tactics would succeed in the limited aims of political fund
raising and recruitment on campus.[212] Similarly, in one
Harris poll, 43% of the militant students attributed the
Kent State deaths to the Nixon administration hostility
toward dissent.[213]

---

[207]Ibid., p. 320.   [208]Ibid., p. 314.

[209]Muller, "A Test...," p. 6.

[210]Those who responded affirmatively to the "use of
disruptive tactics and the destruction of property is often
necessary in order to change the status quo." (Cirese and
Koon, College..., p. 31.)

[211]Ibid., pp. 31-32.

[212]Somers, "Mainsprings...," p. 557.

[213]Harris, "Report May, 1970...," p. 164, cited by
Lipset, Rebellion..., p. 59.

237

Purposes of Violent Political Discontent

Earlier in this paper, a number of purposes as motivations for political conflict and violence were suggested. These purposes are reform, protest, revolution, and fun and profit. It is unlikely that the average participant in political violence has only a single purpose in mind, as these suggested purposes may be only analytically distinct but empirically mixed or even uncertain. Nevertheless, an analysis of expressed purposes may help to test tentatively the chief hypotheses of this study-- that varying degrees of non-support for the regime lead to reformist, radical, revolutionary, and anarchistic purposes as motivations for participation in violent politics. The evidence is very limited, so some reliance will have to be made on inferences.

National

The previous evidence indicates that the white middle and lower-middle class majority almost totally disapproves of the use of political violence, at least if used by blacks and students. In Muller's sample of a single urban community, "whites draw the line at the violent demonstration and property destruction level: none of them also would engage in violent revolution," in addition to peaceful protest and normatively sanctioned political participation.[214] There are, of course, substantial numbers of white racists, super-patriots, and other reservoirs of potential violence, as amply indicated by American history.

Blacks

Several studies of riots in the black community and on campus have shown the purposive character of such violence. Among curfew residents in Watts, 56% said the riot had a purpose; 62% said that purpose was protest.[215]

Fun and profit
Banfield has suggested that a primary motive for young lower class blacks has been fun and profit. These factors may help to explain some participation, particularly under disaster conditions where youthful exuberance and targest of opportunity come readily into play. Yet, in the Campbell and Schuman study of fifteen cities, less than one-fifth of those who said they would join a riot (11%) said

---

[214]Muller, "A Test...," p. 16.

[215]Tomlinson and Sears, "Negro...," pp. 293, 303.

they would "take things from ... stores."[216] Only 2% of
the total sample seemed to indicate their motives were
profit. Most respondents' answers were coded: "would be
likely to break windows of stories that treat Negroes
unfairly" (4% of the total sample), and "would be likely to
burn such stores" (3% of total sample). Thus, profits from
looting seemed less a motive than vengeance against whites.
Indeed, five-sixths of the total sample in one study said
white victims deserved their treatment.[217] The emphasis on
unfairness to Negroes would seem to make fun as well as profit a secondary benefit of rioting. This information provides evidence of mixed motives. Yet fun and profit seem
more likely to be those secondary benefits enjoyed or taken
when the opportunity presents itself. Certainly, the statement that "the highest participating rates were among those
who perceived the riot as a protest directed against people
or groups" seems more accurate than Banfield's analysis.[218]
For blacks, those people and groups were whites.
The arrestees and the self-identified riot participants in
Watts saw the riot as a protest against particular white
people, groups, and institutions.[219] For example, 62% of
the Watts curfew area sample identified white merchants,
stores, or white people in general.[220] These protest motives indicate at least some desire for reform, possibly
even radical reform. The fact that nearly 30% found contact
with whites at a party to be distasteful may indicate separatist motives.[221] The ultimate purposes of such separatist
motives may vary from community control to revolution.
Though motives are mixed, there is more direct evidence of
the most general politial purposes of black violence.

Reform
        In one survey of the black community, the most com-
mon perception was that the purpose of the riot was reform

---

[216]Campbell and Schuman, "Racial...," p. 53.

[217]Fogelson and Hill, "Who Riots...," p. 242, summa-
rizing David O. Sears and Tommy M. Tomlinson, Riot Activity
and Evaluation: An Overview of the Negro Survey ("Riot Ideology in Los Angeles: A Study of Negro Attitudes"; unpublished series written for the U.S. Office of Economic
Opportunity).

[218]Sears and MacConahay, "The Politics...," p. 439.

[219]Ibid.

[220]Merchants and stores-- 38%; white people-- 28%
(Tomlinson and Sears, "Negro...," p. 303).

[221]Murphy and Watson, "The Structure...," p. 196.

(social or economic change). For 26%, rioting was either an instrument to improve conditions, to end discrimination, or to communicate with power structure.[222] According to 41%, rioting called attention to Negro problems, general conditions, and discrimination.[223] At least 42% expected white attitudes to change for the better; 30% expected economic improvement.[224] None of these supposed outcomes would constitute a radical restructuring of American society. Those who were most optimistic (55%) of the outcome were those seeking much more instrumental or reformist purposes, such as reduced discrimination in selected public agencies, such as schools, garbage collection agencies, welfare, fire and parks departments.[225]

Separatism and/or revolution
        Others expressing greater hostility and resentment towards whites were less optimistic (36%) about the outcome of riots.[226] Among these are the potential revolutionaries-- those who are not very optimistic about the effects of mere protest. When asked to label the riot, 38% of curfew area residents used revolutionary rhetoric, calling it a revolt, a revolution, or an insurrection.[227] Among 33%, the purpose of the riot was an expression of hostility, resentment, or revenge, not the instrumentality or reform intentions of the other 67%.[228] Among the militants (the 24% of the total sample who gave positive evaluations of the Black Muslims), 48% used revolutionary language to describe the riot.[229]
        In the Watts riot, of course, the targets of destruction and hostility were generally whites. Among the most militant, 21% sought separatism and/or voluntary segregation from a hated white community.[230] Of course,

---

[222]Tomlinson and Sears, "Negro...," p. 302.

[223]Ibid.   [224]Ibid., p. 307.

[225]Sears and MacConahay, "The Politics...," pp. 443, 447, 448, and 449.

[226]Ibid., p. 449.

[227]Tomlinson and Sears, "Negro...," pp. 293-294.

[228]Ibid., p. 301.

[229]Tomlinson, "Ideological...," JSI, p. 108.

[230]Harris, "Report from Black..." (16% and 9% for separate neighborhoods and separate schools).

the vast majority of the black community continues to prefer integration, or at least desegregation, over segregation. Indeed, 78% wanted desegregation in schools, and 74% wanted desegregation of neighborhoods.[231] Others may sked community control under the slogan of black power.

This antagonism toward whites is also reflected in black evaluations of politicians. In Watts, blacks are more likely to view white politicians as unfavorable than they are to view Negro politicians unfavorably. For example, 53% trusted Negro politicians, while only 14% trusted white politicians. Militant blacks (those who looked upon the Black Muslims with favor) showed twice the hostility toward and distrust of whites than other groups.[232] Militants also expressed greater distaste for social contact with whites; they were more likely to find parties, eating, and inter-marriage distasteful.[233]

> The militants' greater distaste of interacting with whites in social situations appears to be deliberate and ideologically flavored. Thus, to some extent the militant is deliberately renouncing (or denouncing) the white world, and purposefully avoiding contact and interaction.[234]

The militants also expressed greater hostility toward white policemen and institutions than did those in the other groups.[235]

Those blacks seeking revolution probably constitute a small minority in America-. For example, in Muller's black sample, only 4% supported revolution.[236] The predominant concern of blacks appears to be the social equality whites are not yet prepared to give them. Attitudes and political behavior, however, are dynamic, so the revolutionaries might be able to expand their constituency. In any case, a small group of committed revolutionaries may be able to create considerable violence and official reaction.

Students

Campus polls show student interest in reforms are standard. For example, 19% to 54% approve of minimum wel-

---

[231] Ibid.

[232] Tomlinson, "Ideological...," p. 338.

[233] Ibid., p. 339.   [234] Ibid., p. 341.

[235] Ibid., p. 339.

[236] Muller, "A Test...," p. 16.

fare payments.[237] Similarly, 70% advocate ending the war in Vietman.[238] Many students also advocate public subsidies of the arts.[239] Yet, im most cases, campus reform, as opposed to social reform, is probably not a real issue. Indeed, 82% expressed satisfaction with courses and professors at the height of the Berkeley revolution in 1964.[240]

Of greater concern, prospects for a large revolutionary cadre on campus does seem possible. For example, in 1970 42% in some polls beleived America can be changed only by revolution. Similarly, 44% believed "violence is sometimes justified to bring about change in American society."[241] Anywhere from 2% to 11% "would definitely favor a full socialization of all industries," with from 9% to 34% being "somewhat in favor" of such socialization.[242] Those favoring socialization of basic industries is higher: 4% to 34% for definitely in favor, and 20% to 41% somewhat in favor. Ardery provides even further evidence of the growth of radical beliefs among college students. From 1961 to 1970, self-identified radicals increased six fold at some schools (Yale: 3% to 18%) and tripled at others, such as Stanford (5% to 17%), Howard (8% to 29%), Boston (6% to 18%), and Williams (5% to 14%).[243]

Probably most of these students see revolution coming peacefully in the manner of Charles Reich's cultural revolution. For example, although 70% of students supported the anti-war goals of many demonstrations, 64% "took exception to the specific tactics of leaders of the protests"-- disruption and violence.[244] A couple of surveys have attempted to tap directly the percentages seeking varying degrees of political change. For example, Lipset reports that Yankelovich in 1969 found 3% revolutionaries, 10% radical dissidents, 39% reformers, 37% moderates, and 11% conservatives.[245] Among both blacks and students, far more

---

[237]Ardery, "Special...," p. 640.

[238]Harris, "Aversion...."

[239]Ardery, "Special...."

[240]Somers, "Mainsprings...," p. 538.

[241]Gallup, "Four in Ten...."

[242]Ardery, "Special...," p. 643.

[243]Ibid., p. 637.   [244]Harris, "Aversion...."

[245]Lipset, Rebellion..., p. 48. In 1969, Roper found similar figures: 2.5% favored fundamental overhaul; 15.5% suggested many improvements; 71.5% favored some assistance; and 10.5% believed everything to be basically sound and essentially good (Roper Research Associates, A

see political violence and disruption as an effective
tactic for radical reform and change, not for revolution.
Some blacks and students would probably like revolutionary
changes in the social, economi, and political systems, if
they could get them. Realistic recognitions of the costs
of violence and the expectations of coercive regime retalia-
tion probably limit prospects for revolution. It is perhaps
in this context that one can understand the fascist labels
many attach to the existing regime.

Some Speculative Conclusions on Changing
Myths of Democratic Legitimacy and
Their Possible Relationship
to Political Conflict

The Unstable Nature of
Legitimating Myths

Legitimating ideologies exist in the general context
of the particular customs, conditions, or interests of a
particular time and place. If these conditions and interests change, so may the doctrines which attempt to explain
or justify them. Thus, legitimacy beliefs are at best
fragil, vulnerable, and unstable conventions. Periods of
rapid technological, economic, and social change may
threaten myths in "mature"[246] as well as in the so-called
developing nations.[247] During such periods, new myths or
doctrines may arise. These new myths attempt to modify,
reform, revolutionize, or supplant the old legitimating
ideologies. Some recent examples of new myths are the
ideals of the New Left, black nationalists, and the counter
culture. These new myths may also effect the regime's
authority structures and patterns of behavior, which the
old myths had justified. Thus, legitimating ideologies are
dynamic and unstable, even democratic ones.

An Historical Overview of Changes in
American Democratic Legitimacy

The Democratic quest for
perfection
Some modern political scientists have seen democracy

Study of the Beliefs and Attitudes of Male College Seniors,
Freshmen, and Alumni [New York: Roper Research Associates,
May, 1969], cited by Lipset, Rebellion..., p. 54).

[246]See Brzezinski, Between....

[247]Pye, Aspects..., p. 31.

as capable of nearly continuous improvements, progress, and
reform: democracy is perhaps capable ultimately of creating
harmonious human communities-- perfection itself.[248] Faith
in democracy has led perhaps to an expansion, intensification, reinterpretation, and radicalization of the possible
application of the uniquely democratic ideas of equality and
liberty. Cropsey has said, "radicalism is not so much the
antithesis of the previaling regime as the intensification
or radicalization of that regime.[249]

The conflictual nature
of democracy

Schattschneider has suggested that democracy inherently involves high levels of conflict:

> Democratic government is the greatest single instrument
> for the socialization of conflict in the American com-
> munity. The controversy about democracy might be inter-
> preted in these terms also. Government in a democracy
> is a great engine for expanding the scale of conflict.
> Government is never far away when conflict breaks out.[250]

He suggests further that expansions in the meaning and
application of democratic political ideas may aggravate this
tendency toward political conflict:

> Universal ideas in the culture, ideas concerning equal-
> ity, consistency, equal protection of the laws, justice,
> liberty, freedom of movement, freedom of speech and
> association and civil rights tend to make conflict con-
> tagious; they invite outside intervention in conflict
> and form the basis of appeals to public authority for
> redress of private grievances.[251]

---

[248]For comments on this view among the New Left,
see Edward Shils, "Dreams of Plentitude, Nightmares of
Scarcity," Students in Revolt, ed. Seymour Martin Lipset
and Philip G. Altbach (Boston: Beacon Press, 1970), p.
12. Stillman and Pfaff have argued that the ideological
quest for transcendental perfection (the seeking of the
realization of ultimate moral values) have been a major
impetus to the violent character of western civilization,
exemplified by the horrors of total and ideoligical wars--
religious, nationalistic, democratic, etc. (see Stillman
and Pfaff, Politics of Hysteria..., especially pp. 2, 7,
12-13, 18, and 29-30). See also Cohn, Pursuit of the
Millenium....

[249]Cropsey, "Radicalism...," p. 317.

[250]Schattschneider, "Socialization...," p. 134.

[251]Ibid., p. 130 (italics mine).

Schattschneider also says that the political institutions,
which are the vehicles for the practical application of democratic ideals, have actually provided means for conflict:

> The universalization of the franchise, the creation of
> a national electorate and the development of the plebi-
> scitary Presidency elected by a national constituency
> have facilitated the socialization of conflict. Thus,
> modern government has become the principle molder of the
> conflict system.[252]

Many others have argued that important differences
in values are a natural outgrowth of democracy or an "open
society." As Madison said in Federalist No. 10, "liberty
is to faction as air is to fire."[253] Similarly, Tocqueville
warned that the individualism encouraged by equality might
lead to selfishness instead of enlightened self-interest or
"self-interest rightly understood." According to Madison
and Tocqueville, liberty inherently involves the development
of differing interests with conflicting goals. Such conflict need not lead to violence, but as the egalitarian and
libertarian expectations for democracy increase, the potential for violent conflict may also increase.

Eckstein has suggested that increased political
demands may be analogous to economic inflation.[254] Similarly,
both Easton and Deutsch have discussed the problem of political system overloads. According to these writers, when
the regime is incapable of fulfilling the requirements of
these demands, some citizens may perceive this "overload" to
reflect establishment resistance. Many have perceived the
resulting conflict to be a class issue. Class conflict in
politics need not follow the Marxist scenario, but they have
such potential.

The dynamics and evolution of
American politics

It might be useful to approach incessant conflict
over the change of American ideas in the light of important
historical changes in the nature of American political life.
A number of recent American political scientists share the
belief in this dynamic and evolutionary nature of American
politics. For example, Lowi cautions us against a static
view of American politics:

---

[252]Ibid., p. 135.

[253]Hamilton, Madison, and Jay, Federalist..., No.
10, p. 78.

[254]Parsons, "Some Reflections...," p. 63.

Momentary consensus in America has overshadowed debate
that had enlivened public opinion in times past. But
that consensus is superficial and temporary. The issues
and the debates will emerge again because each generation upsets the apple cart one way or another and must
then face all the alternatives in setting it up again.[255]

He has suggested that the contemporary nature of American
political processes varies according to the particular purposes of various governmental arenas. Lowi has designated
these broad policy purposes as: distributive, regulative,
and redistributive.[256]

Distributive policies-- involving the politics of
"logrolling," "pork barrel," patronage, and special clien-
teles-- are "policies in which the indulged and the deprived, the loser and the recipient, never need come into
direct confrontation." Oppositions are disorganized both
because the "deprived cannot be identified," due to multiplicity of interests and individuals, and because nearly
everyone interested in benefits gets them.[257] Regulative
policies-- such as those most often involving the F.C.C.
and F.A.A.-- raise the level of conflict. Such policies
"directly rais[e] the costs and/or reduc[e] or expand ...
the alternatives of private individuals. ... [They] involve
a direct choice as to who will be indulged and who deprived." This results in the politics of shifting coalitions of interests from decision to decision.[258] Redistributive policies have a "much broader [impact], approaching
social classes ... [or] crudely speaking ... [the] haves and
have nots, bigness and smallness, bourgoise and prola-
tariat."[259] Such politics are likely to be ideological--

---

[255]Lowi, Private Life..., p. ix.

[256]Theodore Lowi, "Distribution, Regulation, Redistribution: The Function of Government," Readings in American Political Behavior, ed. Raymond E. Wolfinger (2d ed.;
Englewood Cliffs, N.J.: Prentice-Hall, Inc., 1970), pp
245-256. See also Theodore Lowi, "American Business, Public
Policy, Case Studies and Political Theory," World Politics,
Vol. XVI (July, 1964), pp. 673-715. Emmette S. Redford has
provided considerably detailed analysis of the kinds of
politics present depending on the level of administration
involved in implementing governmental policies. He has
called these kinds of politics micropolitics, subsystem
politics, and macropolitics (Emmette S. Redford, Democracy
in the Administrative State [New York: Oxford University
Press, 1969]).

[257]Lowi, "Distribution...," pp. 245-246.

[258]Ibid., p. 246.   [259]Ibid.

they involve "not equal treatment, but equal possession" of
property.[260] Lowi claims such redistributive conflicts are
stable, because they involve elite, bureaucratic and institutional negotiation and resolution of conflict.[261] This
writer believes that such conflict, in its resemblance to
class conflict, are in fact destabilizing. Some of Lowi's
other work suggests the same.[262]

James Grant has added a fourth policy category to
Lowi's typology of political arenas. This category is
systems maintenance. Grant has suggested that these broad
policy ends of American politics have shifted according to
historical signals of change in the nature of American
politics.[264] For example, Jaffa has written on the ideological issues involved in certain alternative elections.[265]
Burham reveals that third party movements make

> attacks on major parities in the name of democratic-
> humanistic universals against an established political
> structure which was perceived to be corrupt, undemocra-
> tic, and manipulated by insiders for their supporters'
> benefit.[266]

Expanded Meanings and Applications
of American Legitimating Myths

The discussion just completed indicates that
(1) legitimating myths are inherently unstable and (2) democratic regimes are inherently conflictual due to the con-

---

[260]Ibid.   [261]Ibid.

[262]See especially Lowi, Private Life....

[263]James Grant, Ph.D. dissertation (Political
Science Department, University of Chicago, in progress at
time of this writing).

[264]Schlesinger says, "Throughout American history
the political problem has had a series of redefinitions at
the hands of Presidents who responded decisively to the
challenge of their generation." (Schlesinger, Crisis...,
p. 244.)

[265]Jaffa, Equality..., chap. i, pp. 3-41. V. O.
Key's seminal essay on critical elections is also related to
these important changes in American political history (V.).
Key, "A Theory of Critical Elections," Journal of Politics,
Vol. XVII [1955], pp. 3-18). Finally, Burnham's Critical
Elections... also gives some attention to these changes.

[266]Burnham, Critical Elections..., pp. 29-30.

stant redefinition of their legitimating myths. This
section is a discussion of the redefinition of two of the
American democratic legitimating ideologies-- equality and
liberty.

Modifications of equality

Stolz's specific discussion on the ideal of equality
and political conflict is particularly pertinent to this
study. According to Stolz, "the most intense conflicts of
American history-- the Civil War, the period of industrial-
ization and our present situation of 1970 -- are rooted in
disputes concerning equality."[267] Unfortunately, Stolz
neglects to discuss the possibility raised by others that
the idea of equality may have undergone considerable modification of its application from one political conflict to
another. Such negligence also ignores the possibility that
the ends of American politics may have changed as well.
Stolz has recognized, however, that the idea of equality
may encourage extraordinary conflict-- violence. Lowi has
suggested more generally than Stolz that

in a democracy there is a tendency toward expansion
of the public sphere. ... Yet does each and every
public policy produce an increment of public order,
or have some forms of government action proven to
be patently bad for public order?[268]

These works relate to the efforts in this paper to
suggest, tentatively, that at differing periods in American
history, in certain subcultures, or perhaps in "leading
sectors" certain understandings of equality and liberty
have predominated, while other ideas seemed to wait, sometimes violently, in the wings. Essentially, the early
demands for equality were primarily in terms of equal
citizenship-- political equality. According to original
interpretations of the Declaration and the Constitution,
they both seek equality before the law. That is, there
should be no political discriminations between citizens
except by consent of the people to be ruled by their elected
representatives. Recent political thought and legislation,
however, have tended to erode non-political distinctions
among men. Thus, government has assumed the obligation to
provide equality of opportunity by public policies aimed at
breaking down social and economic differences among individuals, groups, and classes. Government is actively promoting equality of opportunity in public accommodations,
housing, employment, education, and other areas.

---

[267]Stoltz, "The Liberal...," p. 28.

[268]Lowi, _Private Life..._, pp. viii and ix.

The recently proclaimed rights to minimum income and health indicate that economic equality may have replaced equality of opportunity. Some form of legislative establishment of such rights to economic equality may be likely before or soon after the 1972 Presidential elections, irregardless of whether or not George McGovern defeats Richard Nixon. Public concern over the quality, as well as the quantity of life, especially with respect to environmental pollution, consumer protection, and governmental subsidies to the arts, may suggest that some citizens may expect government to provide for the aesthetic, as well as the sensual requirement of happiness, rather than merely the pursuit of happiness.[269] In any case, it is difficult to know where the quest for happiness through equality may be leading.

These are perhaps only interesting speculations. Yet they suggest that governmental responsibilities and the scope of American politics may be outpacing the capacity for achievement and perhaps intensifying the potential for political conflict, some of it violent. Several writers suggest that this expansion of the concept of equality from the purely political into other spheres-- such as economic, health, and happiness-- may be very dangerous, especially in view of the fact that government may not be able to keep pace with its promises. The relative deprivation theory of political violence may be quite relevant here, for it recognizes that expectations of social changes may outrace actual regime performance capabilities. Under such conditions, a general awareness of the regime's imperfections (particularly in light of high ideals and expectations) may develop among those groups which are most disoriented and uprooted by rapid change.[270]

Expansion of liberty

Paradoxically, as government expands its efforts to achieve social and economic equality, the demand for more freedom-- less governmental or other restraints-- has increased as well. An expansion of the practical application of the idea of liberty is also occurring. For example, Supreme Court decisions have expanded the concept of freedom of expression to include almost all utterances.[271]

---

[269]On a developing belief in the moral equality of all men, see Shils, "Dreams...," pp. 12-31; and Cropsey, "Radicalism...," pp. 316-318. On the need for psychological equality, see Harold J. Laski, The State in Theory and Practice (New York: Viking Press, 1935); Kaufman, Radical...; and Cleaver, Soul....

[270]Cohn, Pursuit of the Millennium... .

[271]See Harry M. Clor (ed.), Censorship and Freedom of Expression: Essays on Obscenity and the Law (Chicago: Rand McNally and Co., 1971).

Similarly, the result of current thoughts on the meaning of
liberty is the desire to eliminate most social restraints,
for many see self-actualization as a basic human need and
right. This expansionist view of liberty or the prevalence
of "non-authoritarian" or "anti-hierarchial" (anarchist?)
personalities seems most prevalent among the over-privileged
young.

Shils makes an excellent presentation of this
anti-authority/self-actualization phenomenon. According to
Shils, the postwar generation has grown up and has lived in
a society in which "authority has lost its sacredness. ...
Rulers believe that they have to justify themselves by
realizing the desires of their citizenry."[272] The result
has been that

> Sensitivity to the impositions of authority has greatly
> increased, and almost every impingement on it from the
> outside-- unless voluntarily chosen as part of the
> expansion of individuality-- is painful to the point of
> unsupportability. ...
> Institutions-- with their specialized and prescribed
> roles, their restrictions on individual willfulness, the
> crystallization of traditions and their commitments that
> bind the future by the past-- are repugnant to this
> aspiration toward an individuality that creates its
> boundaries only in response to its internal needs.[273]

According to Shils, ultimately

> whatever hampers the fulfillment of whatever happens to
> be desired at the moment-- whether it is a student
> housing arrangement which stipulates the hours of
> visiting in halls of residence ... is repressive. And,
> as such, it is part of an undifferentiatedly repressive
> system.[274]

Thus, unless the regime permits a very high degree of personal freedom, some citizens believe that regime to be
repressive.

Consequences of Changes in American Democratic Legitimating Ideologies

As Smelser indicates, changes in such basic values
as equality and liberty have several implications:

---

[272]Shils, "Dreams...," p. 15.

[273]Ibid., p. 16.   [274]Ibid., p. 13.

A change in the basic definition of values-- for
instance, from free enterprize to socialism-- perforce
implies a revamping of the laws of property, employment,
and contract. Further, such a change would alter radically the organization of authority and control of
economic organizations.[275]

More pertinently for this study, such changes in the legitimating ideologies of American democracy may result in an
"equality Revolution" and the loss of legitimacy for the
present American regime. Such consequences would certainly
be disruptive to the American regime.

The "Equality Revolution"

Herbert Gans suggests that the recent changes in
the interpretations of some American legitimating ideologies
may result in an "Equality Revolution." He argues that in
the American society of the 1960's there were increasing
demands for equality, democracy, and autonomy. "All of
these demands add up to a desire for greater control over
one's life, requiring the reduction of the many inequal-
ities-- economic, political and social."[276] According to
Gans, economic inequalities are readily visible in the fact
that the richest 5% received 20% of the national income,
while the poorest 20% received only 5% of the national
income.[277] Other economic inequalities include the lack of
job security for the non-union wage earner and the fact that
the employee operates in an unequal relationship with the
employer. Lack of economic autonomy is illustrated by the
absence of choice in employment and the resultant low satisfaction with jobs. To correct these economic inequalities,
the wage earner must share in profits and corporate decision
making.

For Gans, political equality requires the application of the principle of "one man one vote," provision of
legal assistance, and broader participation at political
conventions. Gans says one can provide social equality by
treating the young as adults-- as equals in the family and
at schools. Similarly, women must be equal in the family.
Blacks may gain their equality through community control
and recognition that black is beautiful. Lay people must
be allowed to participate in church decision making. Eventually, the principle of equality will apply to high school

---

[275]Smelser, Theory..., p. 33.

[276]Herbert J. Gans, "The Equality Revolution of the
60's," American Politics and Its Interpreters, ed. Louis
Reichman and Barry Wishart (Dubuque, Iowa: William C. Brown
Co., Pubs., 1971), p. 280.

[277]Ibid., p. 281.

students, public employees, teachers, social workers, suburbanites, and consumers.

According to Gans, the equality revolution demands
that a change must take place in American ideologies which
currently give precedence to liberty. The problem is that
presently liberty is only available to the "haves." "Have
nots," such as the blacks, should share in the "distribution
of achievements ... roughly comparable to that of whites."[278]
This quest for equality, however, involves a form of
revolution, for "no one awards equality voluntarily; it
has to be wrested from the 'more equal' by political
pressure and even by force."[279] Thus, the transformation
of American society toward conditions of equality is not
likely to be tranquil, because those with power and privilege will resist.[280] Gans's arguments are compatible with
those of this thesis, except for his optimistic evaluations
that peace will at least ultimately come out of such
expansion of equality and liberty.

The inevitability of conflict arising out of such
expansion of equality is evident in Hallmark's argument
that myths of natural inequality are necessary for social
order.[281] According to Hallmark, "the greater the degree
of equality, the more overtly competitive and prone to
violence a society is likely to become. The more stable
social orders are necessarily not egalitarian," because
competition and aggression usually take place between
"adjacent points in the social rank order."[282] In these
sociological terms, the contemporary battles would be
between the hardhats and the blacks and between the student
culture and the establishment. According to Gans, current
conditions of inequality in American society will result in
an equality revolution. On the other hand, Hallmark
suggests that equality results in political conflict.
Apparently, the ultimate consequence of changes in the
democratic legitimating ideologies of equality and liberty
will be conflict-- perhaps even violent conflict.

The loss of legitimacy

Thus, the modern American democratic regime has
broadened its views so as to be committed to equality across
a wide range of human relations. Such broadened views of
democracy may result in the instability of the regime,
because the new demands placed on the government may go
far beyond the mere preservation of order. With the broad-

---

[278]Ibid., p. 286.

[279]Ibid.   [280]Ibid., pp. 280-286.

[281]Hallmark, "Subcultures...," p. 15.

[282]Ibid., pp. 14-15.

ening of such views, government must take sides in the conflict. At best, government becomes a mediator; even worse
is the possibility of government becoming an arbitrator.
As an arbitrator, government loses its mythological claim to
represent the whole political community. In effect, government becomes another interest group, because it is no longer
impartial. When government becomes an interest group, it
may perhaps lose its legitimacy as well.

Lowi has suggested that such a process may occur if
there is a general belief that the myths of a society are
the property of particular interests or classes. When such
beliefs are prevalent, there is great potential for frag-
mentizing the integrative myths of the regime. Thus, if they
become widely accepted models of politics, the pluralist and
Marxist views of American society-- in that they emphasize
the central role of particular interests and classes in
politics and encourage such partisan interpretations of
mythical systems of belief-- may have disintegrating
effects on the values and myths of the American political
culture. For example, the pluralist or mechanistic view
may delegitimize government authority by seeming to place
government on the same level as almost any other interest
group:

> The zeal of pluralism for the group and its belief
> in a natural harmony of group competition tended to
> break down the very ethic of government by reducing
> the essential concept of government to nothing more
> than another set of mere interest groups.[283]

The Marxian class struggle view of American society may
delegitimize authority by claiming that government represents only the economically privileged part of American
society. Indeed, New Deal attempts to ameliorate or reform
conditions of under-privileged groups may intimately involve
and even solidify government involvement in private disputes and thus may institutionalize racial and class
struggles.[284]

---

[283]Lowi, End of Liberalism..., p. 48. On the
Weimar Republic, see Franz Neumann, Behemoth: The Structure
and Practice of National Socialism, 1933-1944 (New York:
Harper and Row, Publishers, 1966). For the so-called
pluralist view, see particularly Arthur F. Bentley, The
Process of Government (Chicago: University of Chicago
Press, 1908; reprinted in 1935 and 1949 by the Principia
Press of Bloomington, Indiana); Truman, Governmental
Process...; and MacIver, Web....

[284]Lubell, White and Black..., pp. 215-216; and
Schattschneider, Two Hundred....

Summary

Thus, an increase in the responsibilities of government in response to demands to expand the application of liberty and equality makes government merely another interest group. As an interest group, government is no longer impartial and thus loses its legitimate authority. The result may be class struggle. On the other hand, it may be more useful to approach the pursuant conflict in light of the purposes and goals of the various participants (see Chapter IV). The argument of this thesis is that when groups or individuals believe the regime is no longer legitimate, they may develop value systems or myth structures which they believe will promote their political goals. If these groups actually offer their new value systems as alternatives to the imperfect but dominant myths or legitimating ideologies, the result may be political violence. Another possible scenario, that of optimism, is that these groups, even though sometimes violent, represent a brighter future. In the light of such possibilities, subcultural values may actually refect "a pattern of expectations and visions of the future"; a "vanguard of prospective social change"; and "index of development" or the "future of the society"; a "weatherman of revolution"; or even an "anticipatory majority."[285] This writer's vision of the future is less hopeful because "the road to hell is paved with good intentions."

---

[285]Hallmark, "Subcultures...," pp. 7, 10, and 20.

SELECTED BIBLIOGRAPHY

Books

Adorno, T. W., _et al_. Authoritarian Personality. New York: Harper, 1950.

Almond, Gabriel A., and Verba, Sidney. The Civic Culture: Political Attitudes and Democracy in Five Nations. Boston: Little, Brown and Co., 1965.

Apter, David (ed.). Ideology and Discontent. Glencoe, Illinois: Free Press, 1964.

Ardrey, Robert. African Genesis. New York: Dell Publishing Co., Inc., 1961.

Arendt, Hannah. On Revolution. New York: Viking Press, Inc., 1965.

Aristotle. The Politics. Edited and translated by Ernest Barker. New York: Oxford University Press, 1962.

Bachrach, Peter. The Theory of Democratic Elitism: A Critique. Boston: Little, Brown, 1967.

Banfield, Edward C. The Unheavenly City: The Nature and Future of Our Urban Crisis. Boston: Little, Brown and Co., 1968.

Brink, William, and Harris, Louis. Black and White: A Study of U. S. Racial Attitudes Today. New York: Simon and Schuster, 1966.

Buckley, Walter. Sociology and Modern Systems Theory. Englewood Cliffs, New Jersey: Prentice-Hall, Inc., 1967.

Campbell, Angus, _et al_. The American Voter. New York: John Wiley and Sons, Inc., 1960.

Campbell, Angus, _et al_. The Voter Decides. Chicago: Row Peterson and Co., 1954.

Cantril, Albert H., and Roll, Charles W. Hopes and Fears of the American People. New York: Universe Books, 1971.

255

Cleaver, Eldridge. Soul on Ice. New York: Dell Publishing Co., Inc., 1970.

Cohen, Nathan E. (ed.). The Los Angeles Riots: A Socio-Psychological Study. New York: Praeger, 1970.

Cohn, Norman. The Pursuit of the Millennium: Revolutionary Millenarians and Mystical Anarchists of the Middle Ages. New York: Oxford University Press, 1970.

Dahl, Robert A. Modern Political Analysis. Englewood Cliffs, New Jersey: Prentice-Hall, Inc., 1963.

_____. Who Governs? Democracy and Power in an American City. New Haven: Yale University Press, 1961.

Dahl, Robert, and Lindbloom, Charles. Politics, Economics and Welfare. New York: Harper and Row, 1953.

de Grazia, Sebastian. The Political Community. Chicago: University of Chicago Press, 1948.

Dollard, John, et al. Frustration and Aggression. New Haven: Yale University Press, 1957.

Douglas, William O. Points of Rebellion. New York: Random House, Vintage Books, 1970.

Drake, St. Clair, and Cayton, Horace R. Black Metropolis: A Study of Negro Life in a Northern City. 2 vols.; New York: Harper and Row Publishers, Inc., 1952.

Durkheim, Emile. Suicide: A Study in Sociology. Translated by John A. Spaulding and George Simpson. New York: The Free Press, 1951.

Easton, David. A Systems Analysis of Political Life. New York: John Wiley and Sons, Inc., 1965.

Easton, David, and Dennis, Jack. Children in the Political System: The Origins of Political Legitimacy. New York: McGraw-Hill Book Company, 1969.

Eckstein, Harry (ed.). Internal War: Problems and Approaches. New York: The Free Press, 1964.

Feierabend, Ivo K., Feierabend, Rosalind L., and Gurr, Ted Robert (eds.). Anger, Violence, and Politics: Theories and Research. Englewood Cliffs, New Jersey: Prentice-Hall, Inc., 1972.

Ferrero, Guglielmo. The Principles of Power: The Great Political Crises of History. Translated by Theodore Jaeckel. New York: G. P. Putnam's Sons, 1945.

Free, Lloyd A., and Cantril, Hadley. The Political Beliefs
of Americans: A Study of Public Opinion. New York
Simon and Schuster, Clarion Books, 1968.

Freud, Sigmund. Civilization and Its Discontents. New
York: W. W. Norton and Co., Inc., 1961.

Greenstein, Fred I. Children and Politics. 2d ed. revised;
New Haven: Yale University Press, 1969.

Grimshaw, Allen D. (ed.). Racial Violence in the United
States. Chicago: Aldine Publishing Company, 1969.

Gurr, Ted. Why Men Rebel. Princeton, New Jersey:
Princeton University Press, 1970.

Gusfield, Joseph R. (ed.). Protest, Reform, and Revolt: A
Reader in Social Movements. New York: John Wiley and
Sons, Inc., 1970.

Hamilton, Alexander, Madison, James and Jay, John.
The Federalist Papers. Introduction by Clinton
Rossiter. New York: New American Library, 1961.

Hoffman, Abbie. Revolution for the Hell of It. New York:
Pocket Books, 1970.

Kaufman, Arnold S. The Radical Liberal: The New Politics;
Theory and Practice. New York: Simon and Schuster,
a Clarion Book, 1970.

Kroeber, A. L., and Kluckhohn, Clyde. Culture: A Critical
Review of Concepts and Definitions. New York: Random
House, Vintage Books, 1963.

Kunen, James Simon. The Strawberry Statement: Notes of a
College Revolutionary. New York: Avon Books, 1970.

Lane, Robert E. Political Ideology: Why the American
Common Man Believes What He Does. New York: The Free
Press, 1962.

Lasswell, Harold D., and Kaplan, Abraham. Power and
Society: A Framework for Political Inquiry. New Haven:
Yale University Press, 1956.

Lasswell, Harold D., and Lerner, Daniel. World Revolutionary Elites: Studies in Coercive Ideological Movements. Cambridge: M.I.T. Press, 1965.

Lipset, Seymour Martin. Political Man. Garden City, New
York: Doubleday and Company, Inc., 1963.

_____. *Rebellion in the University*. Boston: Little, Brown and Company, 1971.

Lipset, Seymour Martin, and Altbach, Philip G. (eds.). *Students in Revolt*. Boston: Beacon Press, 1970.

Lipset, Seymour Martin, and Wolin, Seldon S. (eds.). *The Berkeley Student Revolt: Facts and Interpretations*. Garden City: Doubleday-Anchor Books, 1965.

Lorenz, Konrad. *On Aggression*. Translated by Marjorie Kerr Wilson. New York: Bantam Books, 1967.

Lubell, Samuel. *White and Black: Test of a Nation*. New York: Harper and Row Publishers, Inc., 1966.

MacIver, Robert M. *The Web of Government*. New York: The Free Press, 1965.

Milbrath, Lester W. *Political Participation: How and Why Do People Get Involved in Politics?*. Chicago: Rand McNally and Co., 1965.

Mills, C. Wright. *The Power Elite*. New York: Oxford University Press, 1956.

Newfield, Jack. *A Prophetic Minority*. New York: New American Library, 1967.

Nieburg, H. L. *Political Violence: The Behavioral Process*. New York: St. Martin's Press, 1969.

Reich, Charles A. *The Greening of America*. New York: Random House, Bantam Books, 1971.

Robinson, John P., and Shaver, Philip R. *Measures of Sociological and Psychological Attitudes*. (Survey Research Center, Institute of Social Research.) Ann Arbor: University of Michigan, 1969.

Robinson, John P., Rusk, Jerrold G., and Head, Kendra B. *Measures of Political Attitudes*. (Survey Research Center, Institute of Social Research.) Ann Arbor: University of Michigan, 1968.

Rubin, Jerry, *Do It*. New York: Simon and Schuster, 1970.

Said, Abdul A. (ed.). *Protagonists of Change: Subcultures in Development and Revolution*. Englewood Cliffs, New Jersey: Prentice-Hall, Inc., 1971.

Scammon, Richard M., and Wattenberg, Ben J. *The Real Majority*. New York: Coward-McCann, Inc., 1970.

258

Schattschneider, E. E. Two Hundred Million Americans in
    Search of a Government. New York: Holt, Rinehart,
    and Winston, Inc., 1969.
Schlesinger, Arthur. Crisis of Confidence: Ideas, Power
    and Violence in America. Boston: Houghton Mifflin,
    1969.

_____. Violence: America in the Sixties. New York:
    Signet Books, 1968.

Smelser, Neil J. Theory of Collective Behavior. New York:
    Free Press, 1963.

Stillman, Edmund, and Pfaff, William. The Politics of
    Hysteria: The Sources of Twentieth Centruy Conflict.
    New York: Harper and Row, Pubs., 1964.

Tocqueville, Alexis de. Democracy in America. Translated
    by Henry Reeve. Edited by Phillips Bradley. 2 vols.;
    New York: Vintage Books, 1945.

Yablonsky, Lewis. The Violent Gang. Baltimore: Penguin
    Books, 1966.

                Articles and Periodicals

Aberbach, Joel D., and Walker, Jack L. "The Meanings of
    Black Power: A Comparison of White and Black Inter-
    pretations of a Political Slogan," American Political
    Science Review, Vol. LXIV, No. 2 (June, 1970), pp.
    367-388.

Aberbach, Joel D., and Walker, Jack L. "Political Trust
    and Racial Ideology," American Political Science Review,
    Vol. LXIV, No. 4 (December, 1970), pp. 1199-1219.

Agger, Robert E., Goldstein, Marshal N., and Pearl, Stanley
    A. "Political Cynicism: Measurement and Meaning,"
    Journal of Politics, Vol. XXIII (1961), pp. 477-506.

Ardery, Philip P. "Special Report: Opinion on the Campus,"
    National Review, Vol. XXIII (June 15, 1971), pp. 635-
    650.

Barton, Allen H. "The Columbia Crisis: Campus, Viet Nam
    and the Ghetto," Public Opinion Quarterly, Fall, 1968,
    pp. 333-351.

Bell, Daniel. "Columbia and the New Left," Public Interest,
    No. 13, Fall, 1968, pp. 61-101.

Brown, Richard Maxwell. "The American Vigilante Tradition," History of Violence in America, ed. Hugh Davis Graham and Ted Gurr. A Report to the National Commission on the Causes and Prevention of Violence. New York: Bantam Books, 1969, pp. 154-217.

Carr, E. H. "Nature of Politics," Readings in World Politics, ed. Robert A. Goldwin, revised by Tony Pearce. 2d ed. revised; New York: Oxford University Press, 1970, pp. 455-460.

Clor, Harry M. "American Democracy and the Challenge of Radical Democracy," How Democratic is America?, ed. Robert A. Goldwin. Chicago: Rand McNally Inc., 1971, pp. 77-108.

Cropsey, Joseph. "Radicalism and Its Roots," Public Policy, Vol. XVIII, No. 3 (April, 1970), pp. 301-319.

Davies, James C. "Toward A Theory of Revolution," American Sociological Review, Vol. XXVII (February, 1962), pp. 5-18.

Diamond, Martin. "Democracy and The Federalist: A Reconsideration of the Framers' Intent," American Political Science Review, Vol. LIII, 1959.

Erskine, Hazel. "The Polls: Demonstrations and Race Riots," Public Opinion Quarterly, Vol. XXXI, No. 4 (Winter, 1967-1968), pp. 655-677.

_____. "The Polls: Textbook Knowledge," Public Opinion Quarterly, Vol. XXVII (Spring, 1963), pp. 137-140.

Finifter, Ada W. "Dimensions of Political Alienation," American Political Science Review, Vol. LXIV, No. 2 (June, 1970), pp. 389-410.

Gallup, George. "Four in Ten College Students Think Change in U. S. Will Come through Revolution." Press release of the American Institute of Public Opinion. Princeton: January 21, 1971.

_____. Gallup Opinion Index, No. 50, August, 1969.

_____. "Public Sees Gun Registration as Most Urgent Step Needed to Curb Violence in America," Gallup Opinion Index, July, 1968.

_____. Special Report on the Attitudes of College Students: Student Disorders-- What's Behind Them? Majority of College Youth Agree with Goal but not Tactics of Militants," Gallup Opinion Index, No. 48, June, 1969.

_____. "Special Survey of College Students." Gallup
Poll release, June 29, 1968.

_____. "The Student Revolution-- A Special Report,"
Gallup Opinion Index, No. 66, June, 1970.

_____. "The U. S. Campus Mood, '71: A Newsweek Poll--
Students Aviod Party Labels: Also Reject Radical
Politics," Newsweek, February 22, 1971, p. 61.

Gans, Herbert J. "The Equality Revolution of the 60's,"
The New York Times Magazine, November 3, 1968.

Harris, Louis. "After the Riots: A Survey," Newsweek,
August 21, 1967, pp. 18-19.

_____. "Aid Programs to Curb Riots are Backed by Both
Races," Philadelphia Inquirer, August 14, 1967.

_____. "Aversion to Vietnam War Reaches High Among
College Students, Harris Survey," Scranton Tribune
(Scranton, Pennsylvania), June 30, 1969.

_____. "Black and White: A Major Study of U.S. Racial
Attitudes Today," Newsweek, August 22, 1966, pp. 12-27.

_____. "College Students 'Radicalized' by Vietnam War,"
Philadelphia Inquirer, June 3, 1969.

_____. "Fifty-two Percent Decry Protests on Cambodia,"
Washington Post, June 1, 1970.

_____. "Most Think Law and Order Has Broken Down in
Nation," Washington Post, September 9, 1968.

_____. "The Negro in America," Newsweek, Vol. LXII, No.
5 (July 29, 1963), pp. 15-22, 25-34.

_____. "Protests Hit a Rut, Harris Survey," Boston
Globe , September I, 1969.

_____. "Report of the May 1970 Harris Survey of
Students," May 20-28, 1970.

_____. "Riots Have Hurt Negro Cause, 87% of America
Believes," Washington Post, August 17, 1964.

_____. "White Fears, Negro Militancy Continue to Show
Steady Rise," Washington Post, June 5, 1967.

_____. "Whites, Negroes Split on Causes of Rioting,"
Philadelphia Inquirer, April 16, 1968.

_____. "A YOung People's Alliance of Whites, Blacks, Growing," Long Island Press, September 11, 1969.

Harris, Louis, et al. "Youth Attitudes for Life Magazine: Year End Issue," Life, November, 1970.

Hayden, Tom. "Manifesto Notes: Problems of Democracy," The New Politics: Mood or Movement?, ed. James H. Burkhart and Frank J. Kendrick. Englewood Cliffs, New York: Prentice-Hall, Inc., 1971, pp. 39-45.

_____. "The Politics of 'The Movement,'" The Politics of the Powerless, ed. Robert H. Binstock and Kathleen Ely. Cambridge: Winthrop Publishers, Co., 1971, pp. 304-311.

_____. "Port Huron Statement," American Radical Thought: The Libertarian Tradition, ed. Henry J. Silverman. Lexington, Mass.: D.C. Heath and Co., 1970, pp. 357-379.

_____. "Post Chicago Interview," Telling It Like It Was: The Chicago Riots, ed. Walter Schneir. New York: New American Library, 1969, pp. 119-133.

Hayden, Tom, and Lynd, Slaughton. "We Are Not at War," American Radical Thought: The Libertarian Tradition, ed. Henry J. Silverman. Lexington, Mass: D.C. Heath and Co., 1970, pp. 226-236.

Hess, Robert D., and Easton, David. "The Child's Changing Image of the President," Public Opinion Quarterly, Vol. XXIV (1960), pp. 632-644.

Hofstadter, Richard. "Reflections on Violence in the United States," American Violence, ed. Richard Hofstadter and Michael Wallace. New YOrk: Random House, Vintage Books, 1971, pp. 3-43.

Hofstetter, Richard C. "Political Disengagement and the Death of Martin Luther King," Public Opinion Quarterly, Summer, 1969, pp. 174-179.

Hovland, Carl Iver, and Sears, Robert R. "Minor Studies of Aggression: Correlations of Lynchings with Economic Indices," Racial Violence in the United States, ed. Allen D. Grimshaw. Chicago: Aldine Publishing Company, 1969, pp. 344-348.

Janos, Andrew C. "Authority and Violence: The Political Framework of Internal War," Internal War: Problems and Approaches, ed. Harry Eckstein. New York: The Free Press, 1964, pp. 130-141.

262

Lieberson, Stanley, and Silverman, Arnold R. "The Precipitants and Underlying Conditions of Race Riots," _American Sociological Review_, Vol. XXX, No. 6 (1965), pp. 887-898.

Lowi, Theodore J. "American Business, Public Policy, Case Studies and Political Theory," _World Politics,_ Vol. XVI (July, 1964), pp. 673-715.

_____. "Distribution, Regulation, Redistribution: The Function of Government," _Readings in American Political Behavior_, ed. Raymond E. Wolfinger. 2d ed.; Englewood Cliffs, New Jersey: Prentice-Hall, Inc., 1970, pp. 245-256.

Lubell, Samuel. "That Generation Gap," _The Public Interest_, Vol. XIII (Fall, 1968), pp. 52-60.

Lyonns, Glen. "The Police Car Demonstration," _The Berkeley Student Revolt: Facts and Interpretations_. ed. Seymour Martin Lipset and Sheldon S. Wolin. Garden City: Doubleday-Anchor Books, 1965, pp. 519-530.

McClosky, Herbert. "Concensus and Ideology in American Politics," _American Political Science Review_, Vol. LVIII (June, 1964), pp. 361-382.

McClosky, Herbert, Hoffman, P., and O'Hara, R. "Issue Conflict and Concensus Among Party Leaders and Followers," American Political Science Review, Vol. LIV (1960), pp. 406-427.

Maslow, Abraham H. "A Theory of Human Motivation," _Psychological Review_, Vol. L (1943), pp. 370-396.

Murphy, Raymond J., and Watson, James W. "The Structure of Discontent: The Relationship Between Social Structure, Grievance, and Riot Support, " _The Los Angeles Riots; A Socio-Psychological Study_, ed. Nathan E. Cohen. New York: Praeger, 1970, pp. 140-257.

Parson, Talcott. "Some Reflections on the Place of Force on Social Process," _Internal War: Problems and Approaches_, ed. Harry Eckstein. New York: The Free Press, 1966, pp. 33-70.

Peterson, Richard E. "The Student Left in American Higher Education," _Students In Revolt_, ed. Seymour Martin Lipset and Philip G. Altbach. Boston: Beacon Press, 1970, pp. 202-231.

"_Playboy's_ Student Survey," _Playboy_, Vol. XVII, No. 9 (September, 1970), pp. 182-184, 236-240.

Prothro, James W., and Griggs, Charles M. "Fundamental
    Principles of Democracy: Bases of Agreement and Dis-
    agreement," Journal of Politics, Vol. XXII (May, 1960),
    pp. 276-294.

Raine, Walter J. "The Perception of Police Brutality in
    South Central Los Angeles," The Los Angeles Riots: A
    Socio-Psychological Study, ed. Nathan E. Cohen. New
    York: Praeger, 1970, pp. 380-412.

Sears, David C., and McConahay, John B. "Riot Participa-
    tion," The Los Angeles Riots: A Socio-Psychological
    Study, ed. Nathan E. Cohen. New York: Praeger, 1970,
    pp. 258-287.

Simon, Geoffrey, and Trout, Grafton. "Hippies in College,"
    The Anti-American Generation, ed. Edgar Z. Friedenberg
    New York: Transaction Books, distributed by Aldine
    Publishing Co., 1971, pp. 19-27.

Somers, Robert H. "The Mainsprings of the Rebellion: A
    Survey of Berkeley Students in November, 1964," The
    Berkeley Student Revolt: Facts and Interpretations,
    ed. Seymour Martin Lipset and Sheldon S. Wolin. New
    York: Doubleday-Anchor, 1965, pp. 530-557.

Tomlinson, Tom M. "The Development of a Riot Ideology Among
    Urban Negroes," American Behavioral Scientist, Vol. XI
    (March/April, 1968), pp. 27-31.

_____ "Ideological Foundations for Negro Action:
    Militant and Non-Militant Views," The Los Angeles Riots:
    A Socio-Psychological Study, ed. Nathan E. Cohen. New
    York: Praeger, 1970, pp. 326-379.

_____. "Ideological Foundations for Negro Action: A
    Comparative Analysis of Militant and Non-Militant Views
    of the Los Angeles Riot," Journal of Social Issues,
    Vol. XXVI, No. 1 (1970), pp. 91-119.

Tomlinson, T. M., and Sears, David O. "Negro Attitudes
    Toward the Riot," The Los Angeles Riots: A Socio-
    Psychological Study, ed. Nathan E. Cohen. New York:
    Praeger, 1970, pp. 288-325.

"The Un-Radical Young," Life, Vol. LXX, No. 1 (January 8,
    1971), pp. 22-30.

Walker, Jack L. "A Critique of the Elitist Theory in
    Democracy," American Political Science Review, Vol.
    LX (June, 1966), pp. 285-295.

Reports

Campbell, Angus, and Schuman, Howard. "Racial Attitudes in
   Fifteen American Cities," Supplemental Studies for the
   National Advisory Commission on Civil Disorders.
   Washington, D.C.: U.S. Government Printing Office,
   July, 1968, pp. 1-67.

Campbell, James S., Sahid, Joseph R., and Stang, David P.
   Law and Order Reconsidered. A Staff Report to the
   National Commission on the Causes and Prevention of
   Violence. New York: Bantam Books, 1970.

Commission on Isla Vista. Report of the Commission on Isla
   Vista. Prepared by a commisson directed by Martin
   Trow. Santa Barbara, Calif.: University of California,
   October 9, 1970.

Fogelson, Robert M., and Hill, Robert E. "Who Riots? A
   Study of Participation in the 1967 Riots," Supplemental
   Studies for the National Advisory Commission on Civil
   Disorders. Washington, D. C.: U.S. Government
   Printing Office, July, 1968, pp. 217-248.

Graham, Hugh Davis, and Gurr, Ted (eds.). The History of
   Violence in America. A Report to the National Commis-
   sion on the Causes and Prevention of Violence. New
   York: Bantam Books, 1969.

Kirkham, James F., Levy, Sheldon G., and Crotty, William J.
   Assassination and Political Violence. A Staff Report
   to the National Commission on the Causes and Prevention
   of Violence. New York: Bantam Books, 1970.

Levy, Sheldon G. "Attitudes Toward Political Violence,"
   Assassination and Political Violence. A Staff Report
   to the National Commission on the Causes and Prevention
   of Violence prepared by James F. Kirkham, Sheldon G.
   Levy, and William J. Crotty. New York: Bantam Books,
   1970, pp. 473-515.

National Advisory Commission on Civil Disorders. Report of
   the National Advisory Commission on Civil Disorders.
   Prepared by a commission directed by Otto Kerner. New
   York: Bantam Books, 1968. (Also known as the Kerner
   Commission.)

National Commission on the Causes and Prevention of
   Violence. To Establish Justice, To Insure Domestic
   Tranquility. Prepared by a commission directed by
   Milton S. Eisenhower, New York: Award Books, 1969.
   (Also known as the Eisenhower Commission.)

President's Commission on Campus Unrest. Campus Unrest.
Report prepared by a commission directed by William W.
Scranton. Washington, D.C.: U.S. Government Printing
Office, 1970. (Also known as the Scranton Commission.)

Unpublished Material

Cohen, Nathan E. "Press Release, August1, 1967." Press
release for the Los Angeles Riot Study. Los Angeles.
University of California, August1, 1967. (Mimeographed.)

Lemberg Center for the Study of Violence. "Six-City Study:
A Survey of Racial Attitudes in Six Northern Cities:
Preliminary Report." Waltham, Mass., Brandeis Univer-
sity, June, 1967. (Mimeographed.)

Muller, Edward N. "A Test of a Partial Theory of Potential
for Political Violence." State University of New York
at Stoney Brook, no date. (Mimeographed.)

Sherrill, Kenneth. "Mass Attitudes Toward Power and Legiti-
macy in the Urban Context." Paper presented before the
American Political Science Association convention, Los
Angeles, California, September, 1970. (Mimeographed.)

Stolz, Matthew F. "The Liberal Paradigm and the Rediscovery
of Violence in America." Paper presented at the Western
Political Science Association convention, Sacramento,
California, April 1-4, 1970. (Mimeographed.)

United Rubber Workers, Research Department. "Membership
Attitudes and Opinion." A Report to the United Rubber,
Cork, Linoleum, and Plaster Workers of America, 1970.
(Mimeographed.)

DATE DUE

JUL 6 1988			